Slave Revolts in Antiquity

Slave Revolts in Antiquity

Theresa Urbainczyk

University of California Press
Berkeley Los Angeles

To the memory of Pauline Watkins

University of California Press, one of the most distinguished university presses in the United States, enriches lives around the world by advancing scholarship in the humanities, social sciences, and natural sciences. Its activities are supported by the UC Press Foundation and by philanthropic contributions from individuals and institutions. For more information, visit www.ucpress.edu.

University of California Press
Berkeley and Los Angeles, California

Published simultaneously outside North America
by Acumen Publishing Limited

© 2008 by Theresa Urbainczyk

Library of Congress Cataloging-in-Publication Data

Urbainczyk, Theresa, 1960–
 Slave revolts in antiquity / Theresa Urbainczyk.
  p. cm.
 Includes bibliographical references and index.
 ISBN 978-0-520-25701-6 (cloth : alk. paper)
 ISBN 978-0-520-25702-3 (pbk. : alk. paper)
  1. Slave insurrections—Greece. 2. Slave insurrections—Rome.
 3. Slavery—Greece. 4. Slavery—Rome. I. Title.
 HT863.U73   2008
 306.3'62—dc22   2008006955

Manufactured in the United Kingdom

17 16 15 14 13 12 11 10 09 08
    10 9 8 7 6 5 4 3 2 1

Contents

Acknowledgements		vii
Chronology		ix
The ancient Mediterranean		xiii
1	The significance of slave revolts	1
2	Preparing for revolt	10
3	Maintaining resistance	29
4	The role of the leader	51
5	The ideology of the slaves	75
6	Sympathy for the slaves: Diodorus Siculus	81
7	The secret of the success of the Spartan helots	91
8	Slave revolts in the ancient historiography	100
	Notes	117
	Bibliography	161
	Index	173

Acknowledgements

I thought a book about slave revolts in antiquity was a great project. I came up with it in 2000 and over the past eight years more colleagues than I care to remember have tried to dissuade me from it. The process of writing and rewriting has been at times extremely dispiriting but I still think the subject deserves several books and am more than happy to have finished this. Consequently, my thanks to those individuals who have encouraged me are more than usually heartfelt. First I must acknowledge with gratitude that University College Dublin allowed me to take two semesters of sabbatical leave, the first spent in Berlin in 2004, the second in Warsaw in 2007. Giving papers in the Free University and the Humboldt University made me rethink my ideas several times and I owe much to the audiences in both places. I am grateful to the Royal Irish Academy and the Polish Academy of Sciences for the grant that enabled me to go to Warsaw for the first time.

Two conferences helped sustain me: one in Galway ("Slave Systems, Ancient and Modern", organized by Enrico del Lago and Constantina Katsari in November 2004); the other in Hull ("Slavery, Unfinished Business", organized by the Wilberforce Institute for the Study of Slavery and Emancipation in May 2007). I would like especially to thank Kevin Bales, Keith Bradley, Douglas Egerton, Vernita Irvin, Constantina Katsari and Orlando Patterson. Their comments on my talks were more helpful than they will ever know.

This book is much better because of the observations of the anonymous readers, and my copy-editor, Kate Williams, for Acumen, and I acknowledge gratefully their contribution to the finished product. Jan Willem Drijvers and Stephen Mennell both read full drafts of this book and were kind enough to tell me to carry on with it. I owe a special debt to Wilfried Nippel, who commented on a late draft very carefully and saved me from many errors. Niall McKeown also read this, and his challenging remarks improved it substantially. Stelios Mallikourtis taught me much about ancient and modern Greece and took an interest in my work when it seemed no one else did. Kieran Allen, Roland Erne and Ireneusz Łada have all, at times, persuaded me to finish this, if only because they did not want to hear about it any more. I shall always be grateful to them whatever their motives. Steven Gerrard saw the possibilities of this book and I am happy that he did. I dedicate this to my mother, who would have thought a book about slave revolts in antiquity was a great project.

Chronology

BCE

Unknown date Slaves rebel on Samos for six years. After their masters are unable to conquer them, they agree a truce and allow them to leave. The slaves board a ship and go to live in Ephesus.

Unknown date After their masters are away on a long campaign, slaves in Scythia take their place; they marry their masters' wives and have children by them.

501 Slave revolt in Rome.

490 Battle of Marathon. Athenians and Plataeans defeat the Persians.

480 Battles of Thermopylae and Salamis; end of Persian invasion of Greece.

464 Taking advantage of an earthquake in Sparta, some helots rebel, and occupy Mount Ithome. After ten years the Spartans still cannot defeat them, so they are allowed to leave the Peloponnese and settle in Naupactus on the Corinthian gulf.

460 Slave revolt in Rome, led by Herdonius the Sabine.

431–404 Peloponnesian War, the war between Athens and Sparta and their respective allies.

Late-5th century Herodotus is writing his *Histories*.

Threat of helot revolt affects Spartan policy during the Peloponnesian War.

425 Athenians land in Pylos on the Peloppenese, hoping to gain the help of the local helots. They score an important victory.

419	Slave revolt in Rome.
Unspecified date	Spartans kill 2,000 helots in an attempt to gain control.
415–413	Slaves desert in Sicily as the Athenians start to lose ground there.
413	20,000 slaves desert from Athens taking advantage of the Spartan occupation of Decelea in Attica.
404	Defeat of Athens. Thucydides is writing *The History of the Peloponnesian War*.
Early-4th century	Xenophon is composing *Hellenica*.
397	Cinadon leads a conspiracy of helots and others against the Spartans.
3rd century	A group of rebel slaves survives in Chios with the leadership of Drimakos, and later without it.
275	The Romans conquer southern Italy.
264–241	First Punic (Carthaginian) War.
259	Slave revolt in Rome.
218–201	Second Punic War.
217	Slave revolt in Rome.
216	Battle of Cannae, victory for Hannibal.
202	Defeat of Hannibal's army at Zama.
198	Slave revolt in Setia in Italy.
197	End of Second Macedonian War. The Romans defeat the army of Philip V of Macedon. Roman territory in Spain is formally constituted into the provinces or Nearer Spain and Further Spain.
196	Slave revolt in Etruria.
192–188	Syrian War. Antiochus III surrenders territory in Europe and Asia Minor to the Romans.
191	Rome completes its conquest of Cisalpine Gaul.
186	Bacchanalian conspiracy involving slaves in Rome and southern Italy.
185	Slave uprising in the region of Tarentum.
184	Slave uprisings in southern Italy.
171–168	Third Macedonian War.
149–146	Third Punic War.
146	Physical destruction of Carthage and Corinth by the Romans. Macedonia becomes a Roman province.

- 141 First slave war starts on Sicily.
- 133 Tribunate of Tiberius Gracchus, who attempts to introduce reforms to remedy the dangerous situation of too many slaves and not enough free people on the land, with a proposal to destribute public land. He and many of his supporters are murdered. King Attalus leaves Pergamum to the Romans in his will. Aristonicus and a following of slaves revolt in Pergamum.
- 132 End of the first Sicilian slave war.
- 129 Annexation of the Roman province of Asia.
- 125 Fulvius Flaccus proposes Roman citizenship for Latins.
- 123 Tribunate of Gaius Gracchus, brother of Tiberius. One of Gaius' reforms is to allow equites to sit as jurors.
- 121 Murder of Gaius Gracchus.
- 107 Marius enlists landless men to the Roman army.
- 104 Decree from Senate to release free citizens of allied states who had been enslaved.
- 104–100 Second slave war on Sicily.
- 91–88 War between Rome and Italian allies, called Social War.
- 89–85 First Mithridatic War, against Mithridates (also spelled Mithradates) VI Eupator Dionysus, king of Pontus.
- 88 Roman general Sulla marches on Rome.
- 87–86 Roman general Marius marches on Rome.
- 83–31 Second Mithridatic War.
- 81 Sulla appointed dictator.
- 77 Pompey is sent to Spain against Sertorius.
- 74–64 Third Mithridatic War.
- 73–71 Slave war in Italy. The slave army is led by Spartacus.
- 71 Defeat by Pompey of army led by Sertorius.
- 71 Defeat of slave army by Crassus and Pompey.
- 71 Pompey allowed to stand as consul, although not qualified to do so.
- 70 Crassus and Pompey are consuls.
- 67 Pompey receives command against pirates in the Mediterranean.
- 63 Conspiracy of Catiline. There are fears that the slaves will join in.

60	Remnants of Spartacus' army are still at large in southern Italy.
49–45	Civil war in Rome.
44	Julius Caesar is murdered.
43–31	Civil war in Rome.
Mid-1st century	Diodorus in composing history.
31	Battle of Actium. Octavian defeats Mark Anthony.
30	Egypt is annexed.
27	Octavian receives the title Augustus. During the reign of Augustus, Livy is composing his history.

CE

14	Death of Emperor Augustus. Strabo is composing his *Geography*.
21	Gladiators join Sacrovir's rebellion.
24	A slave war headed by Titus Curtisius is averted.
61	Gladiators break out of their school at Praeneste. There is talk of another Spartacus.
Late-1st century	Plutarch is composing his parallel lives.
1st–2nd century	Cassius Dio is writing his history.
Early-2nd century	Florus is compiling his eiptome of Livy's history of Rome.
2nd century	Appian is composing his Roman history.
2nd–3rd century	Athenaeus is composing *The Deipnosophistae*.
Early-3rd century	In Italy a group of slaves and others led by Bulla successfully evades capture until betrayal of Bulla to the authorities.
Early-5th century	Augustine is composing his *City of God*. Orosius is composing his *History against the Pagans*.

The ancient Mediterranean

1
The significance of slave revolts

Slaves rebelled in various ways in the ancient world. Sometimes, when they had the opportunity, they ran away. Sometimes they took up arms and fought their masters. Spartacus is a name familiar to many but he was only one of tens of thousands of slaves from antiquity who formed armies to fight for their freedom. We do not have as much information as we should like about these events from the ancient world, but there is more than might be assumed from a quick glance at modern histories.[1] One of the aims of this book is to remind readers that slaves *did* rebel in antiquity; another is to discover why the material that remains has been, to a large extent, ignored or dismissed as historically insignificant. One might reasonably suppose that this attitude simply reflects the ancient texts, and yet one of the results of this re-examination has been the gradual realization that ancient sources accorded far more importance to the actions of the slaves than have modern writers.

While one might expect modern commentators to be more sympathetic toward slaves than their ancient counterparts, the reason for a relative lack of interest in slave rebellion is perhaps not hard to find: slave armies might defeat those of their former masters for a while, even for years, but in the end slavery persisted.[2] There was no abolitionist movement among free people, nor even any text calling for the abolition of slavery. We do not even know that the slaves themselves wanted an end to slavery for other people. It is more likely that, on acquiring their own freedom, they would simply have gone on to become slave-owners themselves. Slaves who took up arms against their masters were simply groups of individuals taking rash, if not downright foolish, action, which could never have succeeded.[3] At the time, it must have seemed threatening to the owners to find their slaves armed and hostile, but with hindsight we can see that such groupings never had a chance of long-term success. And, it might be argued, they had no impact, or only a minimal one, on their own societies.

There are several reasons, however, why it is worth examining slave revolts from antiquity more closely. There is a failure to understand those texts from antiquity that do contain material about revolts if one dismisses the terror they reveal, and indeed it is terror, of rebellious slaves. We also fail to comprehend the true impact that such rebellions had on society at large if we take the view that they were doomed to failure before they even started. The crucifixion of 6,000 slaves along the Appian Way after the defeat of the army led by Spartacus did indeed hold up a gruesome illustration to other slaves of what would happen to them if they so much as had a rebellious thought, but at the same time it was the action of a society that had been terrified by recent events.

A study of slave revolts can thus give rise to a deeper understanding of the ancient societies in which they occurred; it also belongs to the history of slavery. The slaves of antiquity may not have abolished slavery or even wanted to, but their actions, and a history of their actions, is important for slaves of later ages. It is evidence that slaves rebelled, and have always rebelled, against an institution now regarded as unacceptable in a civilized society. Toussaint Louverture was called the black Spartacus, not because he was doomed to failure, but because he had dared to rebel.

At this point, it is worth noting issues raised by Niall McKeown in his provocative work *The Invention of Slavery?*,[4] in which he looks at the works of well-known scholars of ancient slavery and reveals, with a careful precision, the emotional as well as the political attitudes behind their approaches. At the end of his first chapter he comments:

> The problem is not so much that we invent the past as that, when we explore it, we tend to find what we are looking for. Often, when we appear to claim that "this is the way it actually was" we are, in practice, asking the reader to share our ethical ideals, which is something very different.[5]

No historian is free from bias, but it seems that it is more difficult than usual for a detached attitude to be maintained when discussing slave revolts, ancient or modern.[6] Moses Finley comments[7] that ever since Marx and Engels wrote in the *Communist Manifesto* (1848) that all history was the history of class struggle, ancient slavery has been a battleground for Marxists and non-Marxists.[8] This is certainly true of the scholarship on slave revolts, the very essence, one might think, of ancient class struggle for Marxists.[9] In the title of his study of slave revolt in the southern states of the US, *From Rebellion to Revolution*, Eugene Genovese used terms that are key in this debate. His argument is that the particular historical circumstances of, for instance, the rebellion in St Domingue, meant that, unlike their ancient counterparts, these slaves were revolutionary and had revolutionary aims.[10] Until this age of revolution, when ideas about freedom and equality were formulated, slaves merely wished to withdraw from society, not change it.[11] In his Introduction Genovese writes: "The history of slavery and of slave revolts in the Americas corresponds roughly to the transition from seigneurialism to capitalism".[12]

Jacky Dahomay goes even further, writing that the slaves on St Domingue did not even understand the principles of the French Revolution and one cannot call this an anti-slavery revolution; rather, it was an anti-colonial revolution that incorporated anti-slavery uprisings.[13] He goes on to ask: "is revolution thinkable before the advent of modernity?"[14] It seems not and thus my use of the term "revolutionary" will not be in this technical sense, since the concern here is to find out more about the uprisings of slaves, even the more minor ones, in order to discover in what circumstances slaves could rise up. Another consequence of looking for this "revolutionary" content to the revolts is that modern observers tend to emphasize the inevitable failure. What comes across quite strikingly is that for the participants the prospect of escaping slavery overrode fears of a violent death.

The purpose here is partly to indicate the difference in responses between ancient and modern writers, so I have used examples that are better known in order to illustrate this difference more effectively. The nature of the sources, however, has meant that there is a greater focus on the Roman Republic than on other periods and in Chapter 8 I draw some wider conclusions about that particular period of history. The helots of Sparta are sometimes not discussed with other slaves at all, because of their particular nature; I have addressed the issue of their status separately (Chapter 7). I look at the conditions surrounding known episodes of slave resistance so that, by the end of the book, the reader will be more aware not only of ancient and modern attitudes to slave rebellions, but also of the conditions that are beneficial to the successful organization of rebels. This structure was prompted by the following quotation from Finley:

It is a fallacy to think that the threat of rebellion increases automatically with an increase in misery and oppression. Hunger and torture destroy the spirit; at most they stimulate efforts at flight or other forms of purely individual behaviour (including betrayal of fellow-victims), whereas revolt requires organisation and courage and persistence.[15]

Finley highlights the extreme difficulties the slaves had to overcome simply to be in the position of forming an effective army. While it is easy to focus on the ultimate military defeat of the slaves, it is vital not to overlook the successful organization that made a military confrontation possible.

Slavery has been with us since records began and although legal nowhere it has not disappeared from the face of the earth. Orlando Patterson started his book *Slavery and Social Death* with these words:

There is nothing notably peculiar about the institution of slavery. It has existed from before the dawn of human history right down to the twentieth century, in the most primitive of human societies and in the most civilized. There is no region on earth that has not at some time harboured the institution. Probably there is no group of people whose ancestors were not at one time slaves or slaveholders.[16]

In 1999 Kevin Bales documented the slavery that still exists in contemporary society. In the first chapter of his work he stated, "Slavery is not a horror safely consigned to the past; it continues to exist throughout the world, even in developed countries like France and the United States".[17] He estimated that there are currently 27 million slaves in the world.[18]

Although one might argue that chronic persistence does not necessarily entail easy accomplishment, it would not seem illogical to suppose that it is not very difficult to enslave people; indeed, it seems to have been, and still be, shockingly easy. Resisting enslavement is another matter, to which Finley's remark draws our attention. In this book I attempt to illustrate how slaves in antiquity sometimes did succeed in rebelling.

In his book on slave revolts in the New World, Genovese identified conditions in which uprisings were more probable.[19] They were: where the master–slave relationship had deteriorated; where there was economic distress and division between the masters; where there were large slave-holding units, in which slaves heavily outnumbered masters;

where most of the slaves were free-born; where there arose opportunities for slaves to become leaders; and lastly where the geography of the area enabled the slaves to hide.[20] Some of these factors overlap but Genovese's list provides a useful starting-point for this study. As we shall see, many of these conditions hold true for those episodes of slave rebellion in the ancient world about which we have evidence. They are especially true of the period of history during which the most famous episodes took place: the later Roman Republic.

Some issues faced by the historian of antiquity have apparent parallels in the slave revolts of more recent times. Cross-cultural resemblances can be very misleading, and it is easy to draw entirely mistaken conclusions from seemingly similar sets of circumstances. The classicist or ancient historian who teaches both Greek and Roman material is used to remaining conscious of the wide gap between the two societies of Athens and Rome and the dangers of anachronistic assumptions. The difference between antiquity and the New World, for instance, is many times greater and it is beyond question that one must be alert to the perils of drawing simplistic parallels. It cannot be denied, on the other hand, that some issues faced by slaves and slave-owners were not unique to their own historical period, and that therefore it would be unnecessarily restrictive never to refer to, or to consider, other periods of history.[21] Therefore, while remaining conscious of the dangers of looking at modern material in order to speculate about the situation in the ancient world, it is worth remembering that there is a long tradition of scholars of slavery looking at other cultures to help them at least suggest possibilities for the ancient world. Mark Golden's remark is apposite:

> Of course, reports on other cultures cannot in themselves replace missing data for Greece and Rome, but they can be useful all the same in providing models of the working methods of investigators into other cultures, in developing hypotheses, in identifying patterns from scattered scraps, in refuting generalizations.[22]

There was a huge number of armed uprisings by slaves in more recent history and we have quite a substantial amount of information on them. For instance, as Patterson notes in his article about slave revolts on Jamaica in the seventeenth and eighteenth centuries:

> Few slave societies present a more impressive record of slave revolts than Jamaica. During the more than 180 years of its existence as

a slave society, hardly a decade went by without a serious, large-scale revolt threatening the entire system. Between these larger efforts were numerous minor skirmishes, endless plots, individual acts of violence against the master and other forms of resistance, all of which constantly pressed upon the white ruling class the fact that the system was a very precarious one, held together entirely by the exercise, or threat of brute force.[23]

Genovese, surveying the revolts in the Caribbean and South America in his chapter "Slave Revolts in Hemispheric Perspective", was trying to account for why there seemed to have been fewer revolts in the southern states in the United States in the same approximate time period than in these other slave societies.[24] He asked, "Were the slaves in the United Sates unwilling or simply unable to rise in large numbers?"[25] He concluded that there were fewer revolts for a mixture of factors, one of the most important being that the proportion of slave to free in the United States was much lower than in these more volatile places.

Herbert Aptheker's earlier study of American slave revolts had a different focus. While admitting that the huge uprisings seen elsewhere were not present in the United States, he found from his study of the primary sources of the period that there had been more instances of rebellion than had previously been assumed. His meticulous study reveals a heavy reliance on personal letters and contemporary newspapers, exactly the sort of primary source not extant from the ancient world. Even with this type of evidence, the modern historian faces, as Aptheker illustrated, exaggeration, distortion and censorship, which we can see more clearly in the modern world because of the nature of the evidence we do have remaining.[26] Aptheker's conclusions would seem almost as appropriate for the ancient as for the modern world:

> Yet, it is highly probable that all plots, and quite possibly even all actual outbreaks, that did occur, and that are, somewhere, on record, have *not* been uncovered. And the subject is of such a nature that it appears almost certain that some, perhaps many, occurred and were never recorded.[27]

From his examination of these primary sources, Aptheker showed that there were more slave revolts in the United States than had previously been thought and his book is a careful documentation of all the episodes for which he found evidence. He observed that: "The evidence, on the contrary, points to the conclusion that discontent and rebelliousness were not only exceedingly common, but, indeed, characteristic of American Negro slaves".[28]

One is faced with the issue of what counts as a slave revolt. It has been objected that some of the episodes that Aptheker describes are very minor and hardly count as revolts. The bibliography, for example, on Nat Turner, the leader of the slave uprising in Virginia in the 1830s, is considerable and yet we read in a recent book on the topic:

> The revolt was short, *lasting little more than a day*. Although panic spread throughout the South, major violence was confined to Southampton County. The number of people directly involved was limited – 60 to 80 active rebels who killed no more than 57 to 60 whites, and an infuriated white population who retaliated by summarily executing scores, if not hundreds of blacks.[29]

Compared to the ancient revolts, this was a very short-lived insurrection, involving very few slaves. If it had happened in ancient times it is extremely likely that it would not be recorded in any of the texts we have left. And yet for modern historians, Nat Turner's uprising is necessary for our understanding of slavery of the time. To demand a quota for those involved, or a timescale in order to classify revolts and uprisings is beside the point. What Aptheker had wanted to discover was: were the slaves simply content to be slaves or did they try to escape their servitude? His conclusion was that they did indeed take every opportunity to gain their freedom. What Nat Turner's revolt illustrates is that slaves were prepared to take extreme action to gain their freedom, as they have always done when possible.

In antiquity, particularly during the time of the Roman Republic, many (but not all) slaves were prisoners of war, so that they owed their slave status to the fact that they had been defeated militarily. The Romans understood their word for slave as deriving from this fact. The etymology of "servus" is discussed in the compilation of laws, the *Digest*, in the following terms:

> Slaves (*servi*) are so called because commanders generally sell the people they capture and thereby save (*servare*) them instead of killing them. The word for property in slaves (*manicipia*) is derived from the fact that they are captured from the enemy by force of arms (*manu capiantur*).[30]

That is, slaves were people who otherwise would have been killed.[31] This might have led to a psychological situation where they felt much less powerful than slaves who had merely been captured and sold. On the other hand, if they had once been soldiers they would have had more experience in what it took to form and lead armies. The initial band of men who rebelled with Spartacus were trained fighters, that is, gladiators, although the great mass of their army were not. The victories of the Spartacan armies were almost incredible since the Romans had in recent years conquered most of the lands surrounding the Mediterranean, and yet for three years or so, this imperial force was unable to crush the slave rebels who, in massive numbers, marched the length of Italy.

My aim in this book is to look more closely at the organization, courage and persistence identified by Finley in the quotation above, and to see what historical circumstances were most beneficial for an attempt at resistance. In another work, Finley writes:

> In the whole of history there have been only four slave revolts on the scale of a genuine war, with many thousands of men under arms on both sides, with battles between field armies, with the siege and occupation of cities: the three in Sicily and Italy in the period 140–70 BC and the great revolt in Haiti which coincided with, and must be viewed as a by-product of, the French Revolution. Only the latter, headed by free blacks and mulattoes, was successful.[32]

His last sentence might seem to imply that it is the presence of non-slaves that helped the modern rebellion, perhaps indicating that he saw the actions of slaves as ineffective unless aided by the free. His views about the overall failure of the slave rebellions of antiquity reflect a consensus among ancient historians, which has resulted in a general lack of interest or at least lack of attention.

Yet one of the most striking features of this topic is that ancient writers thought the slave uprising were far more significant than modern commentators do. In Chapter 8 I shall discuss how ancient writers viewed the revolts in the Roman Republic and the impact the uprisings had on events at the time. Given the ease with which people have always been enslaved, I wish first to look at how the participants in the revolts not only took action, but maintained their revolt for several years in some cases. Chapter 2, therefore, is on the circumstances of the outbreaks of rebellions and asks whether there are common features discernible in the historical situation that tended to be favourable to slave rebellion like those Genovese observed for the modern world. Chapter 3 deals with how the armies maintained their revolt, and Chapter 4 looks at the leaders that emerged, and how their personalities have been recorded by our historians. Chapter 5 is about the aims of the slaves and the attitudes to freedom and slavery in antiquity that the slaves may be assumed to have shared.

The problem of the interpretation of source material is immense, as will become apparent in the course of this examination. Nevertheless there were some unusual individuals in the ancient world, such as the historian Diodorus Siculus, who, for whatever reason, presented a sympathetic picture of the slaves of Sicily; without his work, any study of slave revolts would be far briefer than this. Chapter 6 concentrates on this unusual writer.

2
Preparing for revolt

In the second half of the second century BCE the Romans virtually lost control of their first overseas province for almost a decade, not to Carthaginians, from whom they had won Sicily in the first place, but to the slaves whom they had imported to work the land. They had won a series of wars against neighbours in the Mediterranean and Rome's rise to power in hindsight looked unstoppable, and yet this valuable source of revenue, the island of Sicily, a great wheat-producing area, was nearly snatched from them, not by a Hannibal or a Mithridates, but by slaves.[1]

The first slave war on Sicily

Diodorus Siculus, who is our main source, tells us that the war started around 141 BCE.[2] He reports that when the servile war started, Sicily had enjoyed about sixty years of prosperity after the destruction of Carthage.[3] The Third Punic War ended with the complete physical obliteration of the city of Carthage in 146 BCE, but he cannot be referring to this. The Second Punic War, which ended the Carthaginian presence in Sicily, had finished in 201 BCE; this is sixty years before 141 BCE. Sometimes 135 BCE is given as the year the war started, but then one must ask why Diodorus did not tell us that it was seventy years after the destruction of Carthage.[4] So our fullest source for the war, Diodorus, who gives us a fairly precise date, would have us believe it started in the late 140s BCE and that it ended about a decade later.

Roman armies were sent out to defeat the rebel slaves and eventually they succeeded. The fact that the uprising took place in Sicily made it especially worrying because the possibility of the whole island being under slave control was a real one and the Roman authority there was certainly greatly threatened. As Diodorus tells the story, the basic outline is as follows. In the first half of the second century BCE, vast numbers of slaves had been imported into Sicily to work the farms and look after animals. There were so many that the masters could not properly provide, or at least had not provided, basic necessities such as food and clothing, so the slaves turned to mugging travellers and took control of many of the roads in Sicily, terrorizing the inhabitants of the island.[5]

Diodorus' narrative describes a split in the ruling class quite clearly and explicitly when giving details of the Roman governors' unhappiness at gangs of slaves roaming the countryside but not daring to remedy the situation because they were scared of the masters. Most of the great landowners were Roman *equites* (i.e. members of the equestrian order) and as *equites* were also jurors in cases against Roman governors accused of maladministration, it was not in the interests of governors to alienate them, writes Diodorus.[6] Gaius Gracchus' reform giving the equestrian order control of the courts was not until 122 BCE, leading modern commentators to dismiss Diodorus' account as simply incorrect.[7] However, the issue of antagonism between the Roman officials and the local landowners might not be inaccurate.

The presence of gangs of slaves at large in the countryside clearly was unsatisfactory from an administrative perspective. Yet from the selfish point of view of the individual slave-owner, providing enough food and clothing for what were clearly large numbers of slaves may have presented problems. In another passage Diodorus relates how those who learnt of the huge numbers of slaves in Sicily could not believe the figures.[8] His description of the situation on Sicily at this time is accepted as generally accurate, since the rapid but enormous expansion of Roman power in the Mediterranean had resulted in a massive influx of slaves into territory controlled by the Romans.[9]

Some slaves in Enna were so badly treated by a particular couple, that they plotted revenge. Diodorus focuses on this Sicilian couple, Damophilus and Megallis, and sees their ill treatment of their slaves as the trigger that started the rebellion.[10] Diodorus tells us that this couple were so brutal that their slaves plotted to kill them. But they seem also to have larger ambitions as they did not simply just murder their masters but went to Eunus, one of the slaves in the area, who was well respected as someone with self-professed connections to the divine, since he was able to perform sleights of hand. They asked his advice about rebelling and he replied that if they proceeded without delay, they would be successful. They did so and were.

After this outbreak, more slaves rose up against their masters on another part of the island, led by Cleon who was from Cilicia. They were also successful and took Acragas (Agrigentum, on the south coast, west of Enna). There followed a series of victories for both sets of rebels, who joined forces, and with each victory attracted more followers.[11] Diodorus tells us that this insurrection on Sicily inspired others: 150 slaves in Rome took up arms; more than a thousand did so in Attica; and there was an outbreak on Delos and "in many other places".[12] We learn from Orosius the names of some of the places in Italy:

> What is more, the contagious disease of the Sicilian slave war infected many provinces far and wide. At Minturnae 450 slaves were crucified. At Sinuessa, an uprising of about 4,000 was crushed by Quintus Metellus and Gnaeus Servilius Caepio. A revolt of slaves in the mines at Athens was repressed by the praetor, Heraclitus. On the island of Delos, slaves who were about to break out in a new revolt were repressed by the preemptive actions taken by the citizens of the island. All of these other incidents were caused by the first source of this evil in Sicily, which scattered the embers, so to speak, that sparked the other fires.[13]

Orosius' account is extremely cursory and he does not say exactly when these other uprisings took place. The late Roman recorder of prodigies, Julius Obsequens, gives uprisings of slaves in Italy for the years 134 and 132 BCE and these may be the ones referred to by Orosius,[14] but it is possible that these are different ones and that slaves had rebelled earlier in these other locations. It makes tactical sense for slaves to take advantage of other slave uprisings or in fact any military activity, to take action themselves. The more fronts on which the Romans had to fight, the more chance of success the slaves had. Livy, for instance, comments on the contemporaneity of events in the early second century: "When these events were taking place in Greece, Macedonia and Asia, a slave conspiracy created great danger in Etruria".[15] In the case of the Sicilians, one may suppose that it was at least in part due to the continued efforts of the slaves on the mainland that the war in Sicily lasted as long as it did. However it seems that the longest lasting of the revolts contemporary with the Sicilian one was in Pergamum.

Julius Obsequens includes the slave wars in his lists of strange happenings.[16] He collected, probably in the fourth or fifth centuries CE, Roman portents for the period 249–12 BCE, although we only have those left for 190–12 BCE. He is thought to have used Livy for this work and thus it may be deemed to be reliable information. The portents include bolts of lightning, volcanoes erupting, hermaphrodites, the birth of deformed children, statues crying and slave revolts.[17]

In Sicily in the 130s BCE, from Diodorus' account, one can observe that there was alienation of the slaves from their masters, large numbers of free-born slaves, a split in the ruling class and leaders ready to present themselves to the slaves: generally, most of the conditions identified by Genovese as present when slaves successfully rebel. The picture drawn by Appian of the period leading to the tribunate of Tiberius Gracchus is one of large landholding units worked by slaves, so we also have the condition of large numbers of slaves in the same workplace, able to communicate with each other and able to organize.[18]

Not only did the slaves succeed in forming an effective army but their cause was supported by free people of Sicily, poor citizens who turned against the slave-owners. Diodorus describes how they welcomed the reversals of the wealthy because for a long time they had resented their wealth and arrogance. He adds that whereas the slaves were careful not to damage property or harvests, and not to harm those working on the land, the free rebels used the slave uprising as a pretext for rampaging over the estates, destroying crops and burning buildings.[19]

For 134 BCE when the consuls were Publius Africanus and Gaius Fulvius Flaccus (the latter being the man Livy reported was sent to Sicily when the praetors could not deal with the war), Julius Obsequens reports that the sun was seen by night, an ox spoke, there was a rain of blood, the tunic of a slave caught fire but when the flames died down there was no trace of a burn, on the Capitol a bird at night groaned like a human being, in the temple of Juno a Ligurian shield was struck by lightning, and finally war broke out in Sicily and another conspiracy of slaves in Italy was suppressed.[20] In his short entry for 132 BCE, he writes that, when Publius Popillius and Publius Rupilius were consuls, many thousands of slaves in Italy were suppressed with difficulty, in Sicily the slaves slaughtered Roman armies and Numantia was razed.[21]

What is to be noted here is that in the entries for both years, he recorded uprisings of slaves in both Sicily and Italy.[22] In both cases, the Italian revolts were crushed, but the Sicilian ones were not. We have far more knowledge of the Sicilian uprising because of the greater success of the slaves on Sicily and because of Diodorus' natural interest in the place, as well as presumably an ease on his part in obtaining information about it. However, it is necessary not to lose sight of revolts elsewhere; those further away from Rome may not have been suppressed as quickly as they otherwise might have been, because troops were dealing with threats even closer to the centre.

Slave unrest in the East

We do not have detailed information about most of the slave revolts that appeared in places other than Sicily and they all seem to have been crushed fairly swiftly. The one other uprising about which we do know more and that does seem to have been more successful than the others was that in Pergamum. Here also we are told that the slaves had the support of free people, as in Sicily, because of the circumstances at the time: the kingdom had been left to the Romans by the king in his will. Consequently, those inhabitants of Pergamum who objected to this would have joined in the revolt. Indeed scholars have recently seen this as more of a nationalist uprising against the Romans than a slave revolt.[23] However, Diodorus quite explicitly states that slaves were involved and would seem to attribute importance to their cause:

> The result [of the maltreatment of slaves in Sicily] was that, without any communication between themselves, tens of thousands of slaves joined forces to kill their masters. Almost the identical thing happened in Asia at the same time, when Aristonicus claimed the kingship that was not rightly his. Because their masters had treated them so terribly, the slaves in Asia joined Aristonicus and were the cause of great disasters to many unfortunate cities.[24]

He makes a direct connection between the activity in Pergamum and the slave war in Sicily. He recorded the first outbreak of the first Sicilian slave war and attributed it to the bad treatment of the slaves by their masters.[25] He comments that as a result they reacted violently when they had the opportunity, and that tens of thousands spontaneously rebelled. In the next sentence he remarks that similar events took place elsewhere, when slaves rebelled in the East. That is, at the same time as the slave war in Sicily, there was one in Asia Minor, although the situation in Pergamum was not exactly the same as Sicily. Diodorus reported, however, quite clearly, that something *similar* happened at the same time, and was quite precise in saying that the slaves rebelled.

The situation arose in the following way. In 133 BCE Attalus III of Pergamum died, leaving his kingdom to the Roman people in his will, while requesting that the city of Pergamum be free. Aristonicus, the illegitimate son of Attalus' father, Eumenes, therefore half-brother of the dead king, took advantage of an uprising of the slaves and formed an army to resist the Romans.[26] Claiming that he was the true heir to the kingdom, for a while he had control of a large part of the area, only to be eventually defeated by the Romans four years later in 129 BCE. The area became the Roman province of Asia.

Even this brief outline has been challenged. For example, Sallust has recorded a different interpretation of the trigger for these events in the letter of Mithridates, in which the misdeeds of the Romans are listed. Mithridates, writing to the king of the Parthians, Arsaces, as recorded by Sallust, attributes only one motive for the actions of the Romans, that is greed for power and money.[27] He then proceeds to list examples of these actions and, in describing the events in Asia Minor, writes:

> Later, having made him [Eumenes] the guardian of a captured territory, they transformed him by means of expense and insults from a king into the most wretched of slaves. Then, having forged an unnatural will, they led his son, Aristonicus in triumph like an enemy, because he had tried to recover his father's rights.[28]

The sources that remain are thus rather critical of Roman conduct in this episode. More importantly for the discussion here, however, both Diodorus and Strabo report that Aristonicus was supported by slaves. It is almost as an afterthought that Strabo records any information about Aristonicus at all since he had not mentioned him in the more obvious place while discussing Pergamum and its kings, where he had related its history as far as the death of Attalus.[29] Instead, we learn about Aristonicus in the description of Leucae, a place for which it would seem Strabo did not have many details, for it is here that we learn about the revolt, and not much else. Strabo writes that, after being defeated in a naval battle, Aristonicus went inland and gathered a large army of poor people and of slaves, whom he enticed with the promise of freedom and whom he called Heliopolitae.[30]

Aristonicus, like other individuals involved in slave uprisings in antiquity, was not a slave; even though Plutarch is derogatory about his birth,[31] he was the illegitimate son of the king's father, Eumenes. Diodorus observes that the slaves were alienated by their maltreatment and joined the rebellion out of anger. In other words, the situation seems to have been that the slaves had already rebelled and that these rebels joined forces with Aristonicus. In any case, the way that Diodorus reports the episode, it is not that Aristonicus recruited slaves because he promised them freedom, but rather they had been badly treated and so joined the revolt.[32] This may or may not be a true analysis but, in his narrative, we see the slaves as active agents, not merely pawns in the power struggle of a weakened dynasty.

In Pergamum, the uprising lasted as long as it did (133–129 BCE) because the ruling class in the region was split between those in favour of the legacy leaving the kingdom to Rome, and those opposing it. In places other than Sicily it would have been the case that all the elements of society, apart from the slaves, were united in putting down the individual revolts. That is, although slaves who rose up against their masters elsewhere helped the rebels in Sicily, they themselves were overwhelmed by the forces against them. In Pergamum the situation was more like that in Sicily in that the region was clearly split between those who supported the Romans, or at least saw opportunities for themselves under their protection, and those who objected to the dramatic last will and testament of their king. This split presented the slaves with an opportunity to exploit, and consequently this particular rebellion was more successful and long-lasting.

Other revolts

The eventual Roman victory over the armies of slaves in the first slave revolt on Sicily did not succeed in crushing the slaves' hopes of freedom, and some thirty years later there was a second damaging slave war in Sicily. The thirty years between the two great wars also saw several episodes of slave rebellion. These seem to have been relatively short-lived but the impression given is that the period was extremely volatile. As observed earlier, revolt, regardless of the final outcome, gives hope to others, often sparking further unrest, and this certainly seems to have been the case here.

Diodorus, who again is the main source of information about this war, reports that at the same time as the Romans had defeated Jugurtha and had had defeats in Gaul against the Cimbri, that is in 104 BCE, news came to Rome of another uprising of slaves in Sicily.[33] Diodorus comments that even before this time there had been indications of unrest. Slaves in Italy had rebelled as if a sign from the gods of what was about to happen: "Even *before* the new uprising of the slaves in Sicily there had occurred in Italy a number of short-lived and minor revolts, as though the supernatural were indicating in advance the magnitude of the impending Sicilian disaster".[34] The first was at Nuceria, south of Nola and west of Pompeii, but only thirty slaves were involved and they were immediately stopped. The second was at Capua where 200 rose up but again they were crushed. The third was bigger, involving hundreds, and Diodorus gives us more details about this one, although not about where it took place. His lack of precision may be due to the fact that it took place in the same area as the previous revolt he had described, that is, Capua.

This third revolt in Diodorus' account, which is reported at most length, is a rather unconvincing tale of a love-sick individual called Titus Vettius Minutius. The son of a wealthy father, he was a young man of the rank of *equites*, who fell in love with a slave and tried to buy her but could not afford her. Since we have already been told that his father was rich, this seems a little strange. As Diodorus writes: "Since he was still ablaze with love for the woman, he did something that was against all reason: he concocted plots against his creditors and began to claim the powers of a king".[35] What is perhaps stronger evidence for his loss of sanity is that he flogged and beheaded his creditors, armed 400 of his own slaves (and again this would seem to imply he had quite substantial wealth himself), and soon acquired a following of more than three and a half thousand rebellious slaves. The Senate sent out one of the praetors, Lucius Lucullus, who took 600 conscripts from Rome and at Capua summoned 4,000 infantry and 400 cavalry. By persuading one of the rebel commanders to betray his own side, Lucullus and his army gained the upper hand and all the rebels cut their own throats.[36]

We can see that the story of this uprising was passed down to us because of the moral nature of it – that is, the dangers of not being able to control oneself, of being a slave to one's emotions – nevertheless, we have the seeds of yet another uprising of slaves, whatever the motives of the leader. The point is that whatever the intentions of Vettius Minutius, arming so many slaves had consequences far beyond one Roman noble either losing his senses from desire, or trying to escape his debts. One might imagine that such a story developed in order for the Romans to understand for themselves why one of their own took up with slaves. They could only understand it if the man was carried away by lust, just as the suggestion was put forward that Spartacus had been trained by the Romans. Only that could explain his huge success.

Keith Bradley makes some thought-provoking remarks concerning Diodorus' narrative about these minor slave uprisings preceding the second big war in Sicily:

> Diodorus, however, saw the three episodes as intimations of the war that was about to come in Sicily soon afterwards, just as he believed that the earlier revolts in Italy, Attica, and Delos were triggered by news of the first war. Similarly, Orosius wrote of sparks flying from Sicily to ignite servile unrest in Attica and Delos. With the benefit of hindsight such connections were easily made. *But they are not credible. Most of the incidents are better understood as purely isolated responses to slavery of the sort that could occur at any time, as indeed had happened in the second century* ....[37]

However, it would seem plausible that when slaves learnt of other uprisings, as they must have, this might give them ideas to attempt the same. Bradley does not put forward any evidence to support his statement and, as Joseph Vogt points out, slaves were generally central to the transmission of news in ancient society, being the messengers both public and private.[38] It is true that if masters had not wanted slaves to know some information then they may have employed free men to transmit certain messages. However, given the ubiquity of slaves in every aspect of life in the ancient world, significant events could not be kept secret from all of them. The isolated responses to slavery that occurred during the second century may well not have been as isolated as our scanty sources might imply.

Another revolt, this time recorded by Athenaeus, also took place at the same time as the second uprising in Sicily.[39] This was again in Laureion, the Athenian silver mines.[40] Athenaeus writes that he acquired this information from Posidonius, who reported that they revolted, murdered their overseers and took the hill of Sunium, and for a long time plundered Attica. He goes on to state that there were many of these uprisings and that more than a million slaves were killed.[41] He adds that Caecilius wrote a treatise on the slave wars that would have included the details of the Athenian uprising, which, according to Posidonius, lasted a long time.[42]

The account for the second war, as preserved by Photius, gives the background information needed to understand the immediate outbreak of revolt in Sicily. It started with Marius' campaigns against the Germanic tribe, the Cimbri, who had been very successful against the Romans. In 105 BCE the Roman army had suffered a terrible defeat against the Germanic tribes. This defeat scared the Romans so much that Marius was given a second consulship to deal with the threat from the north. Marius had been given permission to ask for help from overseas so he approached Nicomedes, the king of Bithynia. Nicomedes refused, saying that he could not comply because most of his countrymen had been enslaved by Roman government contractors.[43] This improbable reply was not taken as a joke but rather seems to have reflected some reality because the Senate passed a decree saying no citizen of an allied state could be enslaved in a Roman province and if they had been, the governors of the provinces were to set them free.[44]

Consequently, the governor of Sicily at this time, Licinius Nerva, immediately set about releasing those who had been free citizens of allied states and, in a few days, freed more than 800 individuals. This encouraged all slaves in Sicily, comments Diodorus.[45] As in the account of the first war, he comments on the split between the Roman authorities and the local elite; the latter objected to seeing their property walking off and protested to the governor, urging him to stop freeing their slaves. Diodorus writes that Nerva was "persuaded by the money [of the slave-owners] or *enslaved* by their patronage".[46] There is hardly a huge difference between being bribed and being forced by the influence of local grandees, except perhaps Diodorus wishes to draw attention again to the "enslavement" of the Romans and the dangerous consequences of it, as he does elsewhere.

Whatever the reason, Nerva did cease his hearings and ordered all the slaves back to their masters. Having had their hopes raised in this way only to be dashed, the slaves fled to the sanctuary of the Palikoi. These were twin gods who avenged perjury and, more importantly here, the shrine of the Palikoi was a traditional place slaves fled to from their masters to escape ill treatment.[47] Here they plotted to revolt.[48]

Diodorus writes that at the shrine they talked about revolt and, in the next sentence, that in many places the daring of the slaves became clear.[49] However, the first slaves to make their bid for freedom were near Halicyae, in the extreme north-west of the island. About thirty slaves, owned by two very wealthy brothers who lived near Halicyae, were the first to rebel, led by a man named Varius. Their numbers escalated.

The governor, being unable to quell the uprising, used the services of a traitor, whom the rebels in their ignorance welcomed because he had a reputation as a friend of the slaves; they made him their commander but he then betrayed them.[50] Those who were not killed in the fighting threw themselves off a cliff and for a short time it looked as if the situation had been contained. But although this first set of rebels had been defeated, the setback, far from dispiriting others, seems rather to have encouraged them to try something similar.

The second slave war on Sicily

The island would have had to have been restocked with slaves after the first war and for once we have a clear statement from our ancient sources that many of the slaves in Sicily had once been free. The original release of 800 slaves gave hope to *all* enslaved on the island, writes Diodorus.[51] It seems improbable that every slave on the island had been a citizen of an allied state of Rome.[52] However, the Senate's decision gives some indication that wrongful mass enslavement had been going on. Given the frequent wars Rome had been engaged in prior to the revolt, it seems safe to say that a dangerously large proportion of the slaves involved in the uprising on Sicily had been free-born. The slaves would have been able to communicate with each other easily if the Romans had not taken care to distribute the different ethnic groups into diverse holdings. We have no evidence that they did, and it seems unlikely that such a division had taken place, given the situation described on Sicily. Consequently, many of the conditions favourable to a successful uprising were once again present on the island.

Diodorus once again describes a split between the governor and the slave-owners, who had put pressure on him in effect to stop enforcing the Senate's decree. Perhaps more importantly the Romans were short of soldiers: they had suffered the damaging defeat at Arausio against the German tribes and in an attempt to meet this threat, and given the shortage of eligible men to enlist, the Roman army was now open to men without the land qualification. To the outsider, to slaves, this must have looked like desperation. And amid these problems, the slaves took their opportunity and took it effectively, rapidly and forcefully.

Again they were successful for a considerable length of time. Diodorus tells us that the second slave war lasted four years (104–100 BCE). Soon after the attempt at rebellion near Halicyae had failed, eighty slaves banded together and killed their master, a Roman knight and started to organize themselves, collecting further recruits.[53] Diodorus' explanation for their success was that the governor, because he had already released his army, did not take swift enough action. The slaves were able to seize on this; they called the governor a coward, incited more to join them and within seven days had armed more than 800 men. Soon after this they numbered 2,000.

When the governor, who was now in Herakleia, realized the numbers involved he sent Marcus Titinius 600 soldiers from the garrison at Enna, but these troops were defeated by the slaves.[54] Diodorus writes that the surviving Roman soldiers saved themselves only by abandoning their weapons and running away from the battle. The slaves thus increased their weapon supply and confidence.

> Now all the slaves were encouraged by the prospect of rebellion. As more and more men turned to rebellion with every passing day, there was a sudden and unexpected increase in their number, with the result that, within a few days, they were more than six thousand.[55]

Once again Diodorus' account describes revolts as giving others the courage to take similar action. Here the slaves had taken swift and effective measures. Diodorus writes that after the slaves near Halicyae had been overcome, the governor disbanded his soldiers. However, in his description of that uprising it seemed that he did not have many in the first place. It was, according to Diodorus, because he could not take the rebel slaves by force that he turned to treachery, persuading a local bandit to help him conquer them. It seems then that the lack of forces had been obvious to other slaves, who took this opportunity to rise up, proclaim the weakness of the Romans and thus quickly draw others to their army with little difficulty. The slaves here showed shrewdness, a correct assessment of the situation and rapid action, which worked.

Opportunity for Spartacus and the gladiators

Thirty years later the Romans were also facing severe problems. They had been engaged in a damaging war against the Italians; had experienced a civil war where one of their best generals, Sulla, and his army marched on Rome; had seen another, Sertorius, set himself up independently in Spain; and, lastly, were facing the threat of a hostile king, Mithridates, in the east.

Against this backdrop, in 73 BCE a small group of gladiators broke out of their gladiatorial school in Capua. In the *Life of Crassus* Plutarch describes how some gladiators were unjustly imprisoned. Because of this treatment, 200 of them had planned an escape, but only seventy-eight succeeded in breaking out. They had armed themselves with kitchen implements but once free came upon wagons containing weapons for gladiators, which they seized.

They elected three leaders, Spartacus, Crixus and Oenomaus. Plutarch writes that Spartacus was the most important and Appian states that he was the main general and the others were his subordinate officers.[56] This band of gladiators was quickly joined by slaves and free men from the area. Their army had a series of major successes against the Roman armies that were sent out to put them down; the slaves acquired more followers and travelled the length of Italy, reaching Mutina in the north and then turning back to the extreme south. Even after the defeat by Marcus Licinius Crassus, and further round-ups by Pompey, there were slaves still alive in 61 BCE, more than ten years later, who were described as the remnants of this rebel army; Suetonius describes the father of the Emperor Augustus as having defeated them.[57]

The remarkable success of this slave army must have been helped by the alienation of the Italians from the Romans. In his account of the Mithridatic War, Appian comments that the Italians had sided with Spartacus, even though he was a wholly disreputable person, against the Romans, so great was their hatred for them.[58] The survival of this slave army for such a length of time, on the Italian peninsula, the core of the Roman Empire, bears witness to the truth of this. The slaves had judged the situation carefully, and one might venture to suggest that this is why they did not leave Italy as they were apparently expected to.

Slaves continued to be caught up in the further unravelling of the Roman political system and we have no way of knowing how many fled, or achieved their freedom, during this troubled time. The concentration of our authors naturally was not on what happened to the slaves, although there are flashes of information, such as Augustus' boast: "I made the sea peaceful and freed it of pirates. In that war I captured about 30,000 slaves who had escaped from their masters and taken up arms against the republic, and I handed them over to their masters for punishment".[59] When free people appealed to slaves to help them, they were drawing on the acknowledged hostility slaves felt for their masters. Slaves often were involved, or seen as a danger, during the clashes between citizens. Sallust tells us that in 63 BCE the Senate ordered that gladiators be removed from Rome and sent to Capua and other outlying Italian cities since they were fearful of the possible use made of them by Catiline and his followers.[60]

In the troubled time of the early 40s BCE, we have evidence again of the perceived danger posed by gladiators. Caesar had sent an ultimatum to Pompey, which was accepted on condition that Caesar withdrew his garrison from towns he had occupied outside his own province. Pompey had Caesar's gladiators distributed to individuals since there were 5,000 of them in a school and they were thought to be planning a breakout. Cicero reporting from Capua in January 49 BCE, wrote a letter about this dangerous situation.[61] Caesar himself refers to this incident and says that the consul Lentulus brought Caesar's gladiators to the forum and tried to bribe them to follow him with promises of freedom and gifts of horses. Because he was criticized for this he changed his mind, and divided up the troupe and distributed them throughout Campania.[62] We are told that in 44 BCE gladiators were on the side of the conspirators and waited at the theatre of Pompey, ready to come to their aid if any senators offered resistance when the attack on Caesar was made.[63]

The increasing split within the slave-holding layer of society of the late Republic resulted in years of civil wars. The change of regime and the establishment of the principate was the solution to this unrest and, after this, there was much greater control over the richer members of the citizen body, the provinces and the armies. The monarchical system ended the relative freedom of the republican system and with it the splits that the increasing wealth of the empire had caused. Also, with the new order came a much slower expansion of the territory of the empire. The tighter control of the imperial bureaucracy resulted in fewer slave revolts. Slaves did still make attempts to escape and resist but with less dramatic results than previously. It may be that the threat that they had posed was recognized and dealt with but, in any event, nothing on the scale of the Spartacan rebellion happened again.[64]

Tacitus tells us that in 21 CE, gladiators were involved in an uprising against Rome. They joined Sacrovir, a Gallic leader, who seized Augustodunum, but this uprising failed, so he retreated and then killed himself.[65] A little later, when describing events for the year 24 CE, Tacitus reports that a slave war, led by one Titus Curtisius, a former Roman soldier, in Brundisium, was only averted by accident.[66] Tacitus finishes his report of this near rebellion saying how much fear this caused in Rome, since the number of slaves had vastly increased, while that of free inhabitants had diminished.

Later, in the *Annals* for the year 61 CE, the same historian tells us of the outbreak of gladiators in Praeneste that was crushed, but that caused alarm and made people talk of Spartacus "in gossip by the people, eager and anxious as ever, for revolutionary disturbances".[67] He goes on to list a series of incidents, the calamity of lost ships, and then, in the following chapter, portents, lightning, a comet and a two-headed baby.[68] One assumes that Tacitus lists all these mishaps to demonstrate just how cursed Nero's reign was. In other words, we learn about slave revolts by accident because they are added to indicate that Nero was a bad emperor, in the same way that we hear about the birth of a deformed child.

Opportunities in Sparta

Slave revolts were not confined to the Roman world, although these are the most thoroughly documented. The most famous example from antiquity of war between masters and their workforce is between the Spartans and their helots, perhaps because Sparta was the enemy of Athens at a time when virtually all our literature comes from Athens. However, the picture drawn is quick action on the part of the slaves, the recognition of a suitable opportunity and the unhesitating readiness to seize it.[69] Indeed, the ancient commentators themselves described this. Aristotle says quite explicitly that the helots who often rebelled lay in wait to take advantage of Spartan misfortune.[70] He goes on to explain that this did not happen in Crete because the Cretans' neighbours did not side with the rebels (presumably being an island was helpful here), whereas Sparta was surrounded by enemies.[71]

Thucydides describes how, in 464 BCE, helots and *perioikoi* took advantage of an earthquake to revolt and he says that the rebels held out for ten years with their centre on Mount Ithome.[72] So here, seeing the chaos caused by an earthquake the helots took their chance successfully to escape their servitude, not temporarily but permanently. The Spartans, because they could not defeat them, appealed to their allies, including the Athenians, to come to their aid. They later sent the latter home again, fearing that they might be persuaded by the helots to help them instead. Not only were the rebels not defeated but the situation was only resolved when they were allowed to leave the area and settle in Naupactus at the entrance to the Peloponnese, where they remained loyal allies to the Athenians.[73] In other words, here we have an example of a successful revolt.[74]

A very similar episode is about a much earlier time, although reported later by Athenaeus, who wrote that someone called Malacus, in his *Annals of Siphnos*:

> tells the story of how some slaves of the Samians, a thousand in number, founded the city of Ephesus. These men had previously withdrawn to the mountain which is on the island of Samos and done the Samians a lot of harm. But as the result of an oracle, the Samians made a truce with these slaves in the sixth year of their revolt, on certain conditions; they were allowed to leave unharmed and sailed away from the island, landing at Ephesus. The Ephesians are their descendents.[75]

We learn here, again incidentally, of a successful rebellion by slaves to escape servitude. One might object that it is probably not true, and it was certainly a long time before Athenaeus' life, but what is of significance here is that this is recorded as if it were a fact that the Ephesians are descended from rebellious slaves. It must have been an occurrence that could have happened for readers to accept this.

Throughout the period of the Peloponnesian War, 431–404 BCE, there were several episodes where Spartan action was affected by the threat of revolt or by actual rebellion on the part of their helots.[76] So again we can see that the helots were aware that external wars could help their cause. The Athenian victory at Pylos in 425 BCE was due to the intervention of the Messenians.[77] The Athenian general Demosthenes wanted to stop at Pylos, as he and his colleagues took their fleet to Corcyra, precisely because of its position. Thucydides states that Demosthenes had thought that: "the Messenians, whose country this used to be, and who spoke the same dialect as the Spartans, were capable, he thought, of doing a lot of damage if they had this place as a base, and would also be a very reliable garrison for it".[78] The Spartans shared his view; once they heard that the Athenians had landed there, they hurried back from Attica after only fifteen days, and immediately (εὐθυς) headed off to regain Pylos,[79] sending orders to the Peloponnesian allies to come as quickly as possible.[80] The Spartans' uncharacteristically prompt action demonstrates the threat that having the Athenians in this area posed for them. The Messenians nearby did indeed help the Athenians, supplying forty hoplites and, at least according to Thucydides, it was their help that won the campaign for the Athenians, because their local knowledge was invaluable for attacking the Spartans.[81] He also comments that once Pylos was garrisoned, the Messenians from Naupactus sent their best troops to the region, and inflicted much damage on the Spartans, partly through their knowledge of their land but again also because they spoke the same dialect: "The Spartans had no previous experience of this type of warfare and as the helots began to desert, they feared the spread of revolution in their country and became exceedingly uneasy about it".[82] Demosthenes' reasoning is presented by Thucydides as being correct and effective, but the overall strength of the Spartans meant that there was no general helot revolt.

The Spartans, although typified in our sources as slow and inactive, took energetic and severe means to prevent a mass revolt. The Athenians had seized Pylos, which was in Messenian territory, and they trapped 120 Spartiates on the island of Sphacteria. By their very presence the Athenians were encouraging neighbouring helots to revolt. The Spartans found this so threatening that they pretended to offer the bravest helots their freedom, and then slaughtered 2,000 of them. Thucydides introduces this episode with the general comment that most of the Spartan institutions were organized with a view to security, which indicates fear rather than confidence in their helots' loyalty.[83]

Later, Xenophon described plans for a coup at Sparta in c. 397 BCE.[84] Given the number of attempts made by helots to rebel, it is perhaps a sign of the immense strength of the Spartans that there were not more successful revolts. For various reasons the number of citizens, the Spartiates, declined dramatically in the fifth and fourth centuries BCE. It is against this backdrop that we learn of the plot described by Xenophon. The would-be leader, Cinadon, led a potential recruit for revolution to the agora, and asked him how many Spartiates he saw. The reply was "about forty" and Cinadon described them as the enemy; the rest of those in the marketplace, who were not Spartiates and were recognizable as such, numbered in the region of 4,000, and these were the allies. When the ephors asked the informant how many were in the conspiracy, he replied that there were not very many, meaning not very many Spartans, because he then went on to say that they were in the plot with everyone else, that is, the various categories of non-Spartiates (helots, *neodamōdeis, hypomeiones* and *perioikoi*), who were permanently in a state of hostility against the Spartans.[85] The last three groups do not concern us at present, but presumably at least the helots were distinguished by their clothes, since there is evidence that this was the case. Athenaeus records that Myron of Priene, in his *Messenian History*, had written that the Spartans made the helots wear a dogskin cap and a leather jerkin.[86] The reason, remarks Xenophon, that the leaders had confidence that they were all potential allies was that whenever anyone mentioned the Spartiate class to them, none of them could hide the fact that they would like to eat them raw.[87]

Shortly after this incident, in 370 BCE, after the battle of Leuctra, the Theban army was urged by Sparta's enemies to invade Laconia. At first, according to Xenophon, the Thebans were reluctant since they considered Laconia to be difficult to invade and they had seen that the easiest routes were guarded.[88] It is interesting to note that Xenophon reports that Oeum in Sciritis was guarded by a band of freed helots. What changed the minds of the Thebans, however, was the promise made by some of the *perioikoi* to rebel if the Thebans entered the territory; they added that they were already refusing to come to Sparta's aid when asked.[89] When they saw the invading army the Spartans made a proclamation to the helots promising them freedom if they took up arms on the Spartans' behalf.[90]

That some helots or, rather, many helots – 6,000 in all – responded to the offer might indicate loyalty towards their masters, but one could also see it as evidence of the attraction of freedom. In any event, the Messenian helots took advantage of the success of the Theban army under Epaminondas in entering the Peloponnese in 370/369 BCE to rise up against their masters and establish the city of Messene, although Xenophon himself makes no mention of this.[91] One might say that as well as staging many revolts that ultimately did not result in their freedom, the helots provided at least two examples of slave revolts that were successful in the long term: the first after the Mount Ithome incident, and the second after Leuctra. In both cases, helots became free.

The helots, being so ready to rebel, forced the Spartans into permanent and open war with them. The main magistrates, the ephors, declared war on the helots every year so that killing them would be lawful.[92] Many of the other conditions seen in the revolts discussed earlier were present: there were vast numbers of helots in comparison to their masters; they spoke the same language and had a shared culture; although they were not born free they had an ideology of a free past; they had leaders; and the geography was suitable for groups of slaves to maintain their independent existence.

Slaves in antiquity rebelled when they could, taking advantage of wars or other slave revolts to take up arms.[93] What does not seem to have deterred them are previous revolts that resulted in death for the participants. If anything, rebellions do indeed seem to have sparked off others, as Orosius commented. We have evidence that such outbreaks were relatively frequent occurrences. What was more difficult was for the slaves to maintain their initial freedom.

3
Maintaining resistance

As seen in the previous chapter, slaves might revolt at any time but the circumstances might not favour continued resistance for one reason or another. There was a good chance of a longer period of success when the slaves' masters were divided or at war. We do not know the circumstances of the breakout of the slaves on Chios, nor the exact date, although it seems probable that it was during the third century BCE. We are told, however, that there were many slaves on Chios because Thucydides comments: "There were many slaves in Chios – more, in fact, than in any other city except Sparta".[1] Here, again, is one of the normal conditions for a successful breakout of slaves, that is, the presence of large numbers of them. It is more the maintenance of the revolt that concerns us here because, for once, we have some information about how the slaves maintained their rebellion. The slaves in Chios, unusually it would seem according to our evidence, entered into an agreement with their former masters to ensure their continued survival as a free group.

Athenaeus preserves this episode. In the voice of his interlocutor Democritus, in *Deipnosophistae* Book 6, he quotes the fourth to third century BCE Greek historian Timaeus of Tauromenium, who had commented that in ancient times (ancient to him, that is) Greeks did not have slaves at all, but used younger members of their families to work for them.[2] He then goes on to quote Plato, who said there were problems with enslaving whole groups of people as the Spartans had, as seen from the frequent revolts of the Messenians. Athenaeus proceeds to quote Theopompus who wrote that the first Greeks to buy slaves were the Chians.[3] Athenaeus' speaker, Democritus, breaks off from quotation and appears to comment in his own voice that the Chians were punished for this practice because they later had a war against their own slaves.[4]

Following this is an extended extract from a work by Nymphodorus of Syracuse called *Voyage in Asia*, which told the story of the rebel slaves of Chios, headed by a man called Drimakos. Nymphodorus, who is thought to have written in the late third century BCE, says that this story was told by the Chians as having happened a little while before his own day.[5] Drimakos, however, had died some time before the narration of the story since at the end of the episode it is commented that after his death runaways continued to bring offerings to his shrine even at the time of writing.[6] So it is thought that the events happened in the first half of the third century BCE.[7]

The extract from Nymphodorus by way of introduction gives the detail that, since Chios was mountainous and wooded, runaway slaves were easily able to find places to hide, and they did. From their hiding places the runaways raided the estates, did much damage and could not be conquered by the slave-owners, who sent out many expeditions against them. A truce was made and an accommodation was reached that the slaves would not steal more than an agreed amount of produce and, having done so, they would seal up the storehouses and leave the property-holders in peace.

The slaves, while limiting their takings, also promised not to accept any runaways into their group other than those who had been badly treated, and who could prove they had been. Nymphodorus records that this condition was observed very strictly and that slaves ran away less often after this because they dreaded being cross-examined by Drimakos. This sounds a little far-fetched but it belongs with the generally paradoxical nature of the story, which presents the slave leader Drimakos as authoritarian. Nymphodorus records that his men were more frightened of him than of their old masters, but presumably they could easily have killed him.

Although this arrangement was kept by both sides, it was nevertheless a victory for the slaves and unsatisfactory for the former owners, who placed a reward for anyone who would capture Drimakos or bring his head. However, Drimakos chose when to give up his command. He was not betrayed by any of his men and, after his death, the masters did not regain control of their ex-slaves; rather, the situation grew worse. Drimakos had, in fact, ameliorated the situation for the slave-owners, and the slaves were in a strong enough position to survive without him and without the agreement. The owners then regretted the loss of Drimakos and set up a shrine to him. The runaways also brought offerings to this shrine so that there emerged a situation where both sides honoured his memory for the benefits he had conferred on them. At the time Nymphodorus was writing, there were still slaves living in freedom; he wrote that they still brought offerings to the shrine.[8]

It seems possible that Nymphodorus enjoyed paradoxical stories and thus included the story of Drimakos in his *Voyage in Asia* for its curiosity value; another piece he wrote was called *On the Wonders of Sicily*.[9] The story of Drimakos might fall into the category of a wonder or a paradox because the final outcome is that slave-owners regretted the passing of a rebel slave leader and both owners and slaves honoured his memory. Drimakos had provided the island with some stability; under his leadership the Chians had come to an agreement with him. However, as the price on Drimakos' head shows, the existence of such groups was humiliating and damaging for the owners, since the slaves had won freedom for themselves and the owners were powerless to prevent this.

The features of this community correspond with similar groups known from more recent times as "maroons", which I shall briefly discuss because from them Bradley has developed a more general argument about ancient revolts.[10] The term "maroon" was used of escaped slaves in the New World.[11] These escaped slaves lived in remote places that they could defend easily and where they could grow food and hunt. They are a well-known feature of slavery from the sixteenth to the nineteenth centuries in the Caribbean and Americas. In an important article on these runaways, Richard Price describes the situation:

> For more than four centuries, the communities formed by such runaways dotted the fringes of plantation America, from Brazil to the southeastern United States, from Peru to the American Southwest. Known variously as *palenques*, *quilombos*, *mocambos*, *cumbes*, *ladeiras*, or *mambises*, these new societies ranged from tiny bands that survived less than a year to powerful states encompassing thousands of members and surviving for generations or even centuries.[12]

Such communities were an embarrassment as well as a danger to the slave-owners and there were drastic punishments not only for running away but also for aiding members of such communities.[13] As Price remarks a little further on:

In a remarkable number of cases throughout the Americas, the whites were forced to bring themselves to sue their former slaves for peace. In their typical form, such treaties – which we know of from Brazil, Colombia, Cuba, Ecuador, Hispaniola, Jamaica, Mexico, and Surinam – offered maroon communities their freedom, recognised their territorial integrity and made some provision for meeting their economic needs, demanding in return an agreement to end all hostilities towards the plantations, to return all future runaways and often, to aid the whites in hunting them down.[14]

Bradley discusses some of the modern episodes in his first chapter of *Slavery and Rebellion in the Roman World 140 BC–70 BC*, before considering whether the ancient slave armies were to some extent maroon communities.[15] When explaining why a comparison with modern maroon communities is fruitful, he writes:

The object, it must be stressed, is not to try to prove a direct equation between the Roman rebellions and later episodes of servile behaviour; it is only to suggest that the ancient events, once set out in detail, can be seen to carry something of a maroon character. In turn, *these correspondences ... may be taken to point up the nonrevolutionary nature of the Roman slave movements. It is in this that the chief pertinence of the modern material lies.*[16]

What would "revolutionary" mean in this case? From this discussion it would seem to entail large personal aims on the parts of the leaders, rather than the more commonplace definition of a situation that is the reversal of the normal state of affairs, which clearly does obtain whenever the slaves take up arms.

Throughout his book Bradley argues that the slaves of the great wars of the Roman Republic were engaged *not* in revolution but rebellion, by which he means they wanted to be free but *nothing more*. They had no plan for a different society and did not want to abolish slavery. He writes, for instance:

The discrete groups of rebellious slaves led by Varius, Salvius, and Athenion rose up in revolt on the lines of a well-established pattern of small-scale resistance and did not *deliberately* aim to engage the whole slave population of Sicily in a more general insurrection.[17]

There are, however, statements in the primary sources that seem to contradict this. In his description of the second Sicilian slave war, Diodorus writes that the slaves rebelled, and collected other recruits *in an active way*, not that others were attracted to them.[18]

About Spartacus' revolt, Bradley observes: "The growth of the rebel movement was *not a deliberately* contrived or *carefully orchestrated* phenomenon, therefore, but an example on the grand scale of traditional patterns of flight and revolt".[19] The argument, then, is that there is a strong connection between the maroon characteristics and the lack of any large aim. However, it does not seem so necessary that there should be such a connection. Those establishing maroon communities may well have had more ambitious plans. Vogt makes a point that relates to Bradley's argument:

> If we ask what were the reasons for this large number of slave revolts, one factor can be excluded immediately. *There was no doctrine current at that time among free citizens which aimed at the abolition of slavery*; the idea that under certain circumstances men could be claimed as chattels by others basically remained unchallenged.[20]

This argument may strike some as surprising. We are being asked to accept that the slaves did not have ambitions because the free people had not developed an abolitionist movement, such as occurred in later times and that preceded the abolition of the slave trade. It might be argued, however, that Wilberforce's abolitionist movement became popular because of the success of the slave revolts at the time, rather than that the slaves took up arms because they heard about the activities of a Member of Parliament for Kingston upon Hull. One might challenge Vogt's thesis and say that the free citizens did not develop a doctrine for the abolition of slavery because the slave revolts were not successful enough.

Bradley also makes the point that we have no evidence of any aims on the part of the slaves apart from their own personal freedom and that we can thus distinguish between their efforts and revolts in the modern world, for instance, on the Engeno Santana of Ilhéus, a large sugar plantation in Brazil in 1789, where slaves sought to improve their conditions. After rebelling for two years they offered terms, saying that they would return as slaves if these were accepted. Unsurprisingly the terms were not conceded but, Bradley adds: "they [the Brazilian slaves] represented all the same a revolutionary threat to the institution of slavery of a kind *that is without parallel* in the Roman world".[21] In other words, the slaves in Brazil were a completely different threat from the slaves in ancient Sicily because they *asked* for certain conditions, not because they achieved them.

The aims of the slaves in Brazil were indeed revolutionary but one can see how they arose from their particular situation since we have a transcript of their demands. The slaves did not demand freedom and an end to their slavery *in those words*, couched in the vocabulary of the French Revolution, for instance, but what they demanded was in reality an end to their slavery.[22] They wanted Fridays and Saturdays to work for themselves, and for their masters to provide them with canoes and nets, proper boats for working and clothes. They did not want to do certain tasks and asked to fix the amount of work for themselves; they asked for proper working conditions; and they wanted to choose their overseers. They wanted to be able to grow their rice wherever they wanted and cut whatever wood they needed and, as Schwartz points out, very importantly they wanted the equipment for their work to remain in their control, "reducing the concept of slavery to a farce".[23] The last clause is perhaps the most striking for the modern reader: "We shall be able to play, relax and sing any time we wish without your hindrance nor will permission be needed".[24]

What the slaves asked for was peculiar to their own situation and yet, what they described, all in all, would have resulted in an end to their slavery, even though they did not couch their demands in these broad, ambitious words. It seems entirely possible that similar events happened in the ancient world about which we no longer have any information. Spartacus, for instance, according to Appian, offered to make terms with Crassus, and we do not know what he offered, except that Crassus refused.[25] If this document from Brazil had not survived, most would never have ascribed revolutionary aims to the eighteenth-century slaves. They did not have their terms accepted; they were defeated and recaptured.

The intentions of the slaves in antiquity are almost certainly lost forever, but it is indisputable that whatever certain individuals may have envisaged at the start of an action, especially war, events can take on their own momentum and make those intentions irrelevant. What starts out as a protest may end in a revolution.

There is, for instance, no evidence that any of the slaves in St Domingue had written or read any revolutionary tracts when they rose up against their masters in 1791. The eventual leader of the first independent black republic outside Africa, Toussaint Louverture, did not join the revolt immediately, so one can hardly assume he had planned the whole course of the rebellion.[26] As Dubois has shown in his history of the St Domingue uprising, the story is immensely complicated. Ideas and aims developed as events unfolded. We know this period is so complicated because we have many more sources to reconstruct the actions and ideas of the different actors. In the ancient world, it is unlikely to have been much simpler, although our insufficient source material might lead us to this impression.

The slaves in St Domingue rebelled because they had the chance, not because they had perfected some strategic plan for an alternative society that they wanted to try out. Their aims in the first instance were for their situation to change, for them to be free, to avenge themselves for their suffering and also to remove the causes of their suffering so they would not have to endure it again. If the slaves in St Domingue had failed, some might call it a rebellion, an attempt for freedom, but probably not a revolution. Once the ex-slaves achieved some freedom they started to think about how they wanted to live, and unsurprisingly concluded that they did not want slavery. This is not such an intellectual feat that the ancient slaves would have been incapable of it.

Maroon communities were clearly a form of open rebellion and it is very probable that there were communities of ex-slaves in antiquity, such as we see in later societies, that were not recorded by texts extant today. Setting up such a community could have been the only aim for the slaves or they could be seen as one stage in a rebellion. When rebels could achieve no more they might remain as maroon communities, preserving their limited victory but not being strong enough to win further ones. It is interesting here to note the terms used for maroon communities in Brazil. The older word used was *mocambo*, which is a Mbundu word meaning "hideout", but a term that came to be used more frequently from the end of the seventeenth century was *quilombo*, which is another Mbundu word, meaning "war-camp".[27] In the slave wars in Sicily and Italy, the insurgents had enough followers to fight on, as did the slaves in St Domingue. It does not seem that one must choose between establishing maroon communities and entering into war; rather, these independent communities were a step towards war. As the authorities recognized, their establishment was an open act of defiance and one that needed to be crushed as soon as possible to restore the power of the masters.

It seems to stretch the term beyond its use, however, to refer to the slaves of the great slave wars as maroon communities when there was no truce with the authorities but the slaves continued fighting and recruiting. We have no evidence that the slaves had wanted only to live in such communities, and perhaps more significantly this is not what they achieved. One may speculate that some of them may have wanted it but one could also suggest that some of them may have wanted to set up slave-free democracy. Building on either speculation is not very fruitful.

As far as we can tell from the evidence, the slaves in Sicily and Italy rose up and fought. They did not try to hide in mountainous hideouts for extended periods of time or seek to reach an accommodation with their former owners. They acquired more and more followers and became increasingly successful as the Romans sent out army after army to fight them.

We have evidence from the ancient world that slaves did take direct action to escape their lives of slavery and live in freedom by running away or taking up arms, or both. At some point they came to the conclusion that a life on the run was preferable to slavery. And there were places where such groups or individuals might find refuge, either whole gatherings of ex-slaves, or independent states, such as that described by Cicero, when governor of Cilicia, in a letter from 51–50 BCE: "The town is on a very high and well-defended site and is inhabited by people who have never given obedience even to kings, which is shown by the fact that they regularly receive runaway slaves".[28] Another possible example is the city of slaves referred to in an inscription from Colophon from the second century BCE, which seems to be referring to a settlement of Aristonicus' followers.[29] The expression δούλων πόλις (*doulōn polis*, city of slaves) could be a term of abuse, but nevertheless describes a community, at least part of which seems to have consisted of slaves.[30]

As always with ancient history, surviving evidence is crucial and one can thus imagine that just as there is not a vast quantity of information generally about slaves, the Greeks and Romans would not have celebrated rebellious slaves in their literary works. For the histories of maroon communities in the Americas, oral history, which naturally does not survive from antiquity in the same manner, is vital. There are oral traditions recording the Saramaka maroon wars for which there are also contemporary Dutch accounts. The accounts differ as much as it is possible to differ in that both sides claim victory for the same battle.[31]

We know of the particular community in Cilicia because Cicero wrote a letter about it, but such places would not reach histories generally.

There was a history written about the slave wars by Caecilius of Kale Akte,[32] but it is perhaps not surprising that we no longer possess his text, just as we do not have the full version of Diodorus' account of the Sicilian slave wars. Generally, such events were not recorded or, even if they were, often not preserved, because the fight against the slaves was seen as shameful. Florus' remarks are typical: "Although we fought with allies – in itself an impious act – yet we fought with men who enjoyed liberty and were of free birth but who could tolerate with equanimity wars waged by a sovereign people against slaves?"[33] We know about Drimakos only because Nymphodorus' account was preserved by Athenaeus, and this was so, one would think, because it is an intriguing story, an exception, an example of a paradox. Athenaeus narrates it in order to show the divine vengeance for buying slaves. He had started the section saying that the Chians were the first Greeks to buy slaves for money (unlike the Spartans and Thessalians who enslaved the native populations, quoting Theopompus). And he adds: "In my opinion God punished the people of Chios for this – for in later times they were engaged in a long war because of their slaves".[34] After giving Nymphodorus' account of Drimakos and his rebellion, Athenaeus adds that their punishment did not end here since later the citizens of Chios were enslaved and given to their own slaves to be resettled in Colchis: "In this way God truly showed how angry he was with them because they were the first people to use human chattels that had been bought, while most people carried out any necessary services by doing the work themselves".[35]

Athenaeus, like Diodorus, does not have a particularly good reputation with historians except as a source for lost works. A volume dedicated to him starts with the words "Few modern scholars admire Athenaeus".[36] However, he, like Diodorus, would seem to have a certain sympathy with slaves, which is not very common in the ancient authors left to us.[37] In the passage just quoted, Athenaeus conveys to the reader that buying slaves for money is wrong. He contrasts the Chians with those who enslaved native populations, which is not, however, held up as being preferable. He quotes Theopompus' *Hellenica*, Book 7, where the latter writes that the conditions of the helot race are in every respect inhumane and horrible. From the overall tenor of his quotations he is warning of the dangers of slavery and especially of having too many slaves.

Helots are a vivid illustration of the danger masters faced every day. In our sources the helots of Sparta are presented as always ready to rebel. The case of the helots on Mount Ithome would also seem to be an example of a very successful maroon community.[38] It was so successful in fact that the Spartans were forced to allow them to leave and become free. However long it lasted, the helots were able to feed and supply themselves for several years and the presence was so damaging to the Spartans that they were forced to concede defeat in the end. The Spartans seem to have felt that this collection of independent helots could have triggered a full-scale rebellion. The Spartans contained them successfully, in that this extension did not happen, but were forced to allow them to leave the Peloponnese and live freely in Naupactus. The helot position, then, was extremely strong.

Maintenance of the armies in the great slave wars

In Sicily the slave revolts were more widespread and there was no possibility for the authorities to contain the rebels in one area. One might argue that because the slaves were not able to reach an accommodation with the slave-owners, they were forced to continue fighting in order to get provisions. Reaching such an accommodation, however, did not necessarily prolong the ability of slaves to hold out. On Chios, after the death of Drimakos, the agreement broke down but the slaves were not recaptured. Nymphodorus relates that the rebels continued to live freely without the calming presence of Drimakos. In fact, for the slave-owners on Chios the position was worse than before because the slaves plundered with no restraint. In Sicily, however, we read not of an attempted agreement, but instead of a steady escalation of numbers joining the slave army. It is possible that the original rebels could not control the development of the army and its rapid increase but at no point do we hear that they were unable to provide for the huge numbers that came to them.

The numbers involved in the first war were reported as being enormous from the beginning. Diodorus tells us that in the first attack 400 slaves rampaged through Enna, and their success attracted a large number of slaves from the city. In three days arms were supplied for 6,000 men and the other followers improvised with the tools of herdsmen and farmers, arming themselves with weapons such as axes and sickles, and cooking spits.[39] They moved around the countryside around Enna collecting more slaves. After their defeat of the first Roman army sent out against them, they attracted vast numbers of followers, so that the rebel slaves numbered more than 10,000.

In another part of the island, more slaves took the opportunity to rise up. Diodorus reports that there were 5,000 involved,[40] whereas Livy recorded a remarkable 70,000.[41] Orosius gives the same figure of 70,000 as the total number of slaves involved in the war.[42] It is impossible now to know how many slaves were involved. Most commentators today would assume Diodorus' figure is closer to the truth, but if the numbers were already into the thousands, this must have seemed quite terrifying to the authorities.[43] The combined forces of slaves would have been even more alarming, and they seem to have had larger aims than merely surviving in an independent community. The slaves seized several cities in Sicily and presumably their food supplies along with them, and looked as if they were about to seize total control of the island, defeating several Roman troops led by praetors and two consular armies. Diodorus (as recorded by Photius) describes the growth in size of the slave army as happening extremely rapidly:

> Soon after, engaging in battle with a general arrived from Rome, Lucius Hypsaeus, who had 8,000 Sicilian troops, the rebels were victorious, since they now numbered 20,000. Before long their band reached a total of 200,000, and in numerous battles with the Romans they acquitted themselves well, and failed but seldom.[44]

The slaves in Sicily were thus quick to respond to the opportunity. Slaves also rebelled outside Sicily but these uprisings were put down. Those in Sicily, however, continued to be successful and the rebels appear to have provided for themselves arms and food and all necessary supplies, without any obvious difficulties.

Diodorus reports that they captured city after city. The two major cities captured seem to have been Enna and Tauromenium, although we also know that they took Acragas and Mamertium.[45] When discussing how the slaves took Acragas, Diodorus gives us a striking detail of how they had staged a play outside the city walls so that the inhabitants could also watch. The play depicted the slaves' own recent past, that is, gaining their freedom and taking vengeance on their masters. Presumably the intention was to strike panic into the hearts of the masters and send hope to their slaves.[46] This is an unexpected insight into the energy and imagination of the slaves during a time of war. Diodorus comments that the slaves abused their masters for their *hybris*, for which they were now being punished.[47] The slaves, supported, we are told, by free people, took over these cities.

Diodorus narrates how even Sicilian citizens, that is the poor free people of Sicily, turned against the slave-owners. They were overjoyed by the misfortunes of the wealthy because for a long time they had resented their wealth and arrogance. He comments that the free were more destructive than the slaves.[48] This is in direct contradiction to Orosius' views of the attitudes of slaves and free. He comments generally that the slaves destroy the country whereas the free try to benefit it: "Inasmuch as it is a rare kind of uprising, an insurrection of slaves is a more dangerous type of rebellion: masses of free citizens are prompted by their aims to increase the strength of their homeland, whereas a mob of slaves is incited to destroy it".[49]

Benjamin Farrington has suggested that the restraint of the slaves with regard to property indicates that they were intending to take over the island.[50] Whatever the intention, Diodorus explicitly writes that the free were more destructive than the slaves. One might view this as part of the punishment inflicted on the wealthy and arrogant landowners, without having to attribute blame to the slaves.

The slaves succeeded in holding the cities and their positions of strength against Roman troops sent out against them, apparently with little trouble. Bradley comments on the three major wars generally:

> Thus it cannot be assumed *that slaves set out to make war*, in any formal manner, against established powers; it can only be said that slaves were prepared to use military tactics to protect and sustain themselves in flight, to make continuous flight and the freedom it represented feasible. Almost paradoxically, however, flight could not bring permanent freedom when so many fugitives were involved. The numerical dimensions of the slave uprisings were therefore the rebellions' fatal flaw.[51]

None of the slaves involved, according to him, wanted war; rather, all of them wanted merely to be free. One might think that the slaves' main hope of success was to continue to attract large numbers of followers and yet Bradley argues that this was their main mistake; if they had remained very few they could individually have escaped. Flight normally implies a direction and whereas the army led by Spartacus certainly did move with an apparent purpose, it is more difficult to say where the Sicilian slaves thought they were going. They do not seem to have attempted to leave the island.

Gerald Verbrugghe's different approach is to say that this was not a slave war and that in fact we should see the events as the province of Sicily in revolt against the imperial power.[52] This may seem an attractive idea but it also necessitates the dismissal of much of the narrative of Diodorus. Verbrugghe criticizes Diodorus' description of Sicily as being dependent on animal husbandry because it is at variance with the testimonies of Livy and Cicero, who say that cereal production was most important.[53] This is a careless reading of Diodorus, since his concern was not (unsurprisingly) to give an economic analysis of Sicily but to explain why the slaves were able to revolt, and he wanted to show that they were able to revolt because of the relatively free situation of those slaves involved in herding animals.

Diodorus also, according to Verbrugghe, wrongly describes Roman knights and Italians controlling most of this husbandry.[54] It is more than probable that Romans and Italians did own land in Sicily and the fact that Diodorus was from Sicily might easily lead him to the impression that there were too many of them. This in turn could quickly be transferred into *most* of the big landowners being Romans and Italians. This is not to say that Diodorus did not make errors. For instance, he attributes the lack of action on the part of the governor of Sicily as being due to the fact that the Roman equites served as jurors in the courts that tried governors for maladministration,[55] whereas equestrian control of the courts was not put in place until the Gracchan legislation of 122 BCE. It is worth noting that it would have been true in the second war but not this one. Another mistake he makes, states Verbrugghe, is in giving figures that are far too large for the numbers of slaves in the revolt since Sicily could not possibly have contained this many slaves.[56] The more usual reaction to surprisingly large numbers in our ancient texts is to challenge them and assume they are exaggerations. However, Verbrugghe boldly assumes that the figures are correct and then, because he thinks there were not so many slaves in Sicily, assumes there must have been a substantial proportion of free inhabitants with them. It is indeed the case that Diodorus writes explicitly that free people did join the rebels, but Verbrugghe's imaginative theory is to make them the bulk of the forces. He also argues that Diodorus is wrong because there was no mass enslavement of Syrians. In fact, Diodorus nowhere writes that most of the slaves were Syrian. He gives us the information that Eunus was from Apamea but says nothing about most of the slaves.

Verbrugghe thus accepts certain details of Diodorus, such as the facts that the leaders did set themselves up as kings and that there were large numbers involved in the rebellion, but cannot accept others, such as the major role played by the slaves. If one challenges so much of Diodorus then one has to justify the parts one accepts since, if he were so abysmally ignorant of the history of his own birthplace, it makes little sense to accept any of his narrative. And if we reject all of it, or even most of it, then we are left with very little at all.

The slave community seems to have adopted some form of monarchical rule and even to have minted their own coins, showing the veiled head of Demeter with a stalk of wheat, so important for Sicily.[57] Here, then, we see signs that the slaves were organized, had definite ideas about how their campaign should proceed and seem to have had long-term plans. Issuing coins is not the action of people hoping either to escape attention or to run off elsewhere. The slaves at least appear to have seen their hope in attracting as many of the slaves of Sicily to their side as possible. There was safety in numbers.

Without Diodorus, our knowledge of the first slave war in Sicily would be very scanty since the accounts in other sources are very brief. The part of Livy that deals with this period is only extant in summary form.[58] The epitomator of Livy makes mention of the war in the summary for Book 56:

> A slave revolt arose in Sicily, and when the praetors could not suppress it, command was assigned to consul Gaius Fulvius. The instigator of this revolt was Eunus, a slave of Syrian nationality; he assembled a force of rural slaves, opened the workhouses and raised his numbers to those of a regular army. Another slave, Cleon, also assembled as many as seventy thousand slaves, and when the forces had joined, they frequently [*saepe*] took the field against the Roman army.[59]

Book 56 covered 136–134 BCE and the account is very condensed; nevertheless, it takes up a third of the summary so the original narrative would probably have been quite substantial. Livy also gives us the names of Eunus, and that he was Syrian, and Cleon, to whose army he attributes 70,000 people.

Although the evidence about the slaves in Pergamum is not abundant, their uprising lasted four years and this group was also able to maintain the rebellion and provide for themselves. Strabo gives the curious detail that Aristonicus called his followers, the poor and slaves, Heliopolitae, Citizens of the City of the Sun, and people have speculated about what this might signify.[60] He does not say that Aristonicus founded a city called Heliopolis, although it is the name of more than one city in antiquity.

Quite remarkably, as mentioned earlier, an inscription found in Claros refers to a "city of slaves" in the region of Colophon, which has been thought to be a reference to a settlement of Aristonicus' followers.[61] Although this term in the inscription may be one of abuse, and might refer to a community such as described by Cicero in Cilicia, that is, one receptive to runaway slaves, some of the individuals in the settlement seem to have been former slaves and so we appear to have more evidence than normal of slave activity. The inscription refers to this community being a nuisance. This may well be a completely different group of slaves, an example of an ancient maroon community. Such communities of runaways may have been quite common but it is possible that we do not hear of them simply because literary sources seldom mention them.

While Strabo and Diodorus mention slaves as being involved in this Pergamene uprising, it was Diodorus who made the direct connection between them and the first Sicilian slave war. In Book 2 he throws some light on the significance of the name Heliopolitae. He had described the Indians, Scythians and Arabians, ending his book with his account of Iambulus' trip to what seems to be a utopia, rather than a real place.[62] Apparently the character Iambulus ends up at the islands of the sun, after which its inhabitants, who live in a state of extreme equality, are called.[63] Diodorus ends Book 2 with a detailed description of the way these extraordinary people lived.[64] The connection between these islands of the sun and the phrase "citizens of the city of the sun" has not gone unnoticed. And indeed the word "Heliopolis", meaning City of the Sun, is not so very common that we are not entitled to enquire into such a connection.

Another factor that has led some to see an ideological aspect to the Pergamene uprising is the fact that we are told Blossius, the Stoic friend of Tiberius Gracchus, fled to help Aristonicus after Tiberius' murder. Some have thought that having worked to influence the reforms of Tiberius Gracchus in Rome aiming at a redistribution of wealth in the form of land, he then moved to Pergamum, where he had similar designs.[65]

The description of events of the second war in Sicily is rather similar to that of the first war in the massive and sudden increase of rebels.

Prior to the second war, after the uprising near Halicyae, it was reported to the authorities that some slaves had murdered their masters and rebelled. At first there were about eighty rebels involved, but their numbers increased rapidly. Diodorus has the story that the governor did march past the area where the rebels were but did not attack them, presumably because he feared he did not have enough troops, having disbanded most of them.[66] However, when it was reported that the number of rebels was more than 800, and soon after that had increased to 2,000, he made Marcus Titinius the commander and sent him with 600 soldiers from the garrison at Enna, but these troops were defeated by the slaves:

> Now all the slaves were encouraged by the prospect of rebellion. As more and more men turned to rebellion with every passing day, there was a sudden and unexpected increase in their number, with the result that, within a few days, they were more than six thousand.[67]

Acquiring adherents is never reported as being a problem in these uprisings. The crucial time is the beginning, the actual breakout, because after a very short amount of time massive numbers of slaves took the opportunity to join in.

After their first success, the victory over Marcus Titinius, the slaves formed an assembly. At this point, they numbered more than 6,000, and elected a leader whom they called a king. Like Drimakos, their leader, Salvius, is described as strict, ordering his followers to avoid cities, since they bred luxury and degeneration. The slave army was well trained and organized; it was split into three groups, each of which had its own commander. They behaved efficiently and effectively and from raiding they soon acquired enough equipment for 2,000 cavalry and 20,000 infantry, and enough supplies to support their substantial army.[68]

The slave army's next move was to attack Morgantina, a city in central Sicily, slightly south-east of Enna. The Roman governor, Nerva, advanced to meet them with 10,000 Italian and Sicilian soldiers and the Romans captured the empty rebel camp, which only had a few guards. The slaves returned, however, and fought back. Photius' narrative tells us that the Roman army started running away, and then reports that Salvius declared that if the Romans dropped their weapons they would not be killed. Most of the Roman soldiers threw down their arms and the slaves retook their camp and gained many new weapons. In Diodorus' narrative the Romans are total cowards and the slaves have their measure. Diodorus adds that because of this humane proclamation (διὰ τὴν τοῦ κηρύγματος φιλανθρωπίαν[69]) only 600 of the Roman army died, while 4,000 were taken prisoner. The word "philanthropia" is quite a remarkable word for an ancient author to use of a slave. One has the sense that the Romans are being criticized here, since they behave in a cowardly way, and the result is a very favourable account of the behaviour of the slaves.

Christian Mileta remarks that this detail of Salvius' offer not to kill Romans who dropped their weapons is not in the *Excerpts* of Constantine, even though the account there is virtually word for word the same as that of Photius.[70] He concludes that the excerptors felt that there was no need to add this, as readers would already know it from their knowledge of Photius.[71] Bradley adds the further comment that the attack on Morgantina is not mentioned by any other ancient author:

> It is somewhat surprising that no other ancient writer ever mentions Salvius and the siege of Morgantina. The reason perhaps is that the new slave king, despite his great success in converting the early insurgents in the west into a coordinated and well-regulated army, never seems to have become as charismatic a figure as the wonderworker Eunus before him.[72]

Another explanation could be that most Roman historians did not want to record such an embarrassing, and for them disgraceful, episode. The Romans not only lost, they lost through cowardice. They fled, threw down their weapons and took up the magnanimous, or contemptuous, offer of the slave leader, and thousands of them were taken prisoner.[73]

The slave army besieged Morgantina and offered the slaves in the city their freedom. These slaves, however, preferred to believe their masters, who also offered them freedom if they helped to defend the city. They were mistaken to do so: the governor rescinded the manumission. The slaves therefore ran away and joined the rebels.[74]

As in the first slave war, there was another uprising of slaves in a different part of the island. Diodorus reports that again the authorities hoped that the two groups of slaves would fight each other but, as in the previous war, they joined forces instead. Diodorus comments: "Fortune, as though intentionally increasing the power of the fugitives, caused their leaders to be of one mind".[75] Athenion, the leader of this second revolt, became Salvius' general, although later Salvius was suspicious of him; Diodorus writes that Salvius ordered Athenion "to be placed in detention".[76]

Maintaining an army in Italy

We can see something similar in the Spartacan outbreak thirty years later. The escaped gladiators and their co-rebels had a rapid series of victories, starting against the Roman army of 3,000 led by a praetor who thought he had trapped the rebels on a hill.[77] But the gladiators twisted vines into ropes, abseiled down the rockface and attacked the Romans from the rear. After this victory, in which the Roman commander's horse was taken by the slaves, the rebel army numbered 70,000, states Appian. Plutarch adds the detail that they were joined by herdsmen and shepherds from the area, although he does not give any indication of the number. Two more praetors (Publius Varinius and Cossinius) were sent out, neither of whom had any luck against the rebels.

The slave army marched northwards. Plutarch and Appian interpret this not as Spartacus intending to avoid the Romans but to cross the Alps. His men, however, had different ideas and preferred to plunder Italy. By this stage the Romans were alarmed, and sent out both consuls to deal with what they considered a major war, writes Plutarch.[78] One of the consuls destroyed the Germans from Spartacus' army but the other was defeated. Crixus, Appian tells us, had 30,000 men under him and two-thirds of these were killed. The rest of the army headed towards Gaul, met Cassius, the governor of Cisalpine Gaul, with 10,000 men, and defeated them too. Plutarch does not say how many men Spartacus had at this point, although we may infer that he was not short of troops. However, Appian, in reporting that their intention was to attack Rome, says that the slave army numbered 120,000 men.

So the numbers involved at this stage were huge and this may explain the apparently aimless marching up and down Italy: the army had to keep moving in order to acquire more food and supplies. Every time they defeated Roman troops they could take their supplies and arms.[79] But also by moving (and continuing to be successful) they could hope to recruit more to their army. Even if the numbers are vastly exaggerated, it is clear that the size of the slave contingent was threatening for their former masters. The ancient sources interpreted the long march as the army intending to cross the Alps but, despite their victories over the

Romans at this point, the army turned around. In order to make sense of it Plutarch presumes that Spartacus' men disobeyed him and decided to stay in Italy to pillage the countryside. Presumably they did pillage the countryside, but this must generally have been how they supplied themselves with food and equipment.

Appian tells the story of the intention to march on Rome. He explains that Spartacus had changed his mind about marching on Rome because he was not ready for such a battle. It seems likely that there was no intention to march on Rome but the Romans were so afraid that they thought this terrible thing was about to happen. Appian also adds that no city had joined the rebels, but only slaves, deserters and riff-raff (although only a few sentences earlier he tells us that Spartacus had refused to accept deserters, and the word αὐτομόλοι is used in both cases[80]). In the next sentence, he reports that the slaves took Thurii, apparently contradicting himself.

The army maintained itself by constantly being on the move, as well as gathering more recruits. It seems that the rebels were allowed to pass through the Italian countryside, not prevented, as they could have been, by the Italians, had they been so disposed. In his account of the Mithridatic War, Appian comments that Mithridates hoped that many of the Italians would join him if he invaded Italy as they had recently been at war with the Romans themselves. The historian adds that Mithridates was encouraged in this hope by the fact that recently the Italians had sided with Spartacus against the Romans, even though he was a wholly disreputable person.[81] The alienation of the Italians from the Romans helps account for the success in the maintenance of the slave army. Appian reports that after taking Thurii the slaves were not allowed by Spartacus to acquire gold or silver and nor could merchants import it into the city. However, they did use iron and copper, and were well stocked with basic materials; when they wanted more they raided, or attacked a Roman army.

After so many humiliating defeats for the Romans, Crassus was given supreme command of the war.[82] He marched against Spartacus with six legions and when he arrived he received in addition the two armies of the consuls, which he decimated for their previous conduct. As Spartacus was heading to Picenum, Crassus waited there and ordered his commander, Mummius, to follow the rebels by another route with two legions, but not to confront them. Mummius thought he knew better and that he had a good opportunity to defeat the slaves, so he attacked them and was duly defeated.

Appian also tells the alternative story of Crassus decimating the whole army, which would have meant killing 4,000 soldiers. He showed his men he was more dangerous than Spartacus and they were victorious in the next engagement, killing two-thirds of the 10,000 rebels in the encounter. According to this narrative, there had been an arrangement with some Cilician pirates to land 2,000 men in Sicily but the pirates broke their agreement and sailed without their cargo of rebels.[83] The slave army marched back from the sea.

Spartacus' intention, thinks Plutarch, was to incite the island, which had recently had a slave war of its own and could therefore easily be encouraged to have another. It may well be that the slaves were going to cross over into Sicily where they might hope to take over the whole island. But, again, it is one of those suppositions about Spartacus' intentions. Was he intending to cross the Alps, to march on Rome or to go to Sicily? All are possible, but we can never know. Crassus had earlier written to the Senate to ask for help from Lucullus and Pompey, but changed his mind and tried to finish the war before they arrived. There was a battle and the Romans killed 12,300 men, writes Plutarch. He states that only two of them were wounded in the back, the others dying fighting the Romans, thus painting a picture of heroism on the part of the slaves.

After the final battle, according to Appian, many of the surviving rebels fled to the mountains and continued to fight until all except 6,000 of them were killed; they were captured and crucified along the road from Capua to Rome. Crassus had finished his task in six months. There were slaves still alive in 61 BCE, more than ten years later, who were described as the remnants of this rebel army; Suetonius writes that the father of the Emperor Augustus defeated them.[84] These individuals, and one must suppose they were quite numerous for this to be remembered of Augustus' father, had survived for *ten* years, presumably in southern Italy, thus showing the possibility that there were more of such groups than we have records for.[85] After all, we hear about these only because of the individual who crushed them, and because they had belonged to such a famous army.

Maintaining themselves does not seem to have been a problem for any of these slave armies. In every case they were defeated militarily. It does not appear to have been the case that they had problems getting supplies or arms; at no point are we told that these aspects are problematic.

Bradley argues that we should not read too much into these slave rebellions:

There can be no reasonable doubt, therefore, that widespread revolt, whether of slaves or of slaves in alliance with other social elements, was not at all the best means by which the gladiators from Capua might hope to convert their act of flight into a state of permanent freedom, for the greater the rebel numbers, the greater the prospect of Roman retaliation in kind.[86]

The Roman retaliation was always going to be severe. The slaves could never have hoped for more lenient treatment if only a few of them had escaped, or had fought back. Bradley argues that the slaves merely wanted to flee, and not to collect large numbers and fight the Romans; he suggests that they could not achieve their aims because there were too many of them. However, he also acknowledges that we know nothing of their aims, and that we cannot know anything because none of our information is from the slaves themselves.[87] Despite this, he affirms that the slaves did not want anything other than flight and he asserts this with surprising confidence: "Within the rebel movement, therefore, a coherent set of objectives never existed".[88]

It is difficult to see what difference the presence of such a purpose or a thought would have made. In any event, we have no way of knowing what they intended. It seems rather presumptuous, however, to say that we know *for sure* that they did not intend a general rebellion. There is no reason why they might not have intended such a thing, however unrealistic it may seem to us today. In fact, it is only hindsight that enables us to judge accurately whether things seem realistic or not. Initially 200 gladiators were supposed to break out, although in the end only about seventy did so. Even seventy is unwieldy if all they wanted to do was run away and melt into the countryside.

There is also the issue that there had been two previous uprisings in living memory, which the sources assume that Spartacus remembered when they suggest that he wanted to cross over to Sicily in order to reignite the flames of rebellion there. Spartacus and his men could very well have known of the revolts in Sicily, and indeed our sources assume that he did.[89] Given this, it is entirely possible that they wished to emulate their predecessors. Certainly other gladiators revolted.

Bradley observes:

Naturally it has to be recognized that the information available on motives comes from nonslave sources – authors who rationalized the behavior of the slave rebels in their own way – and that because the rebels have left no statements of their aspirations and intentions, their views of events, as of all their experiences in slavery must always remain *irrecoverable*.[90]

However, after conceding that therefore all suggestions about the slaves' intentions may be incorrect, he concludes: "As far as can be told, the great escalation of all three movements was unforeseen, unplanned and unexpected".[91]

On this view, the slaves in the second Sicilian slave war had not learned from the first, and Spartacus was ignorant of both. Yet the little evidence we have shows that the slaves did not make very many mistakes – in fact, they were very successful and concerned for the future, and did what they could to succeed – and the slaves in these outbreaks managed to survive for several years. They provided for, and organized, vast armies of followers to the surprise and admiration, however reluctant, of the historians.

Some Roman sources claim that Spartacus achieved success because he had been in the Roman army; they are thereby making the best of a terrible situation – he was good, because they themselves had trained him. A similar approach is to argue, as some have, that the Romans themselves had used slaves in civil wars prior to this, that is, they had used slaves against fellow Romans, so this had given the slaves the idea of fighting Romans for themselves.[92] There may be some truth in this, but it is improbable that Spartacus had no knowledge of the enormous impact of the Sicilian wars, and of the huge numbers involved in both of them, and thus it seems unlikely that he was surprised when similar numbers joined his revolt. It is not credible that this revolt, which required the same number of troops as Julius Caesar was to use to conquer Gaul, was the third in a series of accidents, all of which were unplanned by the individuals who headed them.

4
The role of the leader

The individuals who led the rebel slaves play a large role in the accounts of the better documented slave revolts from antiquity, so it is necessary to look at how these men are represented in our texts. I want to look at how they assumed their role, what kind of characters they had and how effective they were depicted as being. The descriptions we possess almost certainly reflect the prejudices and preconceptions, as well as the ideals, of the writers who portrayed them, but rather than dismiss all accounts as mere fiction, it is interesting to see why some of the individuals are presented as positively as they are.[1] A heroic slave leader might be the norm for a modern writer but it is not what we might expect from ancient writers, who generally, as has often been noted, do not question the necessity of slavery, which is now regarded as unacceptable in a civilized society.[2]

For Spartacus, the most famous slave leader of them all, Plutarch and Appian give different accounts of the start of his command. Plutarch gives us the version that records how at first 200 gladiators had planned to escape but their plan was discovered and only seventy carried it out. Once free and seizing some gladiatorial weapons they chose three leaders, the most important of them being Spartacus. Appian, on the other hand, states that Spartacus, who had been in the Roman army, persuaded about seventy of his fellow gladiators to break out. He had two subordinate commanders, Oenomaus and Crixus. Appian therefore gives a much more active role to the leader, and rather more passive ones to his followers than Plutarch.

We often read of leaders emerging or being chosen after the initial outbreak. One of Genovese's conditions for revolt was the opportunity for leaders to arise, that is, individuals reveal themselves as possible leaders before any outbreak. This does seem to have been true with Spartacus in Appian's account, and is most clearly seen in Diodorus' narrative of the first slave war in Sicily. There the slaves recognized the authority of Eunus and asked him whether they should rebel. He had authority, according to Diodorus, because of his wonder-working skills, which are described as fraudulent but that were effective in giving him influence over others.[3]

One aspect noticeable from the ancient narratives is that they frequently portray the leaders as very able men, markedly superior to the mass of their followers, who are merely slaves. So writers could allow that there might be an exceptional figure in the leader of the slaves but, for the rest, their negative picture of slaves predominated.

In the case of Spartacus, Appian states that he had been in the Roman army, which presumably would help the Romans accept the fact of his victories more easily: they could explain to themselves how it was that he could be so successful.[4] Florus' view that fighting with slaves was disgraceful was a common one and, in a sense, the only way that the slave-owners could accept that they had allowed themselves to get into such a situation was if the slaves were led by exceptional men.[5]

We have this stated explicitly in the case of Bulla Felix in the late empire. In the early third century CE (206–7 CE), in the reign of Septimius Severus, Cassius Dio reports that a group of so-called brigands led by Bulla Felix were at large in Italy.[6] In his narrative of Severus' reign, Dio gave enough information for the reader to see that all was not well in the empire,[7] which might be why he added the episode about Bulla. According to Dio, Bulla led a band of about 600 men and raided Italy for about two years, although forces were sent out against him. Dio describes a romantic figure who uses his brains to escape the authorities, outwitting them at every turn. We do not learn of Bulla's own status, but at least some of those with him had once been slaves. Having tricked a centurion into following him he sent him back with the words: "Tell your masters that they should feed their slaves enough so that they do not turn to a life of banditry".[8] Dio continues: "For most of the men whom Bulla had recruited were slaves from the emperor's household, some of whom had received little remuneration and others who had received no sustenance whatsoever".

The account is very brief but Dio describes Bulla in what could be seen as favourable terms, since he is able to outwit his opponents easily: "Although many men pursued Bulla, and the emperor Severus himself tracked the man zealously, he was never seen when seen, never found when found, never caught when caught. In part this was because of Bulla's great generosity with gifts and his intelligence".[9] The Greek word translated here as "intelligence", is σοφία, which might be rendered as "wisdom". It is a positive and striking term to be used about a rebel. Bulla was able to trick and humiliate the Romans and was defeated not by force of arms, or strategic superiority but by the treachery of a woman. He was put on trial and the praetorian prefect asked him "Why did you become a bandit?", to which Bulla replied "Why did you become a praetorian prefect?". There is no further comment from Dio, but some sympathy for Bulla is clear in this portrait. The message for the emperor and readers is clear, and it is similar to that in Diodorus and Plutarch, our main sources for information about rebellious slaves: treat your underlings well or you will have trouble. The role of the leader, as often in these stories, is crucial; when he was gone the band disintegrated, "so much did the whole strength of his 600 men depend on him alone", adds Dio.[10] This is a rather romantic and surprisingly sympathetic account of a rebel leader, who is portrayed as not only intelligent, quick-witted and resourceful but also very daring. Owing to his personal bravery, the Romans are humiliated. Without him, though, his men, among them runaway slaves, were lost. If any sympathy is presented in our sources, it is usually only for the leaders. They are allowed some abilities but their followers are dismissed and presented critically. In this instance, they need a leader to preserve their group.

By way of contrast, this was not so on Chios after the death of Drimakos, where the rebels carried on in a far less restrained manner than previously. As noted before, Drimakos was described as severe and Athenaeus quotes Nymphodorus as claiming that the slaves were more afraid of him than of their former masters (showing perhaps that terrifying them was the effective way to deal with slaves).[11] Drimakos emerged as leader; we are told that he was a brave man and good in battle and therefore became the leader of the runaways.

It was he who proposed an accommodation with the owners so that they might agree a truce, which would be more beneficial to both sides than the existing situation of continual warfare. He devised weights, measures and a seal and promised that his men would not steal more than a certain amount, and then would seal up the storehouses and leave them in peace. He agreed to return slaves to their masters if they could not show that they had been ill treated. Slaves were apparently less inclined to run away than before because they dreaded his questioning, strange as this may sound. We are also told that his followers obeyed him as a military officer. He punished the disobedient and also refused to allow any plundering apart from whatever he ordered. As narrated in Athenaeus, all this action was his idea and was due to his planning.

He also shows strength of character by choosing the manner of his own death. The Chians had promised a big reward to anyone who brought him or his head to them, so when Drimakos was quite old, he called his lover to him and told him to cut off his head. He said he had lived long enough whereas his lover was young still. After showing some seemly reluctance, Drimakos' lover cut off his friend's head, received his reward, and left for his own country, a free man.[12]

Once Drimakos was gone, Nymphodorus said, the Chians were wronged by their slaves again, that is, all restraint that the slaves had shown with regard to property was abandoned. Although this might seem to be some sort of disintegration, it was only so from the point of view of the property-owners. Without this leader the community of runaways did not disappear;[13] its nature changed but it did not collapse, and one might argue that it became more powerful than before, in that it caused more distress to the slave-owners than previously.

After their initial outbreak, the slaves in the second Sicilian slave war formed an assembly and elected a leader, whom they called a king.[14] This was Salvius, who, like Eunus, had religious associations in that he foretold the future and played the flute at women's religious festivals. Despite these rather peculiar characteristics, he seems to have had good leadership qualities. He is also portrayed as austere; we read that he ordered his men to avoid cities because they were sources of laziness and excess. He trained and organized the slave army efficiently, divided them into three with their own commanders and instructed them to raid and in this ordered manner the slave army soon acquired enough equipment for 2,000 cavalry and 20,000 infantry. Salvius thus behaves very methodically to gain supplies for slaves numerous enough to form a substantial army. Spartacus likewise forbade the importation of gold and silver, distributed his booty equally and did not accept deserters into his camp.[15]

The subordinates are always more shadowy characters. Spartacus' subordinates have often been presented as arrogant, and are described as splitting the army, but there is no direct confirmation for this in the ancient evidence. In the two wars in Sicily Cleon and Athenion showed themselves to be trustworthy lieutenants.

Diodorus, in the narrative preserved by Photius, gives a decidedly unfavourable picture of the leader Eunus, who is not represented as sympathetically as the mass of the slaves, although he was wily enough to impress them; he claimed to tell the future and some of his prophecies turned out to be true thus enhancing his reputation, while those that did not were forgotten, says Diodorus sharply. He tricked people into believing that he could breathe fire by placing some embers in a pierced hollow shell and blowing through it so that sparks and flames burst from his mouth.[16] Just before the war, Eunus claimed that the Syrian goddess had told him he would be a king and the narrative follows this with an episode at a banquet where Eunus is teased by his master and guests about his future kingship and some gave him scraps of food and asked to be remembered for this act of kindness.[17]

Eunus did repay this favour but it is only in *Excerpts* of Constantine that we read what this repayment consisted of: he spared their lives. On being made king he ordered all the slave-owners to be executed, except those who had treated him well in his days of slavery. So Eunus repays a tiny favour in the past, being given scraps of food, by saving their lives. The summary says: "Here was an amazing thing: a sudden small shift in fortune and the fact that a favor granted for such a small thing should be repaid with such a great gift and at such a critical time".[18]

Generally there is a less negative picture of Eunus in Constantine's *Excerpts*; an advisor, Achaeus, objected to the savagery of the slaves towards their ex-masters and declared that they would be punished. Eunus not only did not execute him for his moderation but gave him the house of his former masters as a gift. Bradley comments: "Achaeus understood that continued acts of violence by slaves in revolt would bring retaliation against them as a matter of course".[19] This is a rather surprising explanation for Achaeus' actions. The slaves would all be killed anyway, not for individual acts of violence but because they had revolted. There would be retaliation regardless of the behaviour of the slaves, and this is what makes Achaeus' and Eunus' action all the more remarkable and why, one would think, the excerptors recorded it.

Despite these differences, the overall impression from both versions is that Eunus responded to the slaves, and took advantage of the situation, not that he took the initiative and manipulated them into rebellion. Photius depicts Eunus as having won great authority with his peers through what the reader knows are merely tricks. Eunus was not chosen king, according to Diodorus' narrative in Photius, because of his courage; we find out from his actions at the end of the war that he was a miserable coward, hiding in caves with his cook, baker, bath masseur and master of entertainments at drinking parties. The Romans found him and imprisoned him and he died a horrible death in Morgantina.[20]

Unlike Drimakos or Spartacus, Eunus is not presented as having been chosen for his military abilities but because he was a successful master of illusion and because his name seemed to be a good omen, since the Greek "Eunus" means "friendly", and the slaves hoped he would be "friendly" to his subjects. Eunus then puts on a diadem and takes up other symbols of kingship and calls his partner a queen and also had royal counsellors.[21] We find out at the end of the narrative that he called himself Antiochus when he became king and he called his men Syrians.[22] It seems rather curious that he changed his name, which had been one of the reasons, according at least to Diodorus, for his popularity with the other slaves.

It is usually assumed that most of the slaves were indeed Syrians and that this enabled them to revolt since they had a bond and a common language. Diodorus only tells us that Eunus and his wife were Syrians. Cleon, the other leader, was Cilician and Achaeus, his advisor, was Achaean, says Diodorus. There is another Syrian, Sarapion, who betrayed the slave-held Tauromenium to the Romans,[23] but apart from that we are given no indication of the nationality of most of the slaves.[24]

The other slave leader, Cleon, by contrast, is represented neutrally in Photius' summary, which simply says that on the other side of the island, about a month after the original uprising, Cleon, a Cilician, started another revolt of slaves. We also learn that Cleon had a brother who was captured by the consul Rupilius as he tried to escape Tauromenium.[25] Photius' narrative goes on to tell how Rupilius went from Tauromenium to Enna and besieged it and that Cleon fought heroically (ἡρωικῶς)[26] but was killed fighting. The city was taken, again by betrayal, with the added detail that it could not have been taken any other way because of its fortifications. The detail of Cleon nobly resisting Rupilius' attacks contrasts with the behaviour of Eunus, who in Photius' account fled with a bodyguard of 1,000 men.

In the *Excerpts*, however, Cleon is described as having been a bandit from childhood who, in Sicily, had become a herder of horses, robbed travellers and committed many murders.[27] We learn that: "on hearing the news of Eunus' success, and of the victories of the fugitives fighting with him, he [Cleon] rose in revolt".[28] Although generally the *Excerpts* do not accord such an active role to the slaves, in this instance we see clearly the individual described as using a critical situation to very good effect.

In the second war, the leader, Salvius, is presented as shrewd and effective. When the slaves attacked Morgantina and then the Roman army, which had captured their empty camp, Photius' narrative tells us that the Roman army fled. It is here in the text that it is reported that Salvius announced that if the fleeing Romans dropped their arms they would not be killed. Quite surprisingly most of the Roman soldiers accepted his offer and so only relatively few lost their lives, whereas 4,000 were taken prisoner. The slaves thus regained their camp and acquired more weaponry. Diodorus describes Salvius' offer as humane[29] and the slave leader is thus represented positively and as a good judge of character. His ploy is successful because the Romans are cowards.

After this success, slaves flocked to the rebels, doubling the size of their army, which attacked Morgantina again. Salvius appealed to the slaves in the city to join them but misjudged them because they believed their masters, who promised them freedom if they helped in the defence of the city. Diodorus adds: "When the Roman governor later rescinded these grants of freedom, most of the slaves ran away and joined the rebels".[30]

In the northwestern part of the island around Segesta and Lilybaeum, there was another revolt led by the Cilician Athenion. He too was skilled in predicting the future and was renowned for his bravery (ἀνδρείᾳ διαφέρων), so here we have a positive portrayal of a rebel leader.[31] Athenion was a steward on an estate and certainly seems to have had authority over those who were working for him. He persuaded 200 slaves who worked under him to join him and then recruited slaves on neighbouring farms until within five days he had more than 1,000 with him. Here for once we have evidence for a slave already in a leadership role naturally assuming similar duties on the rebellion, having acquired the authority to persuade others to rebel.

Diodorus also tells us, not that he assumed command, but that the slaves *chose* him as their king, adding:

> Athenion conducted his rule in a manner that was opposite to that of all the other rebel groups. He did not accept all slaves who went into revolt, but turned only the best of them into soldiers. He forced the others to remain at their former tasks and had each of them take care of their own household managerial tasks and work assignments.[32]

Like Salvius, Athenion was a careful and methodical leader. In this way he provided for his soldiers and said that the gods had told him he would be king of Sicily so he wanted to look after the plants and animals as they now belonged to him.[33]

Bradley argues that the outbreak led by Athenion should be seen as completely independent of Salvius' revolt: "There is no evidence whatsoever that the revolts of Salvius and Athenion were anything but uncoordinated, entirely separate uprisings".[34] If we accept Bradley's view of the situation, this might lead us to suppose that outbreaks of slave rebellion are in fact much more frequent than we had assumed. If this was merely a coincidence, then it would seem slaves constantly rose up against their masters and it so happened that two of them coincided and were successful. It seems more likely, however, that Athenion was taking advantage of the Romans being occupied with slaves in a different part of the island and that the events were similar to the previous war, where we are told explicitly that Cleon decided to rebel when he heard about Eunus.[35]

Salvius and his army continued raiding the countryside and acquired more soldiers, the number now reaching over 30,000 men. He announced his change of name to King Tryphon (the name of a recent usurper to the Seleucid throne, but possibly his own name, just as Antiochus, although a common name for Seleucid kings, could have been Eunus' real name, that is, non-slave name) and made contact with Athenion. Diodorus reports that there was the hope that the two leaders would fight each other but, as in the first slave war, they joined forces instead. Diodorus comments: "Fortune, as though intentionally increasing the power of the fugitives, caused their leaders to be of one mind".[36] Athenion became Salvius' general, although later Salvius/Tryphon was suspicious of him, and Diodorus writes that he ordered Athenion "to be placed in detention".[37]

Salvius/Tryphon moved northwards, made his headquarters in Triokala and strengthened its defences. Diodorus describes it as well-placed because it was easy to defend, being on a high rock with fresh water and fertile land around it. Here Salvius/Tryphon built a palace and marketplace and appointed intelligent people to be his advisers. When conducting official business he adopted the trappings of the Roman magistrates, wearing a purple-edged toga and tunic with a broad border, accompanied by lictors with axes.[38] The Senate sent out Lucius Licinius Lucullus with more forces and Diodorus is quite specific here, as if he has access to official documents: 14,000 Italians and Romans, 800 Bithynians, Thessalians and Akarnanians, 600 Lucanians, and 600 others, totalling 17,000.[39]

Salvius/Tryphon released Athenion, who does not appear to have been overly resentful at being detained in that he did not go over to the Romans or betray his own side; however, he did give bad advice.

He suggested fighting the Romans, which they did and lost, Athenion being badly wounded. Twenty thousand of the rebels were killed and the rest were understandably demoralized. The Romans besieged Triokala but then withdrew. Diodorus gives two possibilities for this surprising retreat: either Lucullus was lazy or he had been bribed. He comments that this general was later put on trial and punished for this failure. We are told that the praetor who succeeded Lucullus, Gaius Servilius, also accomplished little. For this lack of action he too was tried and exiled. When Salvius/Tryphon died, (we do not know how), Athenion took over and reigned successfully while Servilius did nothing.[40]

An alternative to the generals being useless is that the Romans were unequal to the task of fighting the slaves. It is entirely plausible that they preferred to blame the commanders than admit the slaves had been too much for them. In 101 BCE the Senate sent out the consul Manius Aquillius (Diodorus calls him Gaius Aquillius),[41] who, we are told, because of his personal bravery, crushed them in a brilliantly conducted battle. He fought a hand-to-hand duel with Athenion, the king of the rebels, and beat him in a heroic contest.

Although wounded himself, Aquillius carried on to fight the rest of the slaves, who numbered about 10,000, and eventually defeated them. Again this seems to have come from an official Roman source, since so much is attributed to the personal valour of the general, and there is even the rather unlikely detail of hand-to-hand combat with Athenion. Diodorus goes on to say that even so, about 1,000 slaves survived, led by Satyros, a leader who had not previously been mentioned. Aquillius negotiated a surrender and took the rebels to Rome to fight as gladiators with wild beasts. Diodorus slightly removes himself from his account of the end by using the phrase "some people say", but nevertheless gives us this version:

> Some people say that they brought their lives to a most glorious end (ἐπιφανεστάτην ... καταστροφήν) when they refused to do battle with the wild animals and instead cut each other down in front of the public altars. Satyros himself killed the last man. Then Satyros took his life with his own hand, dying like a hero (ἡρωικῶς). Thus, the war of the slaves in Sicily, a war that had lasted nearly four years, reached its tragic finale.[42]

Again, it is quite remarkable that Diodorus uses the word "tragic" for the outcome. Clearly for the slave-owners it was not at all tragic, but Diodorus once again shows a sympathy, unusual among ancient writers, for the rebels. Not only that but the slave leaders in the accounts acquitted themselves well in the narratives we have remaining. There is nothing to match the critical comments about Eunus.

Florus has a chapter on the slave wars,[43] and he remarks that the very first uprising of slaves was in Rome under Herdonius the Sabine, in the fifth century BCE. He goes on to observe that Sicily was more devastated in the slave wars than in the Punic War. There is a cursory description of the first war ending with the detail that Perperna crucified all the surviving slaves. Then: "Scarcely had the island recovered when, in the praetorship of Servilius, the command suddenly passed from the hands of a Syrian into those of a Cilician".[44]

Salvius does not appear in Florus' narrative, but much is made of the kingship of Athenion, who, we are told, murdered his master, put on a purple robe and crowned himself:

> He raised an army that was just as large as that of his demented predecessor but he conducted his operations with even greater savagery, on the pretext of avenging him, plundering villages, towns and fortresses, vented his fury with even greater violence upon the slaves than upon their masters, treating them as renegades.[45]

There is no sympathy in Florus' words. Athenion plunders property and murders slaves who refuse to join the rebellion. Only Florus makes a direct connection between the first and second slave wars on Sicily and attributes to Athenion vengeance for Eunus. His men commit suicide rather than surrender and although Athenion himself was taken alive, the crowd around him argued over his arrest and tore his body to pieces.[46] This seems slightly odd but presumably is meant to convey the anger felt by citizens towards someone who had been so threatening to their safety.

In both the Sicilian wars, the leaders assumed monarchical regalia and this has been interpreted as revealing the type of government the slaves had known when they were free citizens. Salvius also adopted the trappings of Roman power, thus taking up symbols of authority from his new situation as well as his old one; presumably Salvius wished to indicate that he had assumed this power for himself.[47]

There were also leaders who were not slaves, such as Aristonicus and Titus Vettius Minutius. The latter is portrayed as completely out of control, as enslaved to his own lust, but it is more difficult to gain a picture of Aristonicus. Both, however, are portrayed as actively taking charge, even though they were exploiting the rebellious nature of the slaves. Neither, of course, were *chosen* as the leaders of their armies; rather, they successfully gathered them and used them for their own ends. But not much detail is given as to how they used their power and here it is simply a question of not having enough material to gain an adequate picture.

Aristonicus, a member of the royal family of Pergamum, in that he was the illegitimate half-brother of the dead king, Attalus III, raised an army when Attalus III left the kingdom to the Roman people in his will. Some of those in that army were slaves. Sallust purports to give the letter Mithridates wrote to the king of the Parthians, Arsaces, which asserts: "Then, having forged an unnatural will, they led his son, Aristonicus in triumph like an enemy, because he had tried to recover his father's rights".[48]

Whether the will was forged or not, the Romans considered that Pergamum was theirs and Aristonicus considered that it was not.[49] The evidence records that his army was successful for a while, that various cities came over to his side, that neighbouring kings took up arms against him, and that he defeated the first Roman troops sent out against him. From a source that has been termed anti-Roman, we have further information about Aristonicus.[50] In his *Epitome of the Philippic History of Pompeius Trogus*, Justin records that the previous king, Attalus, seemed to go mad. He murdered friends and family, alleged that his enemies had killed his mother and wife, took no care with his appearance, started to grow poisonous plants and sent them to his friends.[51] He began building a tomb for his mother but died of sunstroke before finishing it. His total decline is perhaps indicated by the sentence that follows: "In his will the Roman people were named as his heirs". Justin describes what happened next:

> After Attalus' death Aristonicus took possession of Asia, claiming it as his father's kingdom. He fought many successful battles against the cities which refused to yield to him from fear of the Romans, and now seemed to be established as king when Asia was assigned to the consul Licinius Crassus.[52]

The first general sent out against him was Publius Licinius Crassus Dives Mucianus, a distant relative of the more famous adversary of

Spartacus, and also tainted with the charge of avarice.[53] Justin observes of him that he was more interested in Attalus' treasure than in the conduct of the war and that he paid for his greed with his blood. Marcus Perperna, who had recently been successful against the slaves in Sicily, was then sent out. He took Aristonicus prisoner, loaded Attalus' treasure on to ships and sent it to Rome, the implication being that Aristonicus had had possession of it until then.[54] Finally, the consul Manius Aquillius extinguished the remaining sparks of rebellion. Justin finishes the account: "So it was that Asia, made now the property of the Romans, transmitted to Rome its vices along with its riches".[55]

Florus is scathing about Aquillius, who resorted to poisoning the water supply in order to force the rebels to surrender. He also reveals that whole cities were holding out against the Romans, and that the situation was not simply an army of ex-slaves wandering the countryside.

> Aquilius finally brought the Asiatic war to a close by the wicked expedient of poisoning the springs in order to procure the surrender of *certain cities*. This, though it hastened his victory, brought shame upon it, for he had disgraced the Roman arms, which had hitherto been unsullied, by the use of foul drugs in violation of the laws of heaven and the practice of our forefathers.[56]

Our remaining texts describing this episode are thus at the very least ambiguous about the conduct of the Romans. But the information is scanty. Despite the lack of material on Aristonicus, scholars have speculated about his motives. An example of the way Aristonicus has been treated in recent times is the work of Vladimir Vavrinek, who writes:

> Did he [Aristonicus] wish merely to take over the heritage of his forebears and continue ruling with the same means and in the same spirit as they did, or was he a convinced social reformer attempting a radical re-creation of the whole of society with the aim of establishing general justice and equality for all, slaves included?[57]

How can we ever know? It is unlikely that he wished to establish some form of communistic society and, given that he never had a chance to start, it is not even a very interesting question. However, Vavrinek continues: "Was he a revolutionary leader who, conscious of his purpose, placed himself in command of the revolting slaves, or was the freeing of the slave merely a tactical device which he was forced to employ because he lacked other means of achieving his aims?"[58]

The second option is surely much more probable, since the first would make him unique in ancient history, whereas the second has many more examples. Vavrinek concludes that the question of whether Aristonicus was a pretender or a slave leader is a false dichotomy because he was both. But whatever thoughts were in Aristonicus' head, the actions of slaves should not be forgotten. It is unlikely that they were fighting only in order to put another member of the royal family on the throne. One might surmise that they wished to escape their servitude, to win for themselves a better existence, to achieve their own freedom.

We only know about this activity of the slaves from the imperfect preservation of Diodorus' text. Without it the single sentence in Strabo would be just that: a sentence along with others that mention slaves fighting alongside their masters.[59] The evidence for a slave revolt is slight but once again it is Diodorus whose narrative allows us, through his uniquely sympathetic approach, an insight normally lacking in our historians.

Titus Vettius Minutius, as related in the summary of Diodorus by Photius, was a rich young man who fell in love with a slave, tried to buy her but could not afford her. We are told that his father was rich so this lack of money is quite strange, but the picture given is a caracature of a man beside himself because of a woman.[60] When the time came to pay for his girl, he instead killed his creditors and formed an army of 400 of his own slaves, which soon grew to 3,500. A quick response from the Romans, together with treachery on the part of one of Vettius' lieutenants, put an end to this revolt.[61]

In the version from the *Excerpts* that is very similar to that of Photius, a detail is added that helps to explain why Diodorus described this episode at such length: he says about Vettius that he could not pay, "but was now a *very slave* to love, he embarked on an enterprise that passes all comprehension".[62] What is described here, then, is a situation that was extremely dangerous, brought on by a Roman's inability to control himself; he was a slave to his feelings. And the emphasis in the *Excerpts* on advice to rulers also explains why we have this explanatory note in this version; it was important for the readers to see how weaknesses on the part of the owners can lead to terrible consequences.

Spartacus

Spartacus is the most famous of all the slave leaders not simply because he is presented in the most favourable light, which he is, but also because there is more information about him than about the others. This relatively generous allocation of space alone marks him out as a special character, and the sympathetic portrayal increases this impression. For that reason alone, it is worth taking a closer look at why our sources were ready to credit him with heroic characteristics. Spartacus' personal qualities and heroism are often mentioned but any praise is tempered by the overall hopelessness of his task and by the refusal of his followers to accept his wise counsel. A typical modern analysis runs as follows:

> The revolt of Spartacus appears tragic, because the odds were too heavy against him. He was relatively humane and able. His achievement in creating, disciplining and arming from scratch forces that could defeat consular armies was little short of a miracle. But he could not always impose his will on them.[63]

Spartacus has long been regarded as a hero and champion of the oppressed, but one would have thought this is in spite of, rather than because of, the ancient sources. Many would agree with Barry Baldwin that "in general, the ancient accounts are emotionally against the slaves, just as our modern sympathies go out to them for purely emotional reasons".[64] As I have argued briefly elsewhere,[65] this positive depiction of Spartacus is not a purely modern invention but is a product of the portrait painted by Plutarch in his *Life of Crassus*.

Modern scholars have been keen to point out the scanty and unsatisfactory nature of the sources and have argued, quite reasonably, that there is too little evidence for any elaborate theories about this particular individual. J. G. Griffith gives a good example of the response of many, starting his article by commenting that despite the Spartacus legend, "authoritative works in English, the fruits of a long tradition of rigorous historical criticism, say little about him".[66] He concludes, as one might expect, by saying that these works are right to ignore him.[67] There are, however, more sources than one might think from Griffith's introductory remarks, although they are not plentiful. Brent Shaw has recently collected them, as well as those for the previous Sicilian slave wars.[68]

We have accounts from authors contemporary with the event, whose words one might think would be the most valuable but that are not, due to their extreme brevity on the subject. Cicero, Varro, Diodorus and Sallust all refer to Spartacus but only the words of Cicero and Sallust form more than a sentence. The sentence by Varro is favourable: "Although he was an innocent man, Spartacus was condemned to a gladiatorial school". We only know this sentence because it is preserved in the work of a much later author, Sosipater Charisius,[69] who lived in the late fourth century CE. His main concern was grammar, not history, so what this shows is that the tradition of a positive portrait of Spartacus was circulating at this time. Diodorus, our main source for the Sicilian slave wars, uses Spartacus as an example to illustrate that even barbarians return good for good. He writes: "The barbarian Spartacus, on receiving a certain favour from someone, showed him his gratitude. Indeed, nature is self-schooled, even among barbarians, to repay kindness for kindness to those who give assistance".[70] Diodorus, preserved by the *Excerpts*, calls him "the barbarian Spartacus" (ὁ Σπάρτακος ὁ βάρβαρος).[71] Again, we see here the typically Diodoran theme of good behaviour receiving its just recompense. Cicero refers to Spartacus while attacking Verres, in his prosecution of this former governor of Sicily. Given the amount of vitriol Cicero pours on Verres' claim to have prevented the war spreading to Sicily, Verres seems to have made much of this in his defence. Although Verres' character has not survived Cicero's onslaught, Baldwin concludes his article on the Spartacus revolt: "The fact that Spartacus inspired no support from Sicily in Verres' time, or from the many free Italians that had fought the Social War, indicates that Spartacus could not hope to achieve any concrete ideal such as the abolition of slavery – if he ever wanted to".[72] It is not impossible that the failure of any support emanating from Sicily was due to the measures taken by Verres but for our purposes now, it is sufficient to observe that Cicero is utterly hostile to the slave leader.

Sallust (86–35 BCE), who would have been a youth during the war, is considered a very important source because of his closeness in time to the events. However, all that remains of his description of Spartacus are the fragments of his *Histories* and although these have been pieced together to form some sort of narrative the results are frustrating.[73] Some possible glimpses of Sallust's attitude can be had. One is a description ascribed to Spartacus by both editors of the fragments of the *Histories*, B. Maurenbrecher and Patrick McGushin, which reads "of immense bodily strength and spirit".[74] In a later fragment from the same book, it would seem that Spartacus is being held up as giving good advice, but we can only surmise his name; it is not in the manuscript, although later in the same passage we do see him (named) trying to hold his men back.[75]

The best illustration for Sallust's views occurs in a passage in Book 4: "Crassus concerned himself rather with criticizing his colleague than with diligently assessing what was good and what was bad for the people".[76] While this does not belong to the Spartacan narrative proper it gives us an indication of what Sallust thought about Crassus. The negative portrait fits in well with that of Plutarch and also with Sallust's political theory, which was that it was the decline of *virtus* and the rise of *ambitus* and *avaritia* that destroyed the republic.[77] Crassus, according to Plutarch at any rate, is the very embodiment of *avaritia*. The text extant from Sallust is not especially helpful except that it is at least possible that he represented Spartacus in heroic terms and Crassus in not so heroic terms, and that he did write about Spartacus at all. Spartacus appears in other writers briefly, but so briefly as to be hardly useful except as an indication of his fame.

Others did write about Spartacus, but what survives today is so limited that it is difficult to glean much from it. Livy, who witnessed the last stages of civil war and the reign of Augustus, wrote a history of Rome from its foundations to 9 BCE in 142 books. Unsurprisingly the whole of this massive undertaking has not survived and summaries were made, perhaps in the fourth century CE, for those who did not have enough time to read the whole work. It is unclear how reliably they summarized Livy's words and, in the case of Spartacus, the narrative is abbreviated to such an extent that the events are simply mentioned with no attitude discernible. In the fourth century CE Eutropius wrote his *Breviarium* covering 753 BCE–364 CE. For the Spartacan period he is assumed to be using Livy's *Epitome*, but his account differs from our extant version in naming Oenomaus and calling Crassus proconsul.[78] The same can be said for Velleius Paterculus (who lived from 20 BCE until after 30 CE), whose sweeping history in two volumes started with Greek mythology and ended in 29 CE. Frontinus, whose interest was purely military, writing in the late first century CE, describes tricks used by Spartacus and afterwards relates those used by Crassus to defeat the slaves. All of these, apart from Diodorus, wrote in Latin.

On the other hand we have relatively full, and extremely useful sources in the Greek authors Plutarch and Appian, both of whom wrote well over a century and a half after the events they describe.[79]

Plutarch on Spartacus

In his *Life of Crassus* Plutarch describes how, after being ill-treated by those in charge of them, some gladiators planned an escape. They had armed themselves with kitchen implements but, having escaped, they came upon wagons containing weapons for gladiators, which they seized. They elected three leaders, one of whom was Spartacus, a man of great spirit and physical strength as well as intelligence and nobility of character. Plutarch added that when Spartacus was taken to Rome to be sold a snake was seen coiled around his head while he slept and that his wife, who was a prophetess of Dionysus,[80] said it meant he would have a great and fearful power that would bring good fortune.[81]

Plutarch thus credits Spartacus with some sense: he had only wanted to take his followers home, back to Thrace and Gaul, but his men did not listen. He personally had not wanted to face the Romans in battle but those following him became overconfident and overruled him, and he had thought of going to Sicily but had been cheated by the pirates. He fought bravely until the end, always putting the interests of his men first, never deserting them, although they did not listen to him; he was, in fact, the epitome of a great leader, even though he had been a slave. Crassus' leadership skills, on the other hand, depended on instilling fear, not devotion into his army. Plutarch does not mention the crucifixion of survivors, although today this is a well-known aspect of the story, largely owing to the final scene in the Stanley Kubrick film.

That is the narrative as Spartacus appears in it. More than any other single author, Plutarch has contributed to the very positive image the legend was built on. His account should be seen in a larger context. Spartacus features in Plutarch's *Parallel Lives* in the *Life of Crassus*, paired with the Athenian general Nicias. Plutarch's idea of comparing Greek and Roman statesmen in *Parallel Lives* gives us an indication of his intentions. Whatever the purpose of this work, the effect of it would almost certainly have been to show the reader (who, for the most part, would have been Greek, like Plutarch, since that was the language he was writing in) that the Greeks, although now subjects of the Romans, had their own heroes from the past who were equivalent to, or better than, the present or recent Roman ones.

It is quite common for Plutarch to portray both Greeks and Romans as good generals, but the Greeks are more often marked out as also being good men. Generally, and this is surely unsurprising from a

Greek writer, the Greeks are morally superior to their Roman counterparts. Romans from the distant past usually came off better from Plutarch's pen than the more recent ones. Where Romans are praised it is often because they behave like Greeks or show respect to the Greeks and their culture.

For instance, in the comparison of Lycurgus and Numa, Numa is praiseworthy for his treatment of slaves, precisely because he behaved like a Greek:

> Whereas, if we must admit the treatment of the helots to be a part of Lycurgus' legislation, a most cruel and iniquitous proceeding, we must own that Numa was by a great deal the more humane and *Greek-like* legislator, granting even to actual slaves a licence to sit at meat with their masters at the foot of Saturn, that they also might have some taste and relish of the sweets of liberty.[82]

And about Cornelia, mother of the Gracchi, he writes: "She had many friends and kept a good table which was always thronged with guests: Greeks and other learned men frequently visited her, and all the reigning kings exchanged presents with her".[83]

The Romans who show a deep respect for things Greek receive far better press from him than those who despise the Hellenic culture (compare, for example, the *Life of Cicero* with that of Marius).[84] Spartacus was not the subject of a life as he was a mere slave but he appears in a heroic light in the *Life of Crassus*, although not in order to glorify Crassus.[85] It should be noted that Plutarch also describes Sertorius in very favourable terms, a man who was a rebel against the Romans fighting at the same time as Spartacus.[86] Plutarch was not afraid to portray enemies of Rome in a heroic light, and, in turn, not infrequently depicts the Romans as less than virtuous.

Crassus himself is a good example of this. He is described as being excessively greedy in the first paragraph of Plutarch's *Life of Crassus*. He acquires his wealth by buying burning houses in Rome and then repairing them. He owned silver mines and estates and also earned money from the work of slaves. Plutarch comments, "Crassus was not right, however, in thinking and in actually saying that no one could be called rich who could not support an army out of his income".[87]

The life Plutarch describes in parallel to that of Crassus is that of the Athenian general Nicias, whose main fault is that he is excessively pious, a vice, if such it can be termed, hardly on a par with greed.[88]

Indeed, there is an implicit contrast with Nicias in the first paragraph of Crassus' life where we learn that he was suspected of a liaison with a Vestal Virgin. This rumour was a result of the fact that he was pursuing the woman because he wanted her house cheaply. Plutarch says he was acquitted of any wrongdoing with her (presumably sexual) because the judges knew how greedy he was and ends the story saying that he did not cease to pester her until she sold him the house. Nicias, then, is excessively pious and pays too much attention to omens and oracles; Crassus is so impious through his greed that he harasses a Vestal Virgin.

Also early on, while establishing Crassus' character, Plutarch stresses the vast numbers of slaves he possessed, and used as a source of revenue. The stress on the huge numbers of slaves that Crassus owned and exploited appears to be deliberate on Plutarch's part, drawing attention to the irony that he would later find himself fighting them, and indeed hover on the brink of being defeated by them. In the comparison of the Greek and Roman, Plutarch has very little positive to say about the latter.[89] Nicias was also wealthy but used his wealth to serve the public, and this is illustrated in the *Life of Nicias*, where only after hearing of his benefits do we learn that he was wealthy because he owned silver mines, whereas the issue of Crassus' wealth is stressed immediately.

The argument here is not that Plutarch is manipulating facts but rather, owing to his judgement of the two men, putting a different emphasis on their deeds. For him, Nicias' donations were more noteworthy than his excessive wealth. Plutarch does not hide that the Greek was wealthy and that he owned many slaves. In fact, this is important for his parallel with Crassus, but it is the different attitude to wealth that was significant for Plutarch. Nicias has his faults, being too timid and addicted to omens, but whereas Nicias had been reluctant to undertake the Sicilian expedition that was his downfall, Crassus had been eager to go to Parthia. Both were disastrous campaigns but Crassus rushed to his doom and Nicias had to be dragged. Plutarch is thus portraying the Roman in the harshest light and, whatever one thinks of Nicias, no one could come away from Plutarch's *Lives* considering him to be as despicable as Crassus.

Spartacus, a slave and one of the class of men exploited by Crassus in his own household, is held up by contrast. His character is noble; he cares about his men, about honour, about equality. Crassus emerges as the more barbaric character (and notice, as befits such a barbarian, he hates Cicero, who is one of the most favourably portrayed Romans in the *Parallel Lives*[90]). In portraying Spartacus in this way, Plutarch is continuing the negative portrayal of the Roman, since even a slave has more nobility of character than *this* Roman. There is no such negative contrast in the *Life of Nicias*.

In the comparison Plutarch starts by saying that the acquisition of Nicias' wealth was more blameless than that of Crassus. In his discussion of the comparison, Timothy Duff interprets this as follows: "It seems fairly clear in this *synkrisis* that Plutarch's instincts were to prefer Nikias".[91] I would argue that Plutarch's instincts throughout *Parallel Lives* were to prefer the Greeks, as well he might.

Plutarch was using the opportunity of the Spartacus episode to throw light on the character of Crassus. Plutarch liked and used comparisons, not just in the formal sense.[92] For instance, in the *Life of Antony*, Cleopatra, another famous Roman hate-figure like Spartacus, is given extended treatment to highlight Antony's faults. The Roman is putty in her hands; she is clever and manipulative and he is stupid and driven by his passions. For Plutarch's purposes, she was also Greek, as was Alexander. Spartacus, I would argue, had the nobility of character that one would expect from a Roman of Crassus' rank but that Crassus so signally lacked. An indication of Plutarch's intentions in his portrayal of Spartacus is given when he introduces him as a character:

> He not only possessed great spirit and bodily strength (ῥώμην) [*rhōmēn*], but he was more intelligent and nobler than his fate, and he was more Greek than his [Thracian] background might indicate. People tell the following story about him when he was brought to Rome (Ῥώμην) [*Rhōmēn*] to be sold as a slave.[93]

For Plutarch this is praise. Plutarch admired intelligent people, individuals such as Sertorius, Cleopatra and Alexander, but had very little time for the stupid and insensitive such as Marius, Sulla and Antony. Most telling of all is that Spartacus was ἑλληνικώτερος [more Greek] than his people. This is perhaps the most flattering thing from the pen of Plutarch.[94] Plutarch writes well of Cicero too, and much of the praise comes in the form of describing Cicero's respect for Greek culture.

The quotation above mentions him going to Rome, and I have included the last sentence because it is worth commenting on the Greek words. In the original passage the words ῥώμην and Ῥώμην are physically very close to each other. They refer to totally different things but they are the same word. One means strength, the other is the name of the city of Rome, and in Greek one can see the similarity straightaway. That Plutarch was conscious of the meaning of the name can be seen in the opening words of his *Life of Romulus*, where he relates that some say that the Pelasgians named the city Rome because of their strength (ῥώμη) in arms. One thus could say that Spartacus embodies the very essence (ῥώμη) of Rome, although he is only a gladiator. He possessed strength and many other laudable qualities; Crassus on the other hand was despicable in his lust for money and small-minded rivalry with Pompey. Spartacus thinks only of his men and even when they do not listen to him he does not abandon them but does his best. When he realizes all is lost, he stabs his horse and, charging straight for Crassus, kills two centurions and dies fighting surrounded by enemies, even after his own men had fled.[95] There is little doubt where Plutarch's sympathies lay in this story.[96]

Appian's account of the Spartacan war

A near contemporary of Plutarch, Appian lived c.90–c.160 CE, and was also Greek but from Alexandria in Egypt.[97] In his history of the civil wars he describes the revolt of Spartacus, after that of Sertorius.[98] He uses the episode to highlight the tensions between Crassus and Pompey. Spartacus is introduced as having served as a soldier with the Romans but then being taken prisoner and sold for a gladiator, thus arriving in the training school in Capua. He is credited by Appian with the idea of escaping and he and about seventy others do so and flee to Mount Vesuvius.[99] Appian wrote that there were many fugitive slaves and even some free men from the fields who joined them. Spartacus had two subordinates, Crixus and Oenomaus, and because he was a fair leader and divided the plunder equally, he had plenty of men following him. The Roman commanders Varinius Glaber and then Publius Valerius were sent with hastily raised troops but both were beaten.[100]

We also see a more ruthless side to Spartacus than presented in Plutarch's narrative, as Appian describes how he ordered the sacrifice of 300 Roman prisoners on the death of his general, Crixus, killing the rest and the pack animals. He crucified a Roman soldier to set an example to his men and, possibly, the Romans.[101] It may be that for Appian such measures are the sign of a good general, since he also reports that

Crassus had his own soldiers executed. Appian remarked that once he had made his own men realize he was more dangerous than the enemy they beat Spartacus in the next battle. This could either be praise or blame, depending on one's attitude, but the point is that Crassus is ultimately successful and Appian gives him a favourable description. He is described as distinguished by birth and wealth, beats Spartacus brilliantly (λαμπρῶς) and in the next engagement killed 6,000 of the slave army in the morning and the same number again in the evening, losing only three of his own, with seven wounded.[102] Crassus, when facing the prospect of Pompey stealing his victory at the end of this campaign, is the first to offer reconciliation.[103]

The episode of Spartacus comes at the end of Book 1 of Appian's *Civil Wars*, just after a description of Sertorius' activities and Pompey's victory in Spain. The war against Sertorius was against a Roman, who had set himself up independently in Spain after Sulla's victory because earlier he had been on the opposing side. Appian draws a picture of a great general and attributes his failure to him turning to women and drink and alienating his own men so that he was assassinated by his general, Perperna. Appian ends the description saying the war would have lasted longer had Sertorius lived longer.

Appian uses the story of Spartacus to illustrate the burgeoning conflict between Pompey and Crassus. Pompey had been victorious against Sertorius, and Crassus against Spartacus; both now wanted to be consul. There was a stand-off when neither disbanded their army, although Crassus made peace first and war was averted for a while. Overall Appian's account is less favourable to Spartacus than Plutarch's, with fewer gratuitous asides about his noble character.

In our sources, then, Spartacus is credited with sensible plans, and mistakes were only made when his men did not obey him. The Romans could be generous about individuals but not about a whole army. It would seem improbable that much of substance can be gleaned from our sources about the historical slave leaders, but more importantly, perhaps, we can begin to understand how their enemies viewed them; in the case of Spartacus this was as a great general, as befits someone who had caused them so much damage.[104] But the rebellion had to be seen as the creation of an individual who was a virtual genius, not the collective action of the Romans' own slaves.

One individual was built up and heroized so that he could also be demonized and, more importantly, so that their own slaves could be made safe again. The Romans had to live with their slaves after the uprising so it helped them to think that without such a genius as Spartacus to lead them they would be docile and harmless. It makes sense, then, that usually one has a name on which to pin all the threat and the danger.

Helot leaders

It is interesting to contrast the examples we have seen so far with the case of the helots, in which the name of no particular individual is famous beyond all others. This may not be without influence on some scholars, who argue that the helots did not in fact rebel as much as our ancient sources report that they did. Richard Talbert, for instance, goes so far as to cast doubt on the ability of the helots to form any resistance:

> In brief we should expect helots to have been relatively ignorant, simple people, almost without education or awareness of the outside world. Few, if any, can even have gained the chance to develop the skills, let alone the sophistication, to make them natural leaders or agents for change.[105]

This definition of "natural" is a little puzzling since the term "natural leaders" is used by most to mean people who *naturally* are leaders, not ones who have learnt the skills of leadership. One must also remember that Hesychius of Alexandria has a word in his lexicon, μνωιονόμοι, that means leaders of helots. It is a lexicon of rare words, but that does not necessarily mean leaders of helots were rare, just that people did not use the term very often.[106] Talbert completely redraws our picture of helots, observing: "Like the lower orders in many societies throughout human history, helots knew their place within severely limited horizons, clung to it and seldom thought coherently about how to alter it, regardless of how humiliating or undesirable it might seem to others".[107]

This, however, is an unusual view and one not generally accepted by most scholars, who perhaps find it more difficult to ignore what sources such as Thucydides and Aristotle have written.[108] One of the reasons our ancient sources are so critical of the way that the Spartans treated their helots may be not simply that it was brutal but that it did not work, given that the helots were constantly rebelling.

While it is true that we do not learn the names of prominent helots, this may be due to our sources, as well as the famous secrecy surrounding everything Spartan. Usually, however, there is a name on which to attach all sorts of legends and stories. The effect of the nameless leadership of the helots is to accord *all* the helots with an energy and resourcefulness not often attributed to followers in the other revolts. Because we cannot attribute all the success to one particular person, we must acknowledge the role played by all. Similarly, when we have names it is tempting to credit all the success to them, rather than to the group. Certainly in the case of the slaves on Chios, at least, we have evidence that their determination was not due only to the leadership of Drimakos. Similarly, slaves from the Spartacan revolt continued to survive independently for ten years after what is normally termed the final battle.

It has been suggested that often there were religious aspects to the leadership of the slave revolts, and certainly this is true of those who led the Sicilian slave wars, but it is not universal. One can see, however, the importance of religion in binding slaves together although we do not always have enough information to say this was usually the case.[109]

It is difficult to say anything definitive about the individuals who led the revolts, but we can say that the sources attributed to them all the powers, abilities, wisdom and cunning that challenges to the status quo had to have had in order to succeed. This meant that once that individual had gone, the regular slaves need not be feared, or at least not feared more than necessary.

5
The ideology of the slaves

What did the slaves of antiquity think they were doing when they took up arms against their masters? What could they hope to achieve? It is conventional to argue that these revolts were doomed to failure because of the forces marshalled against them.[1] In any case, the slaves could not conceive of a society without slaves. If they fought it would be merely to be masters rather than slaves themselves. Eunus and Salvius set themselves up as kings, indicating that they had no egalitarian aims. What presents a problem is that the slaves seem to have been either suicidal or stupid. How could they hope to defeat the Roman army? How, for that matter, could the lowly helots think they had a chance against the Spartan army?

There are, however, examples even today of people without resources violently resisting others who are much better equipped and armed, and generally more powerful. It is perhaps a mistake to assume that the participants had any long-term plan. Sometimes people have much smaller ambitions and are satisfied merely to inflict damage. It might be that they saw an opportunity and took it, without thinking through all the next moves. The ancients had long recognized how unpredictable events were in wartime. Thucydides put the following expression into the mouths of the Melian speakers as an accepted truth about war:

> Yet we know that in war fortune sometimes makes the odds more level than could be expected from the difference in numbers of the two sides. And if we surrender, then all our hope is lost at once, whereas, so long as we remain in action, there is still a hope that we may yet stand upright.[2]

Rather than look for specific aims that a particular group of slaves may have had, it might be more useful to look at the ideas of slavery and freedom that we do come across in our sources. Our sources were all written by men of the slave-owning class, but they can give us an idea of what might be called the "dominant ideology" of the times. Throughout the classical period, the idea that freedom was desirable and slavery absolutely to be avoided was always current: "Men desire above all things to be free and say that freedom is the greatest of blessings, while slavery is the most shameful and wretched of states", as noted by the Stoic orator, Dio Chrysostom, as he starts his first treatise *On Slavery and Freedom*.[3] He goes on to argue that unfortunately most people do not understand what freedom really is.[4] However, the assumption that the word "freedom" represents something good and desirable was as valid in the ancient world as it is today.[5] This premise, which may appear a truism to many, has important consequences for how we view the ancient world. If freedom is what people want above all else, then one might assume that they would grasp every opportunity to obtain it. From the history of the Atlantic slave trade from the fifteenth to the nineteenth centuries, it is clear from our source material, which is much more copious than that for ancient times, that this was true of the Africans exported to the Americas for their enslavement.[6]

There is also evidence from the ancient world that not only did slaves share this longing for freedom, but also many owners lived under the constant fear generated by this desire. An implication of this premise is that there is a natural enmity between masters and slaves, since the former have deprived the latter of the precious object of freedom, or at least have it in their power to bestow on them this greatest good, but choose not to do so.[7] The assumption of the underlying hostility between masters and slaves is also well documented from ancient times.

In a passage of Plato's *Republic*, where Socrates discusses tyranny with Glaucon, he suggests a parallel between rich men and tyrants.[8] The rich own many slaves but do not fear them, and Glaucon says that this is because the whole city protects the single individual. Socrates agrees, and asks Glaucon to consider the case of a man who owns fifty slaves or more being carried away to some desert island where there is no free man to assist him. What is likely to happen to him? Glaucon answers that the man would be terrified of an uprising of his slaves in which he and his family would be massacred. He would therefore be obliged to be obsequious to his own slaves and to free them even though he did not want to, as the only way of escaping death. Here, the main discussion is not about slavery, since Plato is merely using the example of a rich man and his slaves as a parallel to a tyrant, to show that the slave-owner's security depends on the rest of society; if there were no other citizens to hand, then of course slaves would kill their masters.[9]

In *Hiero*, Plato's contemporary Xenophon describes how the poet Simonides, on visiting the tyrant of Sicily, asked him how life differed from being a private individual. He describes how trust is important for happiness but observes that tyrants do not share the luxury of such trust, wryly commenting that communities put up statues to tyrannicides.[10] Part of the way Xenophon develops the argument is to say one can see trust manifested among ordinary citizens by the way they protect each other from their own slaves.[11] Again, like Plato in the passage mentioned above, Xenophon's main concern is not to discuss the threat posed by slaves to their masters but, taking this for granted, to use it to point out the role of the masters within the community in protecting each other.

When the orator Lysias talked about using slaves as witnesses, he worked from the assumption that the basic attitude the slaves had to their masters was one of hostility:

> To my mind it is surprising that when put to the torture on their own account, they accuse themselves, in the certain knowledge that they will be executed, but when it is on account of their masters, *to whom they naturally have most animosity*, they can choose rather to endure the torture than to get release from their present ills by an incrimination.[12]

The Roman saying "quot servi, tot hostes" is often translated as "all slaves are enemies", the truth of which was disputed by Seneca in the first century CE, followed by Macrobius about 300 years later. These writers urged good behaviour on the part of the masters and commented "non habemus illos hostes, sed facimus" [slaves are not our enemies but we make them so].[13] Yet their very discussion takes place in order to argue against a consensus, and one might add that we learn of this proverb here only because it is being challenged. In the first or second century CE, Quintus Curtius Rufus put the following words in the mouths of Scythians who were asking Alexander not to attack them: "Do not believe that those whom you have conquered are your friends. There is no friendship between master and slave".[14] Even when discussing apparent good will between master and slave, Vogt admits that this was the exception to the rule.[15] In *Ancient Slavery and the Ideal of Man*, he included a chapter on the faithful slave.[16] Many of the examples of servile docility Vogt gives in this context were, however, as he admits, recorded as remarkable events. In the course of describing civil war, in which many of these passages are set, the loyalty of slaves is frequently used to highlight the disloyalty of citizens.[17] In addition, when reading descriptions of great devotion of slaves to their masters, it is necessary to remember that all our sources were from the slave-owning class.[18]

These accounts are all we have left to us. There are no texts extant written by authors who were interested in slave unrest for its own sake. Not only do the ancient authors normally record the activities of the slaves incidentally, but many of the most crucial sources, in the sense of being the fullest, are not in a very good condition, so that we must rely on summaries, excerpts or quotations, often from the works of much later writers. One reason is that those who wrote histories and kept records of events did not wish to confer immortality on the names of rebellious slaves and so either did not mention them, and this would seem to be the largest category, or mentioned them briefly, with great condemnation and, in any case, in the course of some other topic. For example, Cicero often mentions the name Spartacus, but usually only in order to cast a slur on his opponents, to whom he compared him: they were to be considered as great a threat to the *res publica* as Spartacus himself.[19] Cicero was not writing a history but denouncing his opponents and making the most forceful arguments he could. The greatest threat to the state was from Spartacus. This would not have worked as an attack if it did not correspond to his contemporaries' views of the slave war.

The argument that no one in the ancient world, let alone slaves, had been able to form a conception of a society without slaves is not true. Aristotle, for example, writes that some people in antiquity objected to slavery. If one objects to slavery or thinks it wrong, it follows that one is able to imagine a society without it. In *Politics* Aristotle wrote: "*There are others* who hold that controlling another human being is contrary to nature, since it is only by convention that one man can be a slave and another free; there is no natural difference, and therefore it cannot be just, since it is based on the use of force".[20]

Not only could, and did, people challenge the justice of slavery, but it was a commonplace that once, in a golden age, there had been no slavery. In his comparison of Lycurgus and Numa, Plutarch wrote that Numa was a more humane legislator, allowing slaves to taste from freedom at the feast of Saturn, and commenting that in the age of Saturn there was no slavery, when men lived as equals.[21] Herodotus also comments that in the days of the quarrel between the Athenians and Pelasgians there was no slavery.[22] Justin reports that Pompeius Trogus had described the early days of Rome as being without slavery and without private property.[23]

The lack of an extant text that urges the abolition of slavery does not mean such ideas never existed. There is the utopia described by Diodorus, where he apparently reproduces the report Iambulus wrote about the island where men lived in a state of extreme equality.[24] This expression of the inherent injustice of slavery was still there in Roman times; the legal text called the *Digest* has the following statement: "slavery is an institution of the common law of peoples by which a person is put into the ownership of somebody else, *contrary to the natural order*".[25] This is not to suggest that opposition to slavery was widespread, or that it was a dominant view; however, one cannot argue that this opposition did not exist *at all*. In his book on attitudes to slavery in antiquity, Peter Garnsey describes how we first see opposition to slavery as an institution articulated by the theologian Gregory of Nyssa, and he ends with the words: "It will surprise no one that the hero of my narrative is Gregory of Nyssa who, perhaps uniquely, saw that slavery itself is a sin".[26] In an earlier chapter he discusses one of Gregory's homilies, where the bishop had put forward arguments for the abolition of slavery, which Garnsey describes as "unique in the surviving evidence".[27] One cannot assert, and Garnsey is very careful not to, that others had not expressed such views elsewhere; one can only state that such expressions have not survived. It is quite plausible that Gregory was not uttering views that were completely original and disconnected from contemporary thought. It seems more probable that we simply no longer possess evidence of similar views of his contemporaries and predecessors.

The dominant ideology of the time was that freedom was to be preserved and slavery to be avoided. There is no reason to think that the slaves did not share this view and that it did not inform their actions and their intentions. This may seem self-evident but much store is placed on the lack of ideology on the part of the slaves: that they only wanted to be free. There seems no reason to think that slaves were incapable of taking the same step in their thinking as those anonymous people mentioned by Aristotle, who argued that slavery was unjust because it was based on force. They, more than anyone, would have had reason to reflect on the nature of slavery. Had any of the revolts lasted longer, they may well have thought of how they wished their future society to be organized. I do not wish to argue that the slaves did have intentions of this kind, only that we are not entitled to declare definitely that they did not.

6
Sympathy for the slaves: Diodorus Siculus

We know about the slave revolts in Sicily because the first century BCE writer Diodorus, a writer from Sicily (hence his name), wrote about them. Until Kenneth Sacks' reappraisal there was a tendency to dismiss him as a copier, valuable for the most part as a preserver of texts because many of his sources are now lost.[1] The nature of his undertaking was so large, starting with myths earlier than the Trojan War and continuing until the start of Julius Caesar's activities in Gaul in 60/59 BCE, that it has usually been assumed he moved from copying out one text to another.

He himself gives us a great deal of information in his preface to the whole undertaking. He tells us, at some length, why we should read his massive work; that history is useful because we can learn from the mistakes of others; that good deeds are preserved by historians and inspire the readers to emulate them; that history is good but universal history is even better, although it is more difficult to write; that he has worked on his history for thirty years and now finished it; that he did much travelling in order to write his history; that he came from Agyrium in Sicily and that he had much exposure to Latin from his contact with Romans on the island, lived in Rome for a long time and studied the records that were kept there carefully; and that his history covers 1138 years and is divided into forty books (only fifteen of which remain intact today).[2]

His aim, he said, was to help others by writing, since his readers could learn from the lessons of history with no risk to themselves. Diodorus' purpose is perhaps not an original one but a very moral one. By reading history we can learn from the mistakes of the past, and the young can possess the wisdom of the old, direct their lives better and be inspired to emulate the great deeds recorded there. Moreover, historians, he says, are like servants of divine providence (ὥσπερ τινὲς ὑπουργοὶ τῆς θείας προνοίας),[3] since they bring the affairs of the world into an orderly whole. As P. J. Stylianou observes, this moral purpose recurs throughout Diodorus' history, and we often see divine justice bringing down the arrogant.[4] This aspect is quite apparent in the sections dealing with the Sicilian slave wars and the narrative of the Sicilian war is a faithful reflection of the aims expressed in the prologue.[5]

For example, in the opening chapter Diodorus writes about learning from mistakes, and it is clear, as will be shown, that he considered that both the landowners in Sicily and the Roman authorities had made mistakes in their handling of the situation. In the following chapter he discusses the good deeds to emulate, and in the slave war narrative there is the example of the daughter of Damophilus and Megallis who, by her virtuous behaviour towards those weaker than herself, shows the right way to treat them. In describing the difficulties faced by those who would write universal histories, he says that some omitted the deeds of the barbarians.[6] Perhaps one can see the wish for completeness in his description of what happened in Sicily, and clearly he had a personal interest in this, as well as easy access to material about it. A little later he mentions the supremacy of Rome, and the Roman occupation of Sicily and he reveals views on this quite candidly in his later books.[7]

What is noteworthy here is the overall moral purpose for his work and the sympathy that Diodorus has for the slaves. His analysis of the situation absolved them from any notion of vice being innate to slaves and laid the blame firmly at the feet of the slave-owners. They treated their slaves badly and therefore provoked hatred and rebellion from them, in the same way as states that treat their subjects badly will suffer the consequences. Sacks has argued convincingly that Diodorus is critical of the Roman Empire throughout his history and that his description of the slave wars is an example of his antipathy to the Romans and Italians.[8] An illustration of this is when he tells us that the number of slaves on Sicily was so huge that many did not believe such numbers could be true, adding that the Sicilians, who had become so rich, rivalled the Italians in arrogance, greed and villainy.[9]

Sacks argues that Diodorus has been summarily dismissed as simply copying out his sources whereas, in fact, a careful analysis shows that he had very definite ideas of his own, and that one should not simply ascribe everything to the source he was using at the time. For the slave revolt, it is usually assumed that his source was the Stoic writer, Posidonius but, as Sacks demonstrates, in all non-Diodoran parts of Posidonius there is no evidence of anti-Roman sentiment: quite the opposite.[10] Posidonius' work was also on an epic scale: fifty-two volumes, covering probably 146–88 BCE. It has been suggested that Posidonius, who was born about 135 BCE, was interested in the slave wars because he was from Apamea in Syria; Eunus, one of the slave leaders of the first war in Sicily, was Syrian and we know from Athenaeus that Posidonius had written about this episode.

Sacks, however, points out that there are two themes in Diodorus' work through which he criticizes the Romans: one is the degeneration of Rome after the sack of Carthage, and the other is its harsh treatment of the provinces.[11] Here one is reminded that Diodorus was from Sicily and told the reader himself that he had had first-hand experience of Romans in this province.[12] Diodorus thus is someone from the provinces observing the negative aspects of imperial power and recording it, as Plutarch was to later. Diodorus, like Plutarch among others, saw the passage from the early to the more recent Romans as one of decline.[13]

The preservation of Diodorus' narrative

Quite apart from his qualities or lack of them as a historian, there are problems with Diodorus' text concerning the Sicilian slave wars. It survives only in the form of two epitomes made much later in Byzantine times. The two epitomes are not the same as each other and they emphasize different things, but it seems entirely possible, and more than probable, that they both reflect what the authors found in the narrative of Diodorus. In the ninth century, Photius, a patriarch of Constantinople, compiled his own *Bibliotheca*, which was a collection of summaries of all the books he had read, 280 in total, the result running to several volumes.[14] He treated works in different ways and, fortunately for us, gives long summaries of Diodorus; for others he gives only a brief note, sometimes a short biographical sketch of the author and a comment on the literary style as well as content.[15] In the tenth century the emperor Constantine Porphyrogenitus commissioned a work of morally edifying summaries of earlier writers, arranged under topical headings. The extracts of Diodorus in this second compilation are found under the headings "*Excerpta de virtutibus et vitiis*", "*Excerpta de sententiis*" and "*Excerpta de insidiis*".[16]

Mileta has argued that the aims of both these works must be examined in order to assess the information in them and it is certainly true that there are noticeably different emphases in the two summaries, so that, for instance, some modern sourcebooks include both versions.[17] As Mileta has shown, the reasons for compiling the two epitomes have affected the content. Photius' collection had a less overtly political aim than the *Excerpts* of Constantine, which was made to illustrate how to rule satisfactorily. Consequently, in this summary there is much more general moralizing about the faults of the upper classes and less about the actions of the slaves. These, on the contrary, are portrayed primarily as not conspiring to break free but rather reacting to bad treatment and being so oppressed that they could stand their situation no longer. There was a natural interest in Sicily at this time because in the course of the ninth century the Byzantines had gradually lost control of the island to the Arabs, helped, one could say, by mistakes of their own making.[18]

Photius

The description of the Sicilian couple who were the trigger for the first war gives a good example of Diodorus' attitude to slaves and masters. It is from Photius' narrative that we learn the following account of the start of the slave war:

> The origin of the whole slave rebellion was as follows. There was a certain Damophilus, a citizen of Enna, who was an exceedingly wealthy man, but one who had a rather arrogant character. He had maltreated his slaves beyond all tolerable limits. His wife, Megallis, competed with her husband in the punishment and general inhumane treatment of their slaves. Because of this maltreatment, the slaves were reduced to the level of wild beasts and began to plot with one another for rebellion and the murder of their masters.[19]

There is no ambiguity in the account, no suggestion that the slaves were themselves violent, criminal or naturally rebellious. The picture is one of overbearing owners driving their slaves to desperate measures. It was the slaves belonging to this couple who plotted first, according to the narrative, and who then approached Eunus for his advice. Damophilus and his wife were in their country villa so the slaves sent some men to bring them to the city. Damophilus and Megallis received their just deserts: one was both stabbed in the heart and axed in the neck, and the other was tortured then flung off a precipice, but this is recorded only by Photius. We learn from Photius that the ex-slaves Hermeias and Zeuxis killed Damophilus, but only from the *Excerpts* that it was Hermeias who escorted the daughter to safety (see below).

The *Excerpts* of Constantine

In the *Excerpts* there are many more specific details about these two, as one might expect given that the tenor of these extracts is the emphasis of the faults of the ruling class. Damophilus is very wealthy and very arrogant and, says this summary, emulated the Italians in Sicily in the huge numbers of slaves he owned and the harsh way he treated them. He had a very luxurious lifestyle and the power he wielded corrupted his uneducated character: "At first his excessive wealth led to a desire for what would suffice, then it led a violent impulse to acquire more and finally it led to destruction and death for himself and to great misfortunes for his community".[20] The summary gives a highly moralistic judgement of the evils of not being able to control yourself, so it is easy to see why people have been ready to ascribe it to the Stoic Posidonius who, as we know from Athenaeus, had mentioned Damophilus.[21] In his twelfth book, Athenaeus writes:

> Posidonius too in the eighth book of his histories says of the Sicilian Damophilus, who caused the stirring up of the slave war, that he was addicted to luxury and writes as follows: "He was therefore a slave to luxury and vice, driving round about over the countryside in four-wheeled carts, with horses and handsome grooms and a retinue of parasites and lads dressed as soldiers swarming beside him. But later he, with his whole household, ended his life after an outrageous fashion having been grievously outraged by slaves".[22]

Athenaeus appears to be quoting Posidonius directly, and yet the extract is briefer than the account found in the epitome of Diodorus, which is unexpected if the latter took it from the former and elaborated on it. One would have thought that the normal way of working was to summarize sources, not expand on them. This is not to cast doubt that Posidonius really did write this, because the wording is what one would expect of a Stoic: he describes Damophilus as a slave to luxury. However, it should be noted that Athenaeus had quoted Diodorus shortly before this.[23]

The discussion here in Book 12 is about luxury, not slaves, and, in particular, instances of luxury in Sicily. At §541c he mentions the excesses of Dionysius the younger of Sicily, then at §541e he writes that Diodorus reported that the people of Agrigentum had built an enormously expensive swimming pool for Gelon. After a few lines quoting Duris, Silenus and Callias, all of whom could well have been sources for Diodorus since they all wrote on Sicily, Athenaeus moves on to Posidonius. It is possible that Athenaeus took all this material from Diodorus, or at least the sentence by Posidonius. Although Sacks is certainly correct in arguing that Diodorus held firm views of his own that are reflected in his history, there is no reason to doubt that he used Posidonius as a source.

There are more details about Damophilus' neglect of his slaves, such as his refusal to clothe them; when the slaves asked for clothes, his response was to tell them to steal from travellers. The account from the excerptor working for Constantine is unambiguous in its condemnation of this individual: "Because of the stubbornness and cruelty of his character, there was not a day on which Damophilos did not punish some of his slaves, and never for any just cause".[24]

Both versions of Diodorus, preserved by Photius and, a century later, by the excerptors, stress that the cause of the war lay in the bad treatment of the slaves. (As this aspect is in both summaries we can reasonably assume it reflects Diodorus' actual text.) The masters brought it on themselves, and in order to make this even clearer, there is the counter-example of the daughter of this vicious couple. She treated her inferiors well and thus escaped the terrible retribution wreaked on her parents.

The slaves spared the daughter of this villainous couple because she was kind and in both accounts she is used explicitly to illustrate the views that the masters had brought this trouble on themselves. Photius has the following: "From these actions of theirs [i.e. sparing the daughter], it is shown that the violence of the slaves did not stem from an innate disposition toward others, but rather that their actions were only fair repayment for the injustices that had formerly been inflicted on them".[25] This is more fully developed in the *Excerpts*. Again we have more details about her: she was young, of a simple character and very kind, and lived in Sicily (which is an odd detail to include, as one might expect her to). She comforted the slaves beaten by her parents and defended those put in chains, and consequently was loved by everyone. The implications are quite clear: if masters treated their slaves well, and if the Romans were merciful to their subjects, they would be loved not hated. Because she had behaved kindly, this daughter in turn was well treated by the rebellious slaves, who did not rape her but escorted her to relatives in Catania, and in the *Excerpt* that narrates this event we even learn the name of the best of the excellent slaves who escorted her, Hermeias.

A conclusion is then drawn from all this:

> Although the rebellious slaves were wild with rage against all the households of their masters and resorted to uncontrolled violence and vengeance against them, it was clear that this response was not rooted in any innately savage nature. Rather, it was because of the outrages that had previously been committed against them that they now ran wild in the punishment of those who had previously done wrong to them. Even among slaves, human nature is perfectly capable of being its own teacher about what is just repayment, whether it be gratitude or vengeance.[26]

The *Excerpt* even more explicitly lays the blame with the masters, and acquits the slaves of responsibility. They were exacting their own justice for intolerable treatment; when they were well treated, they responded in kind.

Photius has more precise details on the course of the war, with the names of the Roman generals sent out against the slaves, the victories of the slave army and the siege of Tauromenium, which, he says, reduced the slaves to eating their own children and then their wives. We also learn from the patriarch about the strategies of the slaves: how they killed their masters or put them to work to make weapons.

The simultaneous outbreak under Aristonicus in Asia Minor is recorded in the *Excerpts*. Generally, the narrative preserved in Constantine's *Excerpts* is more discursive than Photius' account. There are some general comments on the disasters suffered by the free people of Sicily at the hands of the slaves. We read that if one judged the situation realistically, however, one would see that these things happened with good reason and then the narrative goes into the terrible conditions suffered by the slaves and the cruel treatment they received from their arrogant masters: "Since the maltreatment of the slaves increased in equal proportion to their alienation from their masters, when the first opportunity presented itself, there was a sudden violent outburst of hatred on the part of the slaves".[27] Rather more dramatically than the account in Photius, there is the assertion that without any communication between themselves, "tens of thousands of slaves joined forces to kill their masters".[28]

So the masters bore joint responsibility for the war. He adds that the same thing happened in Asia when Aristonicus claimed the kingship. In the next sentence, he states explicitly that the slaves were treated terribly in Asia as well, so the reader is led to conclude that this was not a specifically Sicilian problem. Following on from this description of the situation in Sicily in the *Excerpts*, there are some generalizations about empire, including:

> Not only in the public realm of power should those in superior positions treat those who are humble and lowly with consideration. But similarly, in their private lives, if they understand their own situation accurately, they should treat their slaves considerately. Just as arrogance and brutal treatment in states leads to social upheaval and strife among the freeborn citizens, in the same way maltreatment procures plots against the masters by the slaves within the household. From this same source, fearsome rebellions are plotted against the state itself. To the degree that cruelty and lawlessness pervert the basic elements of power, to that same degree the characters of subject persons are made savage to the point of despair. For every person who has been made humble by chance or fate and who has willingly treated his superiors with goodness and respect, but who has been deprived of the expected human consideration in return, will become an enemy to those who savagely lord it over him.[29]

Diodorus could hardly be clearer in his expression of his views and it coincides very well with sentiments expressed elsewhere in his work, as discussed earlier. This clear moral tone continues as this excerptor describes how the first rebels set loose slaves in chains, collected 400 others from the vicinity and armed themselves as well as they could. Diodorus, as related by the *Excerpts*, adds one of the most striking sentences: "All of them donned the most powerful weapon of all: a rage that was directed at the destruction of their arrogant and overbearing masters".[30] What gives them most power is their rage at their ill treatment.[31] Treat slaves well and they are disarmed. As we saw with the narrative in the *Excerpts*, Eunus remembered those who had been kind to him as a slave and the slaves also remembered the kindness of the daughter of Damophilus and returned good for good.

As mentioned earlier, while describing the capture of Acragas, Diodorus tells us that outside the city walls, so that the inhabitants of the city could see, the slaves put on mimes from their own recent past depicting them taking their vengeance on their masters. He says that the slaves abused their masters for their *hybris*, for which they were now being punished.[32] He follows this with the following lines about religion:

> As for sudden and unexpected blows of misfortune, there are those who are persuaded that the divine has nothing at all to do with such occurrences. Yet, even so, it is surely to the advantage of the common good of society that fear of the gods should be inculcated in the minds of the great majority of ordinary people. For those who do the right thing because of their personal moral excellence are few in number. The vast majority of humankind refrain from doing wrong only because of the penalties exacted by the laws and the punishments coming from the gods.[33]

This is a slightly unexpected passage; the rather cynical observation being made here is that religion is useful for keeping people in check. However, the broader point seems to be that although Diodorus' readers might consider that the slave war had nothing to do with divine justice, it is not helpful to think that. It is much better for society if one expects to be punished for wrongdoing, because otherwise most people would act criminally. He thinks that the slaves took their own vengeance but is perhaps also suggesting there may be a touch of divine vengeance, which allowed the slaves their success. Clearly, on his point of view there would have been no war if the owners had treated the slaves well, but they were arrogant in the assumption of their superior power, and they showed their *hybris* in relation to their slaves. If they had feared the gods they would not have been tempted to make this error.

One of the *Excerpts* has a mysterious passage that reports that those who ate the sacred fish were punished for their impiety.[34] It is thought that this refers to the fish of the fountain of Arethusa at Syracuse, and that the eaters were the slaves, although the passage does not make this explicit. Diodorus describes this place at some length in Book 5 of his history, which is about the myths of Sicily, and later, in Book 14, describes its desecration by the Carthaginians and their subsequent punishment for this impiety.[35] The passage about the sacred fish appears to have some relation to the slave wars. It says that those who ate the fish were punished by the gods, and that they have also been punished by being abused in the pages of history, and thus have received their just payment for their wrongdoing, echoing his thoughts in the prologue to his whole work, where he says that historians are ministers of divine providence. Such a statement would seem far more consistent with his view of the masters than the slaves, at least from the pages we have extant.

Diodorus, then, is a most unusual historian, showing sympathy for rebellious slaves and critical of the harsh treatment they received at the hands of their Sicilian and Roman masters. He takes the moralistic view that the damaging wars were the result of the selfishness of their wealthy owners, a theory to which we might not subscribe today. Whatever his analysis, however, he gave us an account of episodes about which we would otherwise know very little. Like other historians looking at the Republic, he saw the troubles the Romans suffered from their slaves as connected to their growing wealth. In Chapter 7 I consider briefly some of the views of other writers.

7
The secret of the success of the Spartan helots

The helots of Sparta were remarkably successful in their revolts and are famous for their willingness to take action against their masters, as has been noted in the course of this book. For that reason alone, they merit some attention. It is also worth noting the special circumstances of their condition, which aided their rebellious activities. For some historians the helots are not to be classified as slaves and hence their results cannot be termed slave revolts. That they were not slaves is indicated by the fact that they are generally referred to as "helots". This was not always the case, however. For example, when Athenaeus quotes Theopompus, again with reference to the Chians, he writes: "The Chians were the first Greeks, after the Thessalians and Lacedaimonians, to use slaves, but they did not acquire them in the same way".[1] Theopompus viewed helots as slaves, but as slaves that were acquired differently from those in most other Greek cities. The circumstances of the workforce in Sparta were indeed not identical to those in many classical Greek cities, and were certainly different from those in Athens.

There is a curious passage in Pollux of Naucratis's *Onomasticon* that says that helots (and the Thessalian Penestai and others) are *between* slave and free (μεταξὺ δ'ἐλευθέρων καὶ δούλων οἱ Λακεδαιμονίων εἵλωτες καὶ Θετταλῶν πενέσται).[2] Pollux wrote his *Onomasticon* in the second century CE and the information he gives us here is thought to come from Aristophanes of Byzantium, who lived four centuries earlier. However, the manuscripts that are extant are from a tenth century epitome, possessed and interpolated by Arethas, bishop of Caesarea. One cannot, then, safely deny the helot slave status merely on the basis of this passage, especially in the light of conflicting evidence. As Jean

Ducat comments, this passage of Pollux is contradicted by most of the other ancient texts that deal with the subject.³

The Greeks (and Romans) had a variety of terms to describe their unfree workers.⁴ One of the Greek words for slaves is ἀνδράποδα, which literally means "man-footed", as opposed to τετράποδα, meaning "four-footed". Here we see a very clear indication of the nature of slaves as property where the word distinguishes human from animal stock.⁵ Greeks and Romans owned human beings as they owned horses, dogs, farms and household implements; the slaves worked for them as their farm animals worked for them. In a famous passage Aristotle called them "animate tools": "So a piece of property is similarly a tool needed to live; 'property' is a collection of such tools, and a slave is an animate piece of property".⁶ They did the work of a hammer but could also speak. If there were robots, there would be no need of slaves, as Aristotle went on to say, as if looking forward to the industrial revolution:

> Every assistant is a tool taking the place of several tools – for if every tool were able to perform its particular function when it was given the order or realised that something had to be done … so that shuttles would weave cloth or harps play music automatically, then master craftsmen would not need assistants, nor masters slaves.⁷

Yet Aristotle also saw the authority of a master as like the rule of a king over his subjects, a husband over his wife, or father over children, so that the sense of personhood is present.⁸ In accordance with the acknowledgment of the slave as a "person", in the ancient world killing slaves arbitrarily was not generally sanctioned, although the Spartans evaded this prohibition by declaring war on them every year.

Helots lived in circumstances different from those of many slaves in the ancient Greek world, not least important of which was their shared language, to which Thucydides refers several times, but they seem to have performed very similar work, and performed the same role in society as slaves in other cities. The main difference appears to be their origin and the circumstances of their enslavement, which automatically led to a different situation.⁹ They could all speak the same language, they were living on the land before the arrival of the Spartans and family ties already existed, and would have been difficult to break given the relatively small area in which they lived.

What is striking is the number of ancient sources who *do* refer to them as slaves; for instance, a peace treaty between Athens and Sparta said that Athens had to help in the event of a slave revolt, referring to helots.[10] The term δουλεία, which appears to have been used here to refer to helots, was an official one, since the text appears to contain a verbatim copy of the treaty.

Strabo, who gives us some crucial information, describes the helots as being a form of public slaves. He wrote at the time of the emperor Augustus but had access to reliable sources, one of whom was the Greek historian Ephorus, who lived in the fourth century BCE. Strabo starts paragraph 4 of *Geography* 8.5 with the words "Ephorus says"; he then proceeds to give information on Laconia, including details on helots. He describes how, in the very earliest times, Eurysthenes and Procles took possession of Laconia, and made Sparta their residence and how they subjugated the neighbouring peoples who, although they were subject to the Spartans, had rights of citizenship and access to offices of state. However, the son of Eurysthenes, Agis, required them to pay tribute, and when the people of Helos refused they were attacked and enslaved.[11] This enslavement had certain terms: the owner could not free them or sell them outside the borders. The war was called the war against the helots, Strabo reports, and he adds that one could say that it was Agis and those around him who introduced the whole system of helot slavery, which remained until the time of the Romans. Strabo's reason for explaining helots to his readers as public slaves is that the state allocated them certain places to live and functions to perform.[12]

The picture is one of helots as an indigenous people, who had been subjugated into their present position, but who therefore had a shared history, language and culture and a memory of freedom.[13] They were allowed to keep part of what they produced and could not be sold or freed by an individual but by the polis. They have been called serfs, although this term is normally reserved for the feudal system of the Middle Ages.[14]

Whereas individuals could not free helots, the city could and did, fairly frequently according to our sources and there was also a specific word for these freed helots: *neodamodeis*. If helots could be set free, then logically they were not free before. To say they had more rights than slaves normally had is rather undercut by the fact that they could be killed at any moment; in the Greek world this was seen as something shameful.[15]

In the later Roman Empire, writers, and learned ones at that, continued to view the helots as slaves. Herodian, a grammarian from the third century CE, discusses the derivation of the word "helot". He says that helots are the inhabitants of the Messenian city of Helos and then goes on to state directly that the Spartans called all slaves helots.[16] In a similar vein, in his *Life of Lycurgus*, Plutarch directly contradicts the aforementioned statement by Pollux that the helots were *between* slave and free, when, after discussing the treatment of helots, he writes: "So that it was truly observed by one, that in Sparta he who was free was most so, and he that was a slave there, the greatest slave in the world".[17] In the fourth century CE Libanius wrote a speech called *About Slavery* in which he makes a very similar remark. He quotes Critias as saying that in Sparta men were most free and most enslaved, and Libanius comments wryly that the Spartans in fact were not very free because they were always scared of their slaves.[18]

Plutarch also tells us in his *Life of Cleomenes* that the Spartans had a temple to Fear,[19] and he reports that the Spartans thought that their state was held together by fear.[20] Plutarch was not thinking about helots in particular here, but his depiction of Sparta generally is consistent as being permeated by fear. He related another act of the ephors on entering office (besides declaring war on helots), which was to order all men to shave off their moustaches. Plutarch explains this as showing that the magistrates expected obedience in every aspect of life, however trivial.

Elsewhere, however, Plutarch draws a distinction between slaves and helots. In his comparison of Lycurgus and Numa, he says free men could not earn money so work such as the service at table and in the kitchen was left to slaves and helots.[21] In his dialogue *Alcibiades*, Plato makes Socrates comment that the Spartans are very wealthy, possessing land in their own and in the Messenian country. He says none of the Athenian estates are a match for theirs in size, or in the possession of slaves, especially of helots or of horses or flocks or herds.[22] Here, then, he appears to refer to helots as a subset of slaves.

So although we do possess evidence that uses the term "helot" as being synonymous with "slave", in some passages from ancient writers a distinction is made. One could argue, however, on the evidence above, that this distinction was drawn because of the geographical origin of the helots, and the fact that they are native to the land, not bought from slave markets. Pausanias, for example, explaining the origin of the term "helot", says that the first helots came from Helos on the coast:

Its inhabitants became the first slaves (δοῦλοι) of the Lacedaimonian state and were the first to be called helots, as in fact Helots they were. The slaves afterwards acquired, although they were Dorians of Messenia, also came to be called Helots, just as the whole Greek race were called Hellenes from the region in Thessaly once called Hellas.[23]

According to this explanation, "helot" was originally a term to describe where people came from. All the people from this area became the slaves of the Spartans and later the word became a generic word for slaves, so that slaves from elsewhere might also sometimes be referred to by this name, even though they were not technically helots.

It is useful here to see what Athenaeus has to contribute to this subject. In Book 6 of *Deipnosophistae*, there is a discussion of the matter of whole peoples being enslaved by others, rather than slaves being bought from many different places as was more usual. Athenaeus reports that Masurius Sabinus had said that:

> Philippos of Theangela mentions the Lacedamonian Helots and the Thessalian Penestai and says that in the past, and indeed today, the Carians use the Leleges as their houseboys. Phylarkhos, in book six of his Histories, say that the Byzantines, too exercised mastery over the Bithynians as the Spartans had towards the Helots.[24]

This passage does not necessarily indicate that the legal position of the Bithynians and helots is different from that of ordinary slaves, but is rather pointing to the practice, a relatively unusual feature in the ancient world, of enslaving a whole people. The helots were indigenous to the region, which also meant that they were fellow Greeks, who did not belong to the category of natural slaves.

Athenaeus quotes from Book 11 of Posidonius' histories about the Mariandynians, where there is the following explanation of their subjection:

> Many persons who are unable to manage their own affairs because of the weakness of their intellect, hand themselves over to the service of men who are more intelligent, so that they be looked after by them and provided with whatever they need and may themselves give back to their masters all the service they are

capable of giving through their own work. It was in this way that the Mariandynians placed themselves under the domination of the people of Heraklea, promising to serve them forever, so long as they provided them with what they needed. They added the condition that none of them should be sold beyond the borders of Heraklea, but that they should stay within their own country.[25]

He carries on to say that the people of Herakleia called their slaves "bringers of gifts" (δωροφόροι) to avoid offence, just as the Spartans do with helots, the Thessalians with the Penestai, and the Cretans with their Klarotai. He quotes Ephorus on the Cretans' slaves and explains that they are called the Klarotai because they have been "allotted".[26]

A little later Athenaeus cites a very similar explanation for the Penestai of Thessaly given by Archemachus, who wrote a *History of Euboea*.[27] Whatever the actual origins of the Penestai, Athenaeus is commenting on the practice of a people entering *en masse* into servitude, as opposed to those bought at markets. This is followed by the comment that in the earliest times it was not the Greek custom to buy slaves, and those who did were criticized, the reason given being that it took work away from citizens. There is a quotation from Plato's *Laws* about the system of helots being more controversial than that of the Mariandynians or the Penestai, presumably because, as Athenaeus had just demonstrated, the servitude of the two last-named peoples was (at least according to his sources) voluntary. He remarks:

> This form of property is not easy. This has in actual fact been demonstrated many times – by the frequent revolt of the Messenians, by all the difficulties that have occurred for those states whose citizens keep many slaves who speak the same language and by all the acts of robbery and suffering inflicted by the so-called roving bandits of Italy.[28]

Plato goes on to say (and Athenaeus also reproduces this) that the lesson to be learnt is not to have slaves who come from the same country and to treat those one does possess well. The original passage from Plato's *Laws* is very interesting. He has a short discussion on slavery in Book 6, 776b–778a, in which the Athenian explains to Megillus, a Spartan, and Cleinias, a Cretan, how a society should treat its slaves. The Athenian points out that the Spartan system is the most contentious system as some people approve of it and others disapprove. He goes on to say that in states where slaves speak the same language, and he uses the example of the Messenian helots, the slaves revolt frequently. So, he says, first of all, slaves should not come from the same place and speak the same language and secondly they should be dealt with properly, which means not ill treating them or behaving too leniently. He also has the observation that it is difficult to divide man easily into "slave" and "free".

In any consideration of the helots the most distinctive aspect is the sympathy to be found for them in our sources. The Athenian orator Isocrates described the lot of the helots thus:

> Right from the start these men have suffered severely, and in the present situation they have served Sparta well; yet the Spartan ephors are allowed to execute without trial as many of them as they wish. As far as the rest of the Greeks are concerned it is not holy to pollute oneself by killing even the most useless of one's household slaves.[29]

Plutarch tried to distance his hero Lycurgus from the brutal practice whereby Spartan youths were trained to go out and hunt helots. He nevertheless gives us details in his *Life of Lycurgus*, while describing the arrangements Lycurgus, an early law-giver, made for Spartan society:

> In all of this there is no sign of the injustice and excess for which some find fault with Lycurgus' laws arguing that they make sufficient provision for courage, but are lacking in justice. The so-called krypteia [secret operation] of theirs, if it really was one of Lycurgus' institutions, may be what led Plato as well to that opinion about the system and the man. It operated like this: the leaders of the young men from time to time would send out those who seemed to have the most sense into the countryside in different directions, equipped with daggers and sufficient provisions, but nothing else; by day they made their way in scattered groups to remote places and hid themselves and rested; at night they came down into the roads and slaughtered any of the helots they caught. Often too they journeyed into the fields and did away with the strongest and bravest of them.[30]

Plutarch generally paints a very positive picture of Lycurgus but towards the end of his *Life of Lycurgus* he again discusses the Spartan treatment of helots and he distances his hero from this shameful episode of Sparta's past, writing that it developed after Lycurgus' time and that it was not owing to him. Again, in the comparison of this life with that of Numa, he tries to throw doubt on the idea that the bad treatment by Sparta of the helots was because of Lycurgus:

> whereas if we must admit the treatment of the Helots to be a part of Lycurgus' legislation, a most cruel and iniquitous proceeding, we must own that Numa was by a great deal the more humane and Greek-like legislator, granting even to actual slaves a licence to sit at meal with their masters at the feast of Saturn, that they also might have some taste and relish of the sweets of liberty.[31]

This sympathy can also be seen in the work of Dio Chrysostom:

> Look at the example of the Messenians; after an interval of how many years was it that they got back both their freedom and their country? After the Thebans had defeated the Spartans at Leuctra, they marched into the Peloponnese together with their allies and forced the Spartans to give up Messenia; they resettled all the people who were descended from the Messenians who had previously been the Spartans' slaves and were called Helots. No one says that the Thebans did this unjustly, but rather with great honour and great justice.[32]

Thomas Figueira builds on such comments and argues that the struggle was one of national liberation, which is why the helots are presented differently in our sources.[33] The Greek inhabitants of the Peloponnese had been enslaved by an invading people and they were fighting to regain their freedom. Figueira follows our sources in stressing the distinctive nature of the helots, and is surely right to stress the different nature of these subordinates from others; our sources do seem to have perceived the helots as Greek, as part of their own people, and not one of the "naturally subject" races.[34]

As remarked earlier, it is certainly true that the helots were a special case, that they had different circumstances, and some of those circumstances result in a favourable portrait by historians. One circumstance is that in the end the Messenians won their independence, and Pausanias devotes Book 4 of his *Guide to Greece* to Messenia and their struggles against the Spartans and afterwards. Not only were the entire populations of Messenia and Laconia enslaved but they had certain rights, which other slaves did not have. Again, these circumstances aided their revolt.

Such claims to kinship, one might argue, led to sympathy on the part of observers, who considered that the enslavement of other Greek peoples was wrong, as well as an observation that this was not efficient. It was probably after observing the situation in Sparta that Plato and Aristotle declared it a bad idea to have slaves who spoke the same language as each other. In any case, the ancient sources are sympathetic to helots in a way that is very unusual. I would argue that, indeed, Sparta is a special case and it is precisely due to the special circumstances that we have as much evidence as we do about the attitude and activities of their slaves.

Most of our sources are Athenian and thus, to some extent, anti-Spartan for this period. Athens produced the major literature of the period and many of its aesthetic, political and cultural values were passed down throughout the ages. When we study classical Greece, it is often the society of Athens that is under scrutiny. Much of the Athenian literature has survived, that is, in comparison with other states. Sparta, when Athens was at its height, was its enemy. It is a commonplace that societies make the customs of their enemies "other". Just as Sparta was alien because of the way its women behaved, and were treated, so it was "other" in the barbaric way it treated its slaves. The situation was as different in Sparta and Athens as possible, although given the close geographical proximity, writers could not be too outrageous in their claims. But just as Plutarch later was to contrast how Cato treated his slaves with how the Greeks in general treated theirs (the Greeks treated their animals better than Cato treated his slaves), so the Athenians showed the moral inferiority of their opponents by the way they treated their helots (and their slaves even had a different name). We do not know how much of what the Athenian sources say may be true. It is the fact that it was written down that is important for us here, since normally how slaves had to lead their lives was passed over in silence.

8
Slave revolts in the ancient historiography

What is striking when reading the ancient texts is that their writers considered the damage of slave revolts to be much greater than scholars do with hindsight. In their analyses of the fall of the Republic, the great slave wars were integral to the story. This is not the case in modern books, and indeed the difference between the ancient and modern viewpoints seems to be becoming even more marked. Yet it appeals to common sense that slaves were potentially an enormous threat to the authorities in both Greece and Rome.

Finley observes: "I should say that there was no action or belief or institution in the Graeco-Roman antiquity that was not one way or other affected by the possibility that someone involved *might be* a slave".[1] The first sentence of the section on slave resistance in *The Slavery Reader* is: "The history of slave resistance is the story of slavery itself".[2] Taken together, one can see that if these two propositions have some truth, then the topic of slave revolts is a vital aspect of the study of antiquity. Yet although much has been written on Greek and Roman slavery, the same cannot be said for slave resistance in this period. One reasonable response might be that our sources are inadequate, but this difficulty has been, if not overcome, then courageously addressed by armies of scholars in respect of other aspects of slavery.

As an indication of the scholarly attention to the topic of slave revolts it is interesting to note the differences of treatment of slave wars of the Roman Republic in the first and second editions of *The Cambridge Ancient History*, volume IX.[3] The first edition, from 1932, discussed the first Sicilian slave war in Chapter 1, on Tiberius Gracchus, and the second war in Chapter 3, "The Wars of the Age of Marius"; they were discussed, in other words, in their historical setting, since these wars were 30 years apart.[4] The reader of the second edition, on the other hand, has to search in the subsection "Sicily" of Chapter 2, "The Roman Empire and its Problems in the Late Second Century", to find two pages dealing with both slave wars together.[5] The second edition also puts Spartacus into a subsection of the chapter "The Rise of Pompey", a subsection of some nine pages, entitled "The Wars against Sertorius and Spartacus 79-71", but only two of those pages are about Spartacus.[6] Sixty years earlier, the rebels under Spartacus had had a whole subsection to themselves entitled "The War of the Gladiators".[7]

Spartacus, the only slave leader to be mentioned, has only one reference in the index to a recent textbook, *The Cambridge Companion to the Roman Republic* (which incidentally has no chapter – out of a possible fifteen – with the word "slave" or "slavery" in the title).[8] The reference is to a section entitled "Pompeius" in a chapter on the crisis in the Republic. Of the slave leaders only Spartacus is mentioned, and again only once, in another survey, *A History of the Roman Republic*, although there are five references to slave revolts in that volume.[9] However, each of these refers only to a sentence or so, except for one that refers the reader to a paragraph on the Spartacan revolt. I mention these books only because they represent current attitudes in scholarship to the topic.

Recently, Pierre Piccinin has argued that although there were slaves in Spartacus' army, and although Spartacus and his generals were indeed gladiators, this uprising in 73 BCE cannot be called a slave war. It was rather a war against Rome: a nationalist conflict of Italians against Roman rule.[10] Piccinin admits that his thesis is not new; he is building on the work of Zeev Rubinsohn, among others, who had asked whether this was a servile war and concluded that it was not.[11] As he himself admits, this radical hypothesis means that most of our ancient sources are mistaken.[12] But there are no overwhelming grounds for a total disregard of our ancient evidence, which does in fact present a coherent and consistent account of these episodes.

A large problem for modern scholars has been the intentions of the slaves. What did they want? The line of argument that they *could not have* wanted the abolition of slavery and therefore their uprisings were not important may seem puzzling, but in essence it lies behind many discussions in recent times. Griffith, for example, remarks:

> With the best will in the world I cannot persuade myself that he was a prophet with a social message, dying for a cause for which the time was not ripe. Nor can I see his rising as in any sense a

link in the chain of events leading from republic to empire. He gave the government at Rome a nasty fright but it may be that his influence upon history lies in a very different direction. It was his determined resistance that made it necessary to call in Pompey, on his return from the East, to help finish off ... Had these two men [Pompey and Crassus] been able to work better together in the difficult years that followed history might have taken a very different course.[13]

In other words, according to this view, Spartacus is important because of the role he played in the relationship between Pompey and Crassus. The fate of the Roman Empire lay in the hands of these two individuals, not thousands of slaves. Although an unquestioning acceptance of the statements of some of our sources may give this impression, it seems counterintuitive to imagine that a rebellion of tens of thousands of slaves had no further repercussions.

First, we can never know what the slaves wanted, so to be certain that they could not have wanted the abolition of slavery is impossible. People today work for ends that others see as unrealistic, such as world peace, a nuclear-free world, making poverty history or equality for men and women. Simply because these aims may be unreasonable or even impossible has not stopped our contemporaries having them. One cannot argue that the slaves in antiquity *by necessity* would have been realistic and that they must have seen that there *could* be no end of slavery at that time.[14]

It cannot be denied that the most famous slave revolts of antiquity happened in a relatively short space of time: sixty years or so in the period of the late Roman Republic. The period has always been seen as one of particular disturbance and attracted more comment than others and one might say that its peculiar nature resulted in a peculiar historiography. Those who tended to write about the end of the Republic were often writing in the Imperial period and so were happy to narrate events that perhaps republican historians might not have. Or, on the other hand, one could suggest that the Republic was in such a state of upheaval that the republican historians were also divided and therefore narrated events that in a more stable set of circumstances would not have been reported.

The first of these famous slave wars was the first Sicilian slave war, which broke out maybe in the 140s BCE and certainly carried on until the late 130s. The Spartacan revolt, which was the last great outbreak of this sixty or seventy year period, finished in 71 BCE. These dates alone are significant. In 133 BCE Tiberius Gracchus, who was acting on observations of what was happening in Sicily, that is, the slave war, was murdered for suggesting unpalatable reforms to redistribute to poor citizens the public land, which had sometimes been appropriated by wealthy landowners. In 71 BCE Pompey succeeded in wresting from the Senate a consulship to which he was not entitled, with the slave war having just been finished in Italy. The fact that the Senate allowed him to have this extraordinary consulship cannot be divorced from the extreme threat that had recently faced Rome with an enormous slave army marching the length of Italy defeating Roman armies on the way.

The start and end dates of these major slave wars mark the timespan of *Rome in the Late Republic* by Mary Beard and Michael Crawford, which in turn covers the same period as the first book of the civil wars by Appian.[15] Appian's narrative is central for any study of the period and many modern studies have not strayed too far from his structure, or his analysis. H. H. Scullard starts his classic *From the Gracchi to Nero* with the tribunate of Tiberius Gracchus. This is not chance or laziness. Things in the Roman Republic did change dramatically with the murder of this tribune. As Appian remarks: "The sword was never carried into the assembly and there was no civil butchery until Tiberius Gracchus, while serving as tribune and bringing forward new laws, was the first to fall victim to internal commotion".[16]

According to Appian, the civil war started with the murder of Tiberius Gracchus. With his reforms he was trying to remedy problems caused by the phenomenally fast increase of the conquests of the Romans in the Mediterranean, which included a massive influx of slaves into the Roman system, resulting in the armed uprising on Sicily. Polybius had started his *Histories*: "For who is so worthless or indolent as not to wish to know by what means and under what system of polity the Romans in less than 53 years have succeeded in subjecting nearly the whole inhabited world to their sole government – a thing unique in history?"[17] The fifty-three years in question were 220–168 BCE, that is, from the start of the Second Punic War until the end of the Macedonian monarchy, as he explained.[18] In fact he started earlier than this and went back to the start of the First Punic War, 264 BCE, as he admitted,[19] and continued until the destruction of Carthage and Corinth in 146 BCE. In other words, Polybius, having lived through a large portion of this period, thought the crucial years in the history of Rome were those years immediately preceding the first Sicilian slave war, the years that built up the situation that resulted in tens of thousands of slaves taking up arms against their masters. When in 146 BCE it looked as if Rome had vanquished all its enemies and was at the height of its powers, one aspect of this might was the enormous number of slaves it had taken. It was these that could have been its undoing.

Appian

To ancient writers, then, these years were highly significant, and to them the slave wars were an integral part of the general disintegration of society. With a ruling class divided, there was an opportunity for the slaves. Appian saw the split and wrote his history accordingly. He introduced his *Civil Wars* by saying that, after the murder of Tiberius Gracchus, there were numerous other atrocities ending temporarily in the dictatorship of Sulla; after his death, however, the chaos broke out again until Julius Caesar was made dictator for life. When he in turn was murdered, even worse civil war broke out. Octavius eventually emerged from this conflict to establish a lasting and masterful government that brought peace to the Empire. Appian comments: "So after all sorts of discord, the Roman state returned to harmony and monarchy".[20] The admission that the Romans had a monarch is striking since the Romans were traditionally supposed to hate the very word for king, rex.[21]

Appian drew attention to the increase in the number of slaves used to work the land and stated that the large landowners employed slaves because their labour was more constant; slaves were not conscripted to go and fight as free labourers were. He adds a point often ignored by modern scholars: that the slaves reproduced more than the free precisely because they did not go and fight. He writes:

> At the same time the ownership of slaves brought them [the rich] great gain from the multitude of their progeny, who increased because they were exempt from military service. Thus certain powerful men became extremely rich and the race of slaves multiplied throughout the country while the Italian people dwindled in numbers and strength being oppressed by penury, taxes and military service. If they had any respite from these evils they passed their time in idleness, because the land was held by the rich who employed slaves instead of free men as cultivators.[22]

This is not just a side issue for Appian but is crucial for understanding the problems of the times. It was of central importance, in his eyes, for the campaign of Tiberius Gracchus. In his introduction to him he reported almost immediately: "He [Tiberius Gracchus] inveighed against the multitude of slaves as useless in war and never faithful to their masters, and cited the recent calamity brought upon the masters by their slaves in Sicily ...".[23] He explains that this was because so many had been recently brought on to the island and then comments on the war: "recalling also the war waged against them by the Romans, which was neither easy nor short but long-protracted and full of vicissitudes and dangers".[24] Tiberius Gracchus is supposed to be saying this in 133 BCE so it seems that the war had been going on for some time.

The land law of Tiberius Gracchus, as described by Appian, was an attempt to remedy the situation brought about by the importation of so many slaves and the detrimental effect of this on the Italians. The rich did not like Tiberius' suggestions and brought forward objections, then the poor, he says, complained in their turn. Apart from complaining of poverty, and their military service: "they reproached the rich for employing slaves, who were always faithless and ill-disposed and for that reason unserviceable in war, instead of freemen, citizens and soldiers".[25] In the following chapter, in reporting Tiberius' response to all this, Appian writes that, among other things, he asked whether a citizen was more worthy of consideration at all times than a slave.

According to Appian the start of the civil war was due to the issue of the slaves in the Empire. Slaves were crucial throughout this period, in his eyes. Tiberius Gracchus was murdered at the same time as Aristonicus was leading his uprising in Asia. Appian makes this connection: "These things took place [i.e. the murder on the Capitol] at the time when Aristonicus was contending with the Romans for the government of Asia".[26] He is concerned here with the civil wars so he simply mentions this and passes on, but the reader knows that this trouble also involved slaves. So at the time when the Romans murdered Tiberius Gracchus for trying to solve problems incurred by there being so many slaves in the Empire, there was another uprising on the opposite side of the Mediterranean, which also took some time for the Romans to put down.

Also in Appian's first book we learn about the Social War: the war waged by the Romans against their allies, the Italians, who wanted Roman citizenship. This war is the backdrop to the survival of the army of Spartacus in the Italian countryside but was also a result of the

Gracchan reforms, which were implemented by a commission even though the proposer had been murdered. Italians were losing their land owing to the redistribution, so they tried to protect themselves. One proposal to make the reforms more palatable was to give Roman citizenship to the Italians.

The consul of 125 BCE, Fulvius Flaccus, and one of the agrarian commissioners involved in the redistribution, tried to bring it forward but failed owing to resistance from the Senate. Later Appian goes back to this to explain the origins of the Social War.[27] He sees this as part of the civil wars. As he remarks, it began in Rome and led to terrible consequences. Also related to our concern with slaves, in *Mithridatic Wars* Appian comments that the Italians had allowed Spartacus through their land because they hated the Romans so much. This hatred had its origins in the land reforms and the way the Romans dealt with their concerns, and earlier. When describing the revolt of the inhabitants of Asculum, he remarks that all the neighbouring peoples declared war at the same time and he lists them: "the Marsi, the Peligni, the Vestini, the Marrucini and after them the Picentines, the Frentani, the Hirpini, the Pompeiians, the Venusini, the Apulians, the Lucanians and the Samnites", about whom he commented "all of whom had been hostile to the Romans before".[28] He then goes on to add other people who also joined in.

The Romans, by their maltreatment of their neighbours several decades before, thus aided the revolt of the slaves under the leadership of Spartacus.[29] When the Etrurians and Umbrians started thinking of revolt, Appian reports that the Senate gave in and gave the faithful Italians citizenship to keep them faithful, adding that they made sure their vote was ineffective by enrolling them in the ten new tribes, which voted last; this later became a source of conflict.[30] We also learn in this chapter that there was a shortage of soldiers so that the Romans had to enrol freed men in the army for the first time.

What is interesting about Appian's narrative is that slaves are frequently represented as the deciding factor. When the Marians resisting Sulla in Rome promised freedom to slaves if they fought on their side, no one volunteered,[31] clearly marking out their side as the losing one. And in the next sentence we are told that, in despair after this rejection by the slaves, they fled the city. A little later we are told that Sulpicius and his associates had been exiled from Rome because they had fought against the consuls, and had incited slaves to join them.[32] Appian later describes how Pompey was expected to become a dictator and encouraged this in secret. When the slaves under Milo were rampaging and killing, the Senate also wanted to make Pompey dictator, in order to have protection against the slaves, but in the end they only made him sole consul.[33]

Cinna offered freedom to slaves in Rome but none joined him, so for support he went to the neighbouring towns, the inhabitants of which had recently been given Roman citizenship.[34] He was more successful with them, and after gaining support from them and also from the returning Marius he again asked them to join him. Marius is described as having about 500 slaves with him who had followed their masters. After these successes, and more, Cinna again appealed to slaves in Rome to desert to him, and this time they did, in large numbers.[35] It is immediately after describing this, that is, the desertion by large numbers of slaves, that Appian then narrates that the Senate started to appease Cinna and asked to make peace. In other words, Cinna had had successes but it was once the slaves in Rome deserted that the situation became so critical that the Senate surrendered the city.[36]

On being made dictator, Sulla instituted various reforms, endeavouring to prevent exceptions to the pattern of offices, the *cursus honorum*, and reducing the power of the tribunes. Because so many senators had been killed, he added about 300 equites and, more importantly for us here, added 10,000 slaves to the plebeians. That is, he freed them, gave them Roman citizenship and called them Cornelii after himself. Appian explains the benefits of doing this: "In this way he made sure of having 10,000 men among the plebeians always ready to obey his commands".[37] Later, when describing how Sulla retired, voluntarily laying down his power, Appian explains that he did this because he wanted a quiet life again, not because he was afraid (as one might think, having led such a life and created so many enemies). As Appian explains, he was still strong when he retired, and not only were there 120,000 of his veterans throughout Italy who were loyal to him, but also he could depend on "the 10,000 Cornelii ready in the city".[38] Again, for Appian, slaves play a crucial role in the politics of Rome.

Florus

Florus is another writer in whose construction of the history of the time we can see great importance given to the slave wars. It may be that he reflected Livy's concerns but as Livy is not extant for this period, it is impossible to say. Florus wrote a summary of Livy in two books starting with Romulus and ending with the peace established by Augustus. It is not known exactly when he composed his history. He says that his own time was not far short of 200 years after Augustus:

> From the time of Caesar Augustus down to our own age there has been a period of not much less than 200 years, during which, owing to the inactivity of the emperors, the Roman people, as it were, grew old and lost its potency, save that under the rule of Trajan it again stirred its arms and, contrary to general expectation, again renewed its vigour with youth as it were restored.[39]

Florus' history neatly deals with external and internal enemies of Rome and draws the conclusion that Augustus was a great boon to Rome. The slave wars in Sicily have a chapter in Book 2 to themselves and so does that led by Spartacus.[40] Book 1 is more concerned with external wars, whereas Book 2 has chapters on the revolutions of Tiberius Gracchus ("*seditio Tiberi Gracchi*", 2.2), Gaius Gracchus ("*seditio G. Gracchi*", 2.3), Apuleius ("*seditio Apuleiana*", 2.4) and Drusus ("*seditio Drusiana*", 2.5), the war against the allies ("*bellum adversum socios*", 2.6), the war against the slaves ("*bellum servile*", 2.7), the war against Spartacus ("*bellum Spartacium*", 2.8), again not the *seditio* of Spartacus, then the civil war of Marius ("*bellum civile Marianum*", 2.9), the war with Sertorius, the civil war under Lepidus, the war of Catiline and so on until the Peace with Parthia and the deification of Augustus. This is the first peace in Florus' book. Until then it had been a list of *seditiones* and *bella*. The last chapter is "*Pax Parthorum et consecratio Augusti*":

> It was also discussed in the senate whether he should not be called Romulus, because he had established the empire; but the name of Augustus was deemed more holy and venerable, in order that, while he still dwelt upon earth, he might be given a name and title which raised him to the rank of a deity.[41]

Florus looks back at the Republican period from the imperial period, and sees the late Republic as one of decline, until the arrival of Octavian.

In his introduction Florus explains his view of Rome: he saw Rome as a person passing through childhood, youth, maturity and senility. Its infancy was during the reign of the kings, which lasted nearly 400 years.

Rome's youth, on the other hand, was a mere 150 years when Rome subjugated Italy. The maturity was the 150 years when it conquered peoples further afield and, under Augustus, spread peace to the world. The war against Spartacus thus features in the mature period, but the actual picture presented in the account of the slave wars is one of a decline of sorts. The first book had been about imperial conquest but the second was concerned with internal fighting, and therefore full of condemnation of the actions of the Romans, who consequently needed the strong hand of Augustus to set things straight. In the account of the Social War Florus starts: "Though we call this war a war against allies, in order to lessen the odium of it, yet if we are to tell the truth, it was a war against citizens".[42] He goes on to say that when Italy had been united by the Romans, it became one body, so that for the Romans to fight against the Italians was to fight against fellow citizens.[43] Chapter 7 starts: "Although we fought with allies, in itself an impious act, yet we fought with men who enjoyed liberty and were of free birth; but who could tolerate with equanimity wars waged by a sovereign people against slaves?"[44] And Chapter 8 starts:

> One can tolerate indeed even the disgrace of a war against slaves; for although, by force of circumstances, they are liable to any kind of treatment, yet they form as it were a class (though an inferior class) of human beings and can be admitted to the blessings of liberty which we enjoy. But I know not what name to give to the war which was stirred up at the instigation of Spartacus; for the common soldiers being slaves and their leaders being gladiators, the former men of the humblest, the latter men of the worse, class added insult to the injury which they inflicted upon Rome.[45]

He is hostile to the slaves generally and describes them as rampaging, pillaging and slaughtering, but also presents them as quite disciplined: they formed a regular army and made weapons and armour, using the rods and axes of the Romans they had captured. Spartacus, he says, had begun as a Roman soldier in Thrace, and then deserted, was a bandit and finally a gladiator. He used Roman funeral rights for his generals and then put on gladiatorial games himself.[46] Florus thus gives a picture of a would-be Roman, someone who admired and therefore copied their customs. He says that the slaves fought like the gladiators that they were, that is, to the death. Spartacus died fighting in the front line, like a true general.[47]

Even though the slaves were beaten, the overall situation worsened in Florus' eyes, so that the following chapter about the civil war of Marius begins: "The only thing still wanting to complete the misfortunes of the Roman people was that they should draw the sword upon each other at home, and that citizens should fight against citizens in the midst of the city and in the forum like gladiators at the arena".[48] Whatever Florus says in his introduction, the benefits of maturity occur only with Augustus; until then, things had been going from bad to worse for the Romans. It was a calamity to fight allies, humiliating to fight slaves and even worse to fight gladiators, but worst of all was for Romans to behave like gladiators themselves. In other words, for Florus, the rebellion of the slaves was all part of the degeneration and disintegration of the Republic.

This, however, does not really correspond to what he said he thought about Rome in his introduction. He gives a clearer version of his views of historical causation, and how he planned his work, at the end of his first book. In this interesting chapter he recapitulates what his first book had been about: "Such are the events of the third period of history of the Roman people during which, having once ventured to advance outside Italy they carried their arms over the whole world".[49] Here he departs from his view at the start of the book, or he uses a different division, because he remarks:

> The first hundred years of this period were pure and humane and as we have said a golden age, free from vice and crime while the innocence of the old pastoral life was still untainted and uncorrupted, and the imminent threat of our Carthaginian foes kept alive the ancient discipline. The following 100 years which we have traced from the destruction of Carthage, Corinth and Numantia and the inheritance of the Asiatic Kingdom of Attalus down to the time of Caesar and Pompeius and of their successor Augustus, with whose history we still have to deal, *were as deplorable and shameful owing to internal calamities as they were illustrious* for the glory of their military achievements. For just as it was honourable and glorious to have won the rich and powerful provinces of Gaul, Thrace, Cilicia and Cappadocia as well as the territory of the Armenians and Britons, which though they served no practical purpose, constituted important titles to imperial greatness; *so it was disgraceful and deplorable at the same time to have fought at home with fellow-citizens and allies, with slaves and gladiators and the whole senate divided against itself.*[50]

He continues by saying that it may actually have been better for Rome to forego her acquisitions, and to have been content with Sicily and Africa, or even not to have kept these but to have remained merely in control of Italy, than to increase so much that the Romans were ruined by their own greatness.[51]

According to his view, the wealth produced the trouble:

> For what else produced those outbursts of domestic strife but excessive prosperity? It was the conquest of Syria which first corrupted us, followed by the Asiatic inheritance bequeathed by the king of Pergamon. The resources and wealth thus acquired spoiled the morals of the age and ruined the State, which was engulfed in its own vices as in a common sewer.[52]

He goes on to say that this is why the Roman people demanded more, leading to the revolutions of the Gracchi. More importantly for our understanding of the slave wars, he writes:

> Again what brought the servile wars upon us except the excessive size of our establishments? How else could those armies of gladiators have arisen against their masters, save that a profuse expenditure, which aimed at conciliating the favour of the common people by indulging their love of shows, had turned what was originally a method of punishing enemies into a competition of skill?[53]

He goes on to describe his second book: "We will, therefore now describe in their order all these domestic disturbances as distinct from foreign wars properly so called".[54]

Florus thus saw the imperial expansion as a direct cause of internal unrest; the huge wealth flowing into Rome destabilized that city and the individual fortunes that some of these successful generals gained were the source of trouble.

The slave wars and the decline of the Roman Republic

In a not dissimilar vein, Orosius wrote a very succinct account (he composed a history from the creation to 418 CE), and his was hostile: "Wherever they went the slaves indiscriminately mixed slaughter, arson, theft, and rape".[55] The slaves put on gladiatorial games (at the unlikely event of the funeral of a female prisoner who had killed herself because she had been raped by them), using 400 Roman prisoners. Orosius states explicitly what Florus had only implied: "Those who had once been the spectacle were now to be the spectators".[56] As if realizing that this makes them the equal of the Romans, he adds that they staged them *not* like military commanders but like gladiatorial entrepreneurs. Crassus' decimation is not alluded to, but in the battle the Romans slew 6000 of the slaves and in the next engagement 30,000. In the final battle 60,000 men were killed, 6,000 taken prisoner and a further 3,000 escaped but were later hunted down. There is no mention of any heroism by Spartacus or the final crucifixion of the slaves by the Romans.

Later, at the end of the fifth book, Orosius stresses the importance of this war which might appear insignificant because it was fought against slaves. Orosius emphasizes the disastrous losses for the Romans and the huge numbers involved. He ends: "As for the fugitive slaves themselves, the number of them who were slaughtered in the war surpassed 100,000".[57] The numbers involved had mushroomed by late antiquity. Wars against slaves were terrible to contemplate for the slave-owners. "*Tot servi quot hostes*" [All slaves are enemies]. They had an enemy within.

When ancient writers analysed the fall of the republic they saw the slave wars as being part of the civil wars, fighting their own citizens and slaves. It was a sign of decline to be fighting slaves and, as Florus puts it, the reason the slaves could rebel was that there were so many of them. This is also very similar to the thesis put forward by Diodorus, who tells us most about the Sicilian slave wars.

The works of Appian and Florus, together with Augustine, whose analysis will be briefly discussed later, show that ancient commentators thought the slave revolts were significant. Yet in some sense they had every reason to play down the revolts of slaves. In modern times, the view that one did not advertise slave rebellions for fear the news would get out to other slaves and give them ideas is well documented.[58] The idea, which appeals to common sense, that slaves rebelling was a tremendous threat to the Romans should be taken more seriously: not just the uprising of Spartacus but those in Sicily too, although Spartacus brought the threat even closer to home by being in mainland Italy.

Rome in the Late Republic by Beard and Crawford reveals, perhaps unsurprisingly, that they too see the decline as taking place in the same timescale as our ancient authors: "In some ways, as we have seen, it makes sense to regard Pompey as the first princeps".[59] Whereas Julius Caesar might seem the more obvious candidate for this, Beard and Crawford point out that Pompey was the turning point for the Republic:

> The example of Pompey was of particular importance. His early career, built entirely upon military success, *culminated in 71*: outside Rome and in command of his army, he obtained from the senate (no doubt with the unspoken threat of violent intervention) permission to stand for a consulship before holding any other elected office and a triumph. He proceeded later in the east to yet more striking forms of dominance, acting frequently without reference to the senate and occupying an almost royal position; coins were minted carrying his portrait; cities were named after him; religious cult was offered to him. Away from Rome, Pompey had gone far beyond what might now seem the tentative steps of Sulla. It was left only for Caesar, after the civil war, to apply these principles in Rome itself.[60]

So they suggest that we view 71 BCE as a crucial date; Pompey gets a consulship the following year, that is, out of turn. Why was he allowed to acquire this? Because the Senate was terrified not only of Pompey's army, but because the war against the slaves had only at that point been brought to an end.

The starting-point for this decline for most commentators is the tribunate of Tiberius Gracchus in 133 BCE. This coincides with the first Sicilian slave war, which was of course part of the motivation for Gracchus' reforms anyway. Ancient writers described the slave wars as part of the disintegration of the system, as a symptom of the decline and indeed it may have been owing to this that they recorded them at all. They wanted to show the terrible dangers that the state had been in, and from which it had been rescued. Therefore they painted it in colours as dark as possible, which meant for once reporting the actions of slaves. That there were so many slaves was a direct result of the prosperity of the Romans, as Florus accurately described, as mentioned earlier.

One of the problems of ancient history is that our remaining sources for the most part come from a very small segment of the total population and it is very difficult to reconstruct other voices and other opinions or alternative explanations. The Christians often took over the attitudes of their classical forebears but had strong reasons for sometimes providing a different interpretation of events. In Book 4 of the *City of God*, Augustine mentioned Spartacus, as he wanted to demonstrate what a great threat this rebellion was to the Romans. As he points out, the Roman Empire was at its height when a few gladiators threatened it:

> What I want to say is that when the Roman Empire was already great, when she had subjugated many nations and was feared by all the rest, this great Empire was bitterly distressed and deeply alarmed, and had the utmost difficulty in extricating herself from the threat of overwhelming disaster, when a tiny handful of gladiators in Campania escaped from the training school and collected a large army. Under three commanders they wrought cruel havoc over a wide area of Italy. Would our opponents tell us the name of the god who assisted them, so that from a small and contemptible gang of thugs they developed into a kingdom inspiring fear in the Romans for all Rome's great resources and all her strongholds?[61]

He goes on to say that the gladiators must have had divine help since:

> They broke the chains of their servile condition; they escaped; they got clean away; they collected a large and formidable army; and in obedience to the plans and orders of their "kings" they became an object of dread to the soaring might of Rome. They were more than a match for many Roman generals; they captured much booty; they gained many victories; they indulged themselves at will, following the prompting of every desire; in fact they lived in all the grandeur of kings, until their eventual defeat, which was only achieved with the greatest difficulty.[62]

Augustine had started Book 4 saying that even though the Roman Empire was longlasting it did not mean the gods favoured it, so he wanted to depict the troubles they had. He also wanted to show that the Roman Empire may have been big and it may have lasted a long time but it existed without justice (because it was pagan). Before mentioning the great achievements of the gladiators, he has a short chapter commenting that empires without justice are simply criminals on a large scale, which many today might find a sympathetic judgement. He illustrated his point with the following story:

> For it was a witty and truthful rejoinder which was given by a captured pirate to Alexander the Great. The king asked the fellow,

"What is your idea, infesting the sea?" And the pirate answered, with uninhibited insolence, "The same as yours, in infesting the earth! But because I do it with a tiny craft, I'm called a pirate: because you have a mighty navy, you are called an emperor."[63]

Notes

1. The significance of slave revolts

1. It is commonplace but worth stating again that none of our ancient evidence comes from slaves. Jean Andreau and Raymond Descaut comment at the start of their recent work that we only hear about slaves from their masters and then they only talk about those they know personally. They remark that slaves are some of the forgotten people of history (*Esclavage en Grèce et à Rome* [Paris: Hachette, 2006], 9). This is true, but in the case of slave revolts even our small amount of evidence is not given the attention it deserves.
2. Although see Keith Bradley's invaluable *Slavery and Rebellion in the Roman World 140 BC–70 BC* (London: Batsford, 1989), to which I shall refer many times in the course of the following examination. The size of my debt to his work will be apparent and if I disagree with some of his observations, the scholarship contained in his volume has made my own task much easier.
3. This might remind some readers of the observation in the UK Home Office White Paper *Crime, Justice and Protecting the Public*, Cm 965 (London: HMSO, 1990) that it was "unrealistic to construct sentencing arrangements on the assumption that most offenders will … base their conduct on rational calculation. Often they do not" (quoted by Phil Harris in his *An Introduction to Law*, 7th edn [Cambridge: Cambridge University Press, 2007], 328).
4. Niall McKeown, *The Invention of Ancient Slavery?* (London: Duckworth, 2007).
5. *Ibid.*, 29. McKeown's warnings about our preconceptions colouring our approaches are apposite but they should clarify our thoughts not paralyse us. It is not a question of taking the middle ground between those who accept the reports by the masters of their own good behaviour and those who see ill treatment everywhere. With regard to questions such as whether slaves were well or badly treated (see e.g. McKeown, *The Invention of Ancient Slavery?*, 30–51), it must be that some masters treated their slaves well; it may be that vast numbers of them did. This, however, does not make the institution of slavery more acceptable. What interests me are the actions of those slaves who fought

against their masters, and therefore against slavery, in open armed warfare, and how the reports of those actions have been passed down to us today.
6. For similar difficulties in the study of the modern phenomenon, see John Bracey's foreword to Herbert Aptheker, *American Negro Slave Revolts*, 6th edn (New York: International Publishers, [1943] 1993), 3–10.
7. Moses I. Finley, "Was Greek Civilisation Based on Slave Labour?", *Historia* **8** (1959), 145–64, esp. 160; reprinted in his (edited) *Slavery in Classical Antiquity: Views and Controversies*, 53–72 (Cambridge: Heffer, 1960).
8. The *Communist Manifesto* starts:
    The history of all hitherto existing society is the history of class struggles. Freeman and slave, patrician and plebeian, lord and serf, guildmaster and journeyman, in a word, oppressor and oppressed, stood in constant opposition to one another, carried on an uninterrupted, now hidden, now open fight, a fight that each time ended, either in a revolutionary reconstitution of society at large, or in the common ruin of the contending classes.
    It seems that many modern commentators on slave wars subscribe to this view since they say that the slave wars resulted in no change of society, and therefore are not significant. On the other hand, the ancient sources, as discussed in Chapter 6, did see the slave wars as part of a process in the Roman Republic that certainly did end in a revolutionary reconstitution of society, the principate. The approach here is, less ambitiously, a re-examination of these episodes as worth studying in their own right.
9. Finley, "Was Greek Civilisation Based on Slave Labour?", 160 (*Slavery in Classical Antiquity*, 68). On the other hand, the subject has been ignored by some historians because they have seen the important class struggle as being between poor and rich, not slave and free. For example, de Ste Croix quotes a passage from the preface to the second German edition of 1869 of Marx's *The Eighteenth Brumaire of Louis Bonaparte*: "In ancient Rome the class struggle took place only within a privileged minority, between the free rich and the free poor, while the great productive mass of the population, the slaves, formed the purely passive pedestal for these conflicts" (quoted in G. E. M. de Ste Croix, *The Class Struggle in the Ancient Greek World: From the Archaic Age to the Arab Conquests* [London: Duckworth, 1981], 61). Ste Croix professes not to subscribe to this definition but in this work gives surprisingly little attention to the fight between slave and free.
10. Eugene Genovese, *From Rebellion to Revolution: Afro-American Slave Revolts in the Making of the Modern World* (Baton Rouge, LA: Louisiana State University Press, 1979), xix.
11. *Ibid.*, xiv, xxi.
12. *Ibid.*, xviii.
13. Jacky Dahomay, "Slavery and Law: Legitimations of an Insurrection", in *The Abolitions of Slavery: From the L. F. Sonthonax to Victor Schoelcher, 1793, 1794, 1848*, M. Dorigny (ed.), 3–16 (Oxford: Berghahn, 2003), 4.
14. *Ibid.*, 12. See also David Brion Davis, *The Problem of Slavery in the Age of Revolution* (Ithaca, NY: Cornell University Press, 1975), 137–48, on events in

St Domingue. Although the ideological background is so different, one can see parallels with the late Republic, since France was involved in both internal and external wars thus offering an opportunity to the slaves, which they took.
15. Finley, "Was Greek Civilisation Based on Slave Labour?", 159 (*Slavery in Classical Antiquity,* 67).
16. Orlando Patterson, *Slavery and Social Death: A Comparative Study* (Cambridge, MA: Harvard University Press, 1982), vii.
17. Kevin Bales, *Disposable People: New Slavery in the Global Economy* (Berkeley, CA: University of California Press, 1999), 3.
18. *Ibid.*, 8. See also Kevin Bales, *Understanding Global Slavery: A Reader* (Berkeley, CA: University of California Press, 2005) and *Ending Slavery: How We Free Today's Slaves* (Berkeley, CA: University of California Press, 2007). Estimates vary and people dispute the conditions that justify the term slavery, but no one denies that people around the world are being deprived of their liberty illegally and that this is very profitable. The United Nations Office on Drugs and Crime announced the launch of its Global Initiative to Fight Human Trafficking in March 2007. Andreau and Descaut start their study of ancient slavery by distinguishing ancient legal slavery from the modern illegal condition (*Esclavage en Grèce et à Rome,* 7–8).
19. Genovese, *From Rebellion to Revolution,* 11–12. I have adapted his words to fit the ancient context. He expressed the conditions thus:

(1) The master–slave relationship had developed in the context of absenteeism and depersonalization as well as greater cultural estrangement of whites and blacks; (2) economic distress and famine occurred; (3) slaveholding units approached the average size of one hundred to two hundred slaves, as in the sugar colonies, rather than twenty or so, as in the Old South; (4) the ruling class frequently split either in warfare between slaveholding countries or in the bitter struggles within a particular slaveholding country; (5) blacks heavily outnumbered whites; (6) African-born slaves outnumbered those born into American slavery (creoles); (7) the social structure of the slaveholding regime permitted the emergence of an autonomous black leadership; and (8) the geographical, social and political environment provided terrain and opportunity for the formation of colonies of runaway slaves strong enough to threaten the plantation regime.

He carries on to observe

the list may be extended, refined and subdivided but taken together, these conditions spelled one: the military and political balance of power. Slave revolts might anywhere, anytime flare up in response to the central fact of enslavement; no particular provocation or condition was indispensable. But the probabilities for large-scale revolt rested heavily on some combination of these conditions. (*Ibid.,* 12)

20. Paul Cartledge, "Rebels and Sambos in Classical Greece: A Comparative View", reprinted in his *Spartan Reflections,* 127–52 (London: Duckworth, 2001) took these factors and applied them to Greek history. In his discussion of the first point, Cartledge remarks: "We are plunged straight into the fundamental but

predictably contentious area of slave ideology and psychology" (*ibid.*, 135). Later he returns to this and, after commenting that Genovese had not ranked these items in order of importance, remarks: "But I think he would not be unwilling to accept that (1) the factor that may be shortly summarised as slave ideology was at bottom the most decisive of them all" (*ibid.*, 146). As we shall see, this is not the view put forward here.

21. For a full discussion of the issue, see Ingomar Weiler, *Die Beendigung des Sklavenstatus im Altertum. Ein Beitrag zur vergleichenden Sozialgeschichte* (Stuttgart: Franz Steiner, 2003), 73–111.

22. Mark Golden, "The Uses of Cross-cultural Comparison in Ancient Social History", *Classical Views/Echos du monde classique* **36**(11) (1992), 309–11, esp. 311. Keith Bradley, *Slavery and Society at Rome* (Cambridge: Cambridge University Press, 1994), 180, makes a similar point.

23. Orlando Patterson, "Slavery and Slave Revolts: A Socio-Historical Analysis of the First Maroon War, Jamaica 1655–1740", *Social and Economic Studies* **19**(3) (1970), 289–325, esp. 289.

24. Genovese, *From Rebellion to Revolution*, 1–50. For those not familiar with the history of these slave societies, the success of some maroon communities, that is, groups of runaway slaves living independently of their masters, may seem remarkable. For an overview, see Richard Price, "Maroons and their Communities", in *The Slavery Reader*, G. Heuman & J. Walvin (eds), 608–25 (London: Routledge, 2003), and Stuart B. Schwartz, "Resistance and Accommodation in Eighteenth-century Brazil", also in *The Slavery Reader*, 623–34. For slave revolts in Latin America see Leslie B. Rout, *The African Experience in Spanish America: 1502 to the Present Day* (Cambridge: Cambridge University Press, 1976), 99–125. On Brazil, see also Stuart B. Schwartz, *Slaves, Peasants and Rebels: Reconsidering Brazilian Slavery* (Urbana, IL: University of Illinois Press, 1992), 103–36. The maroon community of Palmares lasted virtually for the whole of the seventeenth century, 1605–94, and is thought to have been made up of more than 20,000 people. One might think that the authorities must have turned a blind eye to its existence but in fact it fought to survive and was attacked yearly for some of its history. Despite the apparent defeat of the community at the end of the seventeenth century, fugitive slaves headed there as late as 1746 (*ibid.*, 124). For forms of resistance including maroons in Bourbon in the second half of the eighteenth century, see Prosper Ève, "Forms of Resistance in Bourbon, 1750–1789", in *The Abolitions of Slavery: From the L. F. Sonthonax to Victor Schoelcher, 1793, 1794, 1848*, M. Dorigny (ed.), 17–39 (Oxford: Berghahn, 2003).

25. Genovese, *From Rebellion to Revolution*, 7. Involved in this question is the issue of how slaves were treated. Those wishing to put a favourable gloss on what might be considered a shameful episode in the history of the United States had argued that the American masters treated their slaves better than masters in the Caribbean or Brazil. However, Aptheker, *American Negro Slave Revolts*, revealed that there *were* continual attempts on the part of slaves to resist their slavery, rather as Patterson had described being the case in Jamaica. Genovese's contribution was to point to the different ratio of slaves to free in these societies.

26. Aptheker, *American Negro Slave Revolts*, 150–61. Winthrop D. Jordan's *Tumult and Silence at Second Creek: An Inquiry into a Civil War Slave Conspiracy* (Baton Rouge. LA: Louisiana State University Press, 1993) is an excellent example of how evidence of rebellious slaves can remain hidden, and yet what a fascinating story can be told if a historian has the will to investigate. I am grateful to Kevin Bales for alerting me to this work.
27. Aptheker, *American Negro Slave Revolts*, 161. It is far less likely that there are records of outbreaks from antiquity that are completely unknown. But it seems probable that many instances were never recorded or, if they were, these records are now lost.
28. *Ibid.*, 374.
29. Kenneth S. Greenberg (ed.), *Nat Turner: A Slave Rebellion in History and Memory* (Oxford: Oxford University Press, 2003), xi, emphasis added.
30. *Digest*, 1, 5; Thomas Wiedemann, *Greek and Roman Slavery* (London: Routledge, 1981), 15.
31. For discussion see Patterson, *Slavery and Social Death*, 38–45.
32. Moses I. Finley, *Ancient Slavery and Modern Ideology* (Harmondsworth: Penguin, 1980), 113–14. He goes on to write that the reason for the ancient wars was the crisis of Roman society and the presence of newly enslaved men, many educated and of high enough social status to be leaders. This restriction of slave wars to the three in the Roman Republic is echoed by many scholars. For instance, Peter Green remarks: "The Roman slave revolts of the second and first centuries BC were unique. Nothing like them had ever happened before, and after the final suppression of Spartacus in 70 BC no comparable uprising ever took place again" ("The First Sicilian Slave War", *Past and Present* **20** [1961], 10–29, esp. 10). Joseph Vogt has a similar start to his chapter on slave rebellions: "Everyone who considers the great slave revolts of the ancient world will be struck by the fact that they all occurred in the relatively short period of time between 140 BC and 70 BC" (*Ancient Slavery and the Ideal of Man*, T. Wiedemann [trans.] [Oxford: Blackwell, 1974], 39). And Keith Bradley introduces his book on the topic with the following remark:
   > In the seventy years between 140 BC and 70 BC Rome was confronted by three major insurrections of slaves .... This series of events was unique in Rome's history, for slave uprisings on such a dramatic scale had never been known beforehand and similar episodes were never to recur despite the long endurance of slavery in the Roman world.
   >
   > (*Slavery and Rebellion*, xi)

   It is by no means clear that this is the case since one could argue that our knowledge of these events merely reflects the survival of a limited number of ancient texts.

2. Preparing for revolt

1. See Geoffrey Rickman, *The Corn Supply of Ancient Rome* (Oxford: Clarendon Press, 1980), 104–6, on the importance of Sicily as a supplier of corn for

Rome during this period and later. Even before this time, in the first half of the second century BCE in Italy, there had been a series of incidents that had involved slaves, to quell which Rome had sent several armies. There is not much evidence remaining, however, only some paragraphs in Livy (Livy, *History of Rome*, 32.26.4–18; 33.36.1–3; 37.2.1, 6–7; 37.50.13; 38.36.1; 39.8.3– 9.1, 17.4–6, 18.7; 39.29.8–9; 39.41.6–7; 40.19.9–10) and an inscription (*Corpus Inscripionum Latinarum* [*CIL*] [Berlin: Berlin-Brandenburgische Akademie der Wissenschaften, 1863–], I2, no. 581). Maria Capozza wrote a study of early revolts for which we have evidence from the period 501–184 BCE: *Movimenti servili nel mondo romano in età repubblicana. I. Dal 501 al 184 a. Cr.*, Università degli Studi di Padova, Istituto di Storia antica, 5 (Rome: Università degli Studi di Padova, 1966). She looked at eight uprisings that took place in 501, 460, 419, 259, 217, 198, 196 and 185–4 BCE.

2. The state of Diodorus' text, however, is not unproblematic. See Chapter 6 for the state of Diodorus' narrative about the slave wars and its preservation, albeit in abbreviated form, in the ninth century CE by Photius and in the tenth by the composers of the *Excerpts* of Constantine. The Loeb edition of Diodorus' *Bibliotheca* (or *Library of History*), volume 12 (for Books 33–40), indicates which passages come from which summary.

3. Diodorus, 34/35.2.1.

4. Discussed by Karl Bücher, *Die Aufstände der unfreien Arbeiter 143–129* (Frankfurt: C. Adelmann, 1874), 121–32. See also Green, "The First Sicilian Slave War", 28–9, with a reply by W. G. G. Forrest and T. C. W. Stinton, "The First Sicilian Slave War", *Past and Present* **22** (1962), 87–92. Brent D. Shaw, *Spartacus and the Slave Wars: A Brief History with Documents* (Boston, MA: Bedford/St Martin's, 2001), 79, accepts Green's preference for 135 BCE, and Bradley, *Slavery and Rebellion*, 59, does not commit himself.

5. Diodorus, as reported in the *Excerpts* of Constantine, narrates that naked slaves approached their brutal master, Damophilus to ask him for clothing and he suggested that they take supply themselves by taking their clothes from those travelling through the country! (Diodorus, 34/35.2.36).

6. Diodorus, 34/35.2.3.

7. See, for instance, F. R. Walton's note in Diodorus Siculus, *Library of History*, 12 vols, F. R. Walton (trans.), Loeb Classical Library (Cambridge, MA: Harvard University Press, 1967), vol. 12, 57 n.2, and Shaw, *Spartacus and the Slave Wars*, 81, n.1. Appian, *Civil Wars*, 1.22, describes the reforms.

8. διὸ καὶ τοσοῦτο τῶν οἰκετῶν ἐπέκλυσε πλῆθος ἅπασαν Σικελίαν, ὥστε τοὺς ἀκούοντας τὴν ὑπερβολὴν μὴ πιστεῦσαι (Diodorus, 34/35.2.27).

9. I return to the circumstances of the revolt in Chapter 8, in the discussion of the place of the revolts in ancient historiography.

10. Diodorus, 34/35.2.9–10.

11. The role and strategy of the two leaders will be discussed in Chapter 4.

12. καὶ κατ' ἄλλους πολλοὺς τόπους (Diodorus, 34/35.2.19).

13. Orosius, *History against the Pagans*, 5.9.4–8.

14. Julius Obsequens, *Book of Prodigies*, 27, 27b.

15. Livy, 33.36.1. In introducing an earlier revolt he wrote, "Although Gaul was

more peaceful than expected that year, slave insurrections broke out in regions close to the city of Rome" (32.26.4).
16. Julius Obsequens, *Ab anno urbis conditae DV prodigiorum liber*.
17. Slave revolts appear to be rather different from such phenomena as crying statues, but it would seem that in the period Julius Obsequens was writing, there was a perception that certain events were unusual, that is, contrary to the normal order of things, and a sign of a general malaise of society. Augustine, concerned to show the chaos that preceded the birth of Christ, is a good indicator of how the stories of the slave revolts were seen in later times. His chronology is subservient to his argument but the overall impression he gives is that these were very damaging events. After describing how Mithridates massacred all the Romans in Asia, he had a chapter on the internal disasters the Romans had undergone and he lists the social wars, the servile wars and the civil wars. He goes even further than our other historians and tells us:

> For before the allies of Latium rose against Rome all the animals which had been tamed to serve men's needs – dogs, horses, asses, oxen and all the other cattle which were under men's domination – suddenly turned wild, forgot the gentleness of domesticity, left their quarters and roamed at large, shunning the approach not only of strangers, but even of their owners; they threatened danger and even death to any who risked closing in on them to round them up. (Augustine, *City of God*, 3.2)

After describing the horrors of the period of the Gracchi, and mocking the Romans for erecting a temple of Concord, saying they should rather have built one to Discord, Augustine narrates the period of wars that followed. He finishes Chapter 26 of Book 3 with a variant on the usual accounts of the slave wars:

> The servile war [referring to the one in the 70s BCE] was started by a mere handful of gladiators, less than seventy, in fact, and think of the huge number finally involved and the bitterness and ferocity of their struggle; remember the Roman generals defeated by that multitude, the cities and districts devastated and the manner of the devastation. The adequate description of it has baffled the powers of the historians. And this was not the only Servile War. Before this the bands of slaves had depopulated the province of Macedonia; later they devastated Sicily and the maritime coast. Who could find words to match the gravity of the events – words adequate to express the horrors of their acts of brigandage at the beginning and their wars of piracy later? (*Ibid.*, 3.26)

Zvi Yavetz, *Slaves and Slavery in Ancient Rome* (New Brunswick, NJ: Transaction Books, 1988), 41, n.5, wonders if Augustine has muddled Aristonicus' revolt in 132 BCE in Asia, with that of Andriscus in 149 BCE, in which case it is worth noting that Augustine saw Aristonicus' revolt as a slave war. On the other hand, it is entirely possible that the slave trouble in Macedonia is a different incident, about which there is little or no evidence remaining. Augustine himself comments that historians have not been up to the task of giving the full details.
18. Appian, *Civil Wars*, 1.8. For a further discussion of Appian and his view of the period, see Chapter 8. The dangers of slaves being able to talk the same language had been noted much earlier by thinkers such as Plato; see Plato, *Laws*

6, 777C, quoted by Athenaeus, *Deipnosophistae*, 6.264d–e, and by Aristotle, *Politics*, 1.5.6.
19. Diodorus, 34/35.2.48.
20. "Fugitivorum bellum in Sicilia exortum, coniuratione servorum in Italia oppressa" (Julius Obsequens, *Book of Prodigies*, 27).
21. "In Italia multa milia servorum quae coniuraverant aegre comprehensa et supplicio consumpta. In Sicilia fugitivi Romanos exercitus necaverunt. Numantia diruta" (Julius Obsequens, *Book of Prodigies*, 27, 27b).
22. There had been uprisings in Italy in the first half of the second century. Unfortunately our sources for these are brief, as noted earlier, although see Capozza, *Movimenti servili nel mondo romano*.
23. Although both Vogt, *Ancient Slavery and the Ideal of Man*, 93–102, and Yavetz, *Slaves and Slavery in Ancient Rome*, 45–66, discuss the rebellion of Aristonicus as if it were a slave uprising, Aristonicus' name does not even appear in the index to Bradley, *Slavery and Rebellion*. More recently Andreau and Descat, *Esclavage en Grèce et à Rome*, 236–7, comment on the timing of the rebellion but agree that it should not really be counted as a slave uprising. The event is also not included in Wiedemann's chapters "Resistance" (*Greek and Roman Slavery*, 188–97) and "Rebellion" (*ibid.*, 198–223). Wiedemann had explained in his introduction that:

> this war should not be seen so much as slave rebellion than as an instance of slaves being promised their freedom in return for fighting on behalf of someone who saw himself as a legitimate ruler threatened by a foreign power. There is no evidence that Aristonikos envisaged the permanent abolition of slavery as an institution. (*Greek and Roman Slavery*, 13)

Diodorus himself, however, viewed this, as well as the later episode of Titus Minutius Vettius (Diodorus, 36.2a), as a slave revolt. Shaw did not even feel the need to justify his exclusion of it from his sourcebook, *Spartacus and the Slave Wars*. For an entertaining and informative overview of the earlier literature, which accords greater claims to the intentions of Aristonicus, see Thomas W. Africa, "Aristonicus, Blossius and the City of the Sun", *International Review of Social History* 6 (1961), 110–24. See also Christian Mileta, "Verschwoerung oder Eruption? Diodor und die byzantinischen Exzerptoren ueber den Ersten Sizilischen Sklavenkrieg", in *Dissertatiunculae criticae, Festschrift fuer Guenther Christian Hansen*, C.-F. Collatz et al. (eds), 133–53 (Würzburg: Königshausen & Neumann, 1988) for a discussion of the contemporaneity of the uprisings in Sicily and Pergamum.
24. τὸ παραπλήσιον δὲ γέγονε καὶ κατὰ τὴν Ἀσίαν κατὰ τοὺς αὐτοὺς καιρούς, Ἀριστονίκου μὲν ἀντιποιησαμένου τῆς μὴ προσηκούσης βασιλείας, τῶν δὲ δούλων διὰ τὰς ἐκ τῶν δεσποτῶν κακουχίας συναπονοησαμένων ἐκείνῳ καὶ μεγάλοις ἀτυχήμασι πολλὰς πόλεις περιβαλόντων (Diodorus, 34/35.2.26). The verb συναπονοέομαι is quite unusual and means "to share in folly with". A more common verb, and one that in this context makes more sense, is συμπονέω, which simply means "to toil with, suffer with".
25. Summarized in the *Excerpts* of Constantine, 34/35.2.25–6.
26. Attalus I (ruled 241–197 BCE) was succeeded first by his oldest son Eumenes

II (ruled 198–158 BCE), then by his second son Attalus II (ruled 158–138 BCE). The next king was Attalus III (ruled 138–133 BCE), the son of Eumenes II.
27. "cupido profunda imperi et divitiarum" (Sallust, *Letter of Mithridates*, 5).
28. "Post, habitum custodiae agri captivi, sumptibus et contumeliis ex rege miserrumum servorum effecere, simulatoque impio testamento filium eius Aristonicum, quia patrium regnum petiverat, hostium more per triumphum duxere" (Sallust, *Histories*, 4.69.8–9).
29. Strabo, *Geography*, 13.4.2.
30. εἰς δὲ τὴν μεσόγαιαν ἀνιὼν ἤθροισε διὰ ταχέων πλῆθος ἀπόρων τε ἀνθρώπων καὶ δούλων ἐπ᾽ἐλευθερίᾳ κατακεκλημένων, οὓς Ἡλιοπολίτας ἐκάλεσε (*ibid.*, 14.1.38). Albert Forbiger, the German translator of Strabo's *Geographica*, suggests that this name was used because most of the slaves came from Heliopolis near Sardis, but there is no evidence to support this (*Strabo: Geographica* [German translation and notes] [Wiesbaden: Marix, [1855–98] 2005], 921, n.98). There were cities in existence called Heliopolis, but what is curious is that we see Aristonicus naming his followers this way.
31. "Aristonicus of the family of a common musician, upon the reputation of being the son of Eumenes, filled all Asia with tumults and rebellion" (Plutarch, *Life of Flamininus*, 21.6). Florus, on the other hand, writes that he was of royal blood: "Aristonicus, regii sanguinis ferox iuvenis" (*Epitome of Roman History*, 1.35).
32. In the summary of Book 58, Livy discusses Tiberius Gracchus, his land reforms and his murder. It ends with a description of how his body and the bodies of others killed at the same time were thrown into the Tiber. The next sentence records that this book contained an account of campaigns in Sicily against the slaves: "Res praeterea in Sicilia vario eventu adversus fugitivos gestas continet". At the start of the summary of the next book there is a sentence about the Scipio Africanus' victory over Numantia and then one saying that the consul Publius Rupilius ended the slave war in Sicily: "P. Rupilius consul in Sicilia cum fugitivis debellavit". The next sentence of the summary mentions the uprising of Aristonicus in Pergamum. It seems then that Livy had also placed these events together because they were contemporaneous, but the connection of the involvement of slaves may also have been a further connection, and a reason for Livy discussing these events together, as had Diodorus.
33. Diodorus, 36.1–2. His interest is not surprising given that he was from Sicily and is often referred to as Diodorus Siculus.
34. πρὸ δὲ τῆς κατὰ τὴν Σικελίαν τῶν δούλων ἐπαναστάσεως ἐγένοντο κατὰ τὴν Ἰταλίαν πλείους ἀποστάσεις ὀλιγοχρόνιοι καὶ μικραί, καθάπερ τοῦ δαιμονίου προσημαίνοντος τὸ μέγεθος τῆς ἐσομένης κατὰ τὴν Σικελίαν ἐπαναστάσεως (Diodorus, 36.2.1, emphasis added in English translation).
35. Diodorus, 36.2.3
36. Diodorus, 36.2.6. Betrayal by their own side recurs in slave revolts, or at least the narrative of them. It should be seen as a result of a weakening of the revolt, that is, if the slaves had not already lost strength the betrayal would not have been decisive. Sarapion, for instance, in the first slave war betrayed slave-held Tauromenium to the Romans (*ibid.*, 34/35.2.21); Titus Vettius Minutius

was betrayed by one his own commanders (*ibid.*, 36.1.1–2); the slaves led by Varius were betrayed by an infiltrator sent in by the Romans (*ibid.*, 36.3.1–3). The bandit Bulla was betrayed by his lover (Cassius Dio, *Roman History*, 77.10.6–7).
37. Bradley, *Slavery and Rebellion*, 73, emphasis added.
38. Vogt, *Ancient Slavery and the Ideal of Man*, 88.
39. Athenaeus, *Deipnosophistae*, 6.272f.
40. Slaves in Attica had rebelled at the same time as the first slave war, we hear from Diodorus, as seen earlier. Few scholars pay much attention to the numbers in Athenaeus. All that is important for the discussion here is that Posidonius, if the quotation is not exact, indicated that very many slaves were involved.
41. πολλαὶ δε αὗται ἐγένοντο, καὶ ἀπώλοντο οἰκετῶν ὑπὲρ τὰς ἑκατὸν μυριάδας (*ibid.*).
42. ἐπὶ πολυν χρόνον (*ibid.*).
43. Silvia Bussi, *Economia e demografia della schiavitù in Asia Minore ellenistico-romana* (Milan: LED, 2001), 117, suggests that these enslaved Bithynians were in fact *laoi*, whose free but tied status the Romans did not understand.
44. Diodorus, 36.3.1–3.
45. *Ibid.*, 36.3.2.
46. ὁ δ' εἴτε χρήμασι πεισθεὶς εἴτε χάριτι δουλεύσας (*ibid.*, 36.3.3).
47. See *ibid.*, 11.89.1–8, for the power of this shrine. Diodorus comments that it honoured its protection of slaves to show its capacity, in other words, that it was such a holy place that *even* slaves were protected by it.
48. Later Salvius sacrificed here to thank the gods for his victory after Morgantina (*ibid.*, 36.7.1).
49. *Ibid.*, 36.3.4.
50. The man's name was Gaius Titinius, and he was also called Gadaios, writes Diodorus (36.3.5).
51. *Ibid.*, 36.3.2.
52. There had been plenty of wars of conquest to provide slaves after the recent campaigns in Gaul, the Balkans, Spain and Sardinia and against Jugurtha.
53. κατέσφαξαν ὀγδοήκοντα ὄντες, καὶ ὅτι πλῆθος ἀγείρουσι (*ibid.*, 36.4).
54. T. Corey Brennan, *The Praetorship in the Roman Republic*, 2 vols (Oxford: Oxford University Press, 2000), 478, points out that the garrison was probably put there after the first war.
55. Diodorus, 36.4.4.
56. Plutarch, *Life of Crassus*, 8; Appian, *Civil Wars*, 1.116. These and other authors and their attitudes to the topic of slave revolts are discussed in Chapters 4, 6 and 8.
57. Suetonius, *Life of Augustus*, 3.1.
58. Appian, *Mithridatic War*, 109: 519–20. Barry Baldwin, "Two Aspects of the Spartacus Slave Revolt", *Classical Journal* **62** (1967), 289–94, esp. 294, cites the lack of Italian support as the reason why Spartacus' enterprise was doomed from the start. I have not dealt with the Bacchanalian conspiracies from the early second century BCE as reported by Livy because the evidence is so slight. The authorities thought that slaves were involved and, given the outbreaks in

the south of Italy, one might suppose that here again, in a region that had chafed against the domination of the Romans, slaves successfully escaped their lot. That is, slaves took advantage of the division between the local landholders and the Romans to seize the chance to rebel.
59. Augustus, *Res Gestae*, 25. Augustus alludes here to his defeat of Sextus Pompeius, whom the sources portray as employing slaves in his army; see P. A. Brunt and J. M. Moore, *Res Gestae Divi Augusti: The Achievements of the Divine Augustus* (Oxford: Oxford University Press, 1967), 66. See also Anton Powell and Kathryn Welch (eds), *Sextus Pompeius* (London: Duckworth, 2002).
60. Sallust, *Bellum Catilinae*, 30.7.
61. "Eruptionem facturi fuisse dicebantur" (Cicero, *Letters to Atticus*, 7.14.1–2). He then goes on to report that women were sent out of Rome.
62. Appian, *Civil War*, 1.14.
63. Cassius Dio, *Roman History*, 44.16.1–2.
64. "Clearly this is partly accounted for by the strengthened military and bureaucratic apparatus of the Empire, which was more able than the Republican regime had been, to combat open insubordination" (Elena M. Štaerman, "Der Klassenkampf der Sklaven zur zeit des roemischen Kaeserreiches", *Jahrbuch fuer Wirtschaftsgeschichte* 2 [1971], 307–35, esp. 311, my translation). Ste Croix describes the Augustan success as follows:
> How, then, did Augustus reconcile the senators to the Principate? I would say that the Roman aristocracy wanted five things above all: (1) Peace, (2) Prosperity, (3) Position, (4) Patronage, and (5) Power; and that it was only the last of these that Augustus was unwilling to allow the senators to pursue to their hearts' content.
> (*The Class Struggle in the Ancient Greek World*, 363)
65. Tacitus, *Annals*, 3.43.1–2; 3.46.
66. "eadem aestate mota per Italiam servilis belli semina fors oppressit" (*ibid.*, 4.27.1–2). See E. Groag, A. Stein, L. Petersen, *et al.* (eds), *Prosopographia Imperii Romani Saeculi* I, II, III, 2nd edn (Berlin: Walter de Gruyter, 1933), where Curtisius is described as "quondam praetoriae cohortis miles, dux belli servilis" (*c.*1606). I am grateful to Matthaeus Heil for this reference.
67. Tacitus, *Annals*, 15.46.
68. *Ibid.*, 15.47.
69. We also have evidence from elsewhere in the Greek world of slaves resisting. For example, slaves deserted in enormous numbers from Athens when the enemy army established themselves very close to the city and fortified Decelea in Attica during the Peloponnesian War. Thucydides states that 20,000 slaves, most of whom were skilled craftsmen, ran away (*History of the Peloponnesian War*, 7.27).
70. ἥ τε γὰρ Θετταλῶν πενεστεία πολλάκις ἐπέθετο τοῖς Θετταλοῖς, ὁμοίως δὲ καὶ τοῖς Λάκωσιν οἱ Εἵλωτες ὥσπερ γὰρ ἐφεδρεύοντες τοῖς ἀτυχήμασι διατελοῦσιν (Aristotle, *Politics*, 2.6.1269a36–9).
71. This is reminiscent of the comment in Xenophon, *Hiero*, 3.4.3.
72. One might term this a maroon community, although the issue of maroon communities will be dealt with in Chapter 3. The term refers to slaves who

escape and form communities that can survive independently. As A. W. Gomme, *A Historical Commentary on Thucydides, Volume 1: Introduction, and Commentary on Book 1* (Oxford: Oxford University Press, 1945), 302-3, remarks, this figure of ten years is one of the most disputed numbers in Thucydides. Gomme reasonably states that Ithome must have been the headquarters of the rebels, and not that they were shut up there for years (*ibid.*, 299). On the revolt, and for a discussion on the debate of how long the rebels held out, see Pavel Oliva, *Sparta and her Social Problems* (Prague: Academia, 1971), 152-63. See also Simon Hornblower, *A Commentary on Thucydides, Vol. 1* (Oxford: Oxford University Press, 1991), 157-61. Plato, *Laws*, 698D, refers to a Messenian revolt at the time of the battle of Marathon earlier in the fifth century BCE, although Herodotus is silent on this. See discussion by George Huxley, *Early Sparta* (London: Faber, 1962), 87-96.
73. Thucydides, *History of the Peloponnesian War*, 1.101-103. Thucydides refers to the ancestors of the rebels as having been "enslaved": οἱ τῶν παλαιῶν Μεσσηνίων τότε δουλωθέντων ἀπόγονοι. See Nino Luraghi, "Becoming Messenian", *Journal of Hellenic Studies* **122** (2002), 45-69.
74. One recent textbook misleadingly reports the incident thus: "A helot revolt did indeed break out in Messenia in 464 BC, after a severe earthquake and it took the Spartans almost four years – and a great deal of effort – to suppress it" (Lukas de Blois and R. J. van der Spek, *An Introduction to the Ancient World* [London: Routledge, 1997], 99).
75. Athenaeus, *Deipnosophistae*, 6.627b
76. Thucydides observes that the Spartans had not been quick to go to war before and were restricted by wars of their own, presumably referring to that against the helots (*History of the Peloponnesian War*, 1.118.2). The issue of the status of helots is discussed in Chapter 7.
77. *Ibid.*, 4.36.
78. *Ibid.*, 4.3.3.
79. *Ibid.*, 4.3.8.
80. *Ibid.*, 4.8.2.
81. *Ibid.*, 4.36. Thucydides even goes as far as to say the struggle would have continued indefinitely had the Messenians not stepped forward to help.
82. Τῶν τε Εἰλώτων αὐτομολούντων καί φοβούμενοι μὴ καὶ ἐπὶ μακρότερον σφίσι τι νεωτερισθῇ τῶν κατὰ τὴν χώραν (*ibid.*, 4.41).
83. αἰεὶ γὰρ τὰ πολλὰ Λακεδαιμονίοις πρὸς τοὺς Εἴλωτας τῆς φυλακῆς πέρι μάλιστα κατειστήκει (*ibid.*, 4.80).
84. Xenophon, *Hellenica*, 3.3.5-7.
85. Αὐτοὶ μέντοι πᾶσιν ἔφασαν συνειδέναι καὶ εἵλωσι καὶ νεοδαμώδεσι καὶ τοῖς ὑπομείοσι καὶ τοῖς περιοίκοις (*ibid.*, 3.3.6).
86. Athenaeus, *Deipnosophistae*, 14.657c-d.
87. Ὅπου γὰρ ἐν τούτοις τις λόγος γένοιτο περὶ Σπαρτιατῶν οὐδένα δύνασθαι κρύπτειν τὸ μὴ οὐχ ἡδέως ἂν καὶ ὠμῶν ἐσθίειν αὐτῶν (Xenophon, *Hellenica*, 3.3.6).
88. *Ibid.*, 6.5.24.
89. *Ibid.*, 6.5.25.

90. *Ibid.*, 6.5.28. In response to this proclamation, about 6,000 helots came forward, which at first alarmed the Spartans, but once other allies arrived, reducing the proportion of helots to the total force to a more acceptable size, the Spartans were less fearful.
91. The establishment of Messene was an event that was, Cawkwell remarks, "the most important achievement of the campaign" (Xenophon, *A History of My Times*, Rex Warner [trans.], George Cawkwell [intro. and notes] [Harmondsworth: Penguin, 1979], 351, note on ch. 6.5.52).
92. Plutarch, *Life of Lycurgus*, 28.7. Another Athenian source, Isocrates, from the fifth/fourth century BCE, describes the lot of the helots thus: "Right from the start these men have suffered severely, and in the present situation they have served Sparta well; yet the Spartan ephors are allowed to execute without trial as many of them as they wish. As far as the rest of the Greeks are concerned it is not holy to pollute oneself by killing even the most useless of one's household slaves" (*Panathenaicus*, 181).
93. Sometimes they resorted to mass desertion, as illustrated by the Athenian slaves in the Peloponnesian War in 413 BCE, but the present discussion is concerned with armed revolt.

3. Maintaining resistance

1. Thucydides, *History of the Peloponnesian War*, 8.40. Thucydides mentions slaves in Chios at this point late in the Peloponnesian War because he goes on to say that they did great damage to their owners because many of them deserted and, going over to the Athenians, provided the enemy with very useful information.
2. Athenaeus, *Deipnosophistae*, 6.264c.
3. *Ibid.*, 6.265b.
4. In connection with the debate about maroon communities later, it is perhaps worth noting that Athenaeus describes the episode as a *war* (ἐξεπολεμήθησαν διὰ δούλους) (*ibid.*, 6.265c). All in all, Athenaeus' character, Democritus, gives a very sympathetic picture of slaves.
5. μικρὸν δὲ πρὸ ἡμῶν (*ibid.*, 6.265d).
6. καὶ αὐτῷ ἔτι καὶ νῦν οἱ δραπέται ἀποφέρουσιν ἀπαρχὰς πάντων ὧν ἂν ὑφέλωνται (*ibid.*, 6.266d).
7. Alexander Fuks, "Slave War and Slave Troubles in Chios in the Third Century BC", *Athenaeum* **46** (1968), 102–11.
8. Athenaeus, *Deipnosophistae*, 6.266d.
9. *Ibid.*, 13.588f–589a. Nymphodorus is included in A. Giannini's *Paradoxographorum Graecorum Reliquiae* (Milan: Istituto Editoriale Italiano, 1966), 112–15, and Antonius Westermann's collection of paradoxographical writers, ΠΑΡΑΔΟΞΟΓΡΑΦΟΙ: *Scriptores Rerum Mirabilium Graeci* (London, 1839), 177–8. It is interesting to note, since Diodorus is another important source on slaves, that P. J. Stylianou, *A Historical Commentary on Diodorus Siculus, Book 15* (Oxford: Oxford University Press, 1998), 4–5, comments on Diodorus'

predilection for the sensational, using paradoxographers as sources for his history.
10. Wiedemann, *Greek and Roman Slavery*, does not put the Drimakos episode in his chapters on "Resistance" or "Rebellion" but in "Status Symbol or Economic Investment?". Shaw, *Spartacus and the Slave Wars*, includes Drimakos along with runaways in a chapter entitled "Fugitive Slaves and Maroon Communities". Bradley gives the definition of these communities: "communities of fugitives and slaves in revolt organised in hideouts on a paramilitary basis as a way of creating an alternative life to the one previously spent in slavery" (*Slavery and Rebellion*, 4).
11. It was thought that it was a derivation from the Spanish "*cimarrón*", which means "wild" or "untamed" but, as Richard Price remarks in the new introduction to his *Maroon Societies: Rebel Slave Communities in the Americas* (Baltimore, MD: Johns Hopkins University Press, [1979] 1996), xii, it has been argued that it in fact derives from an Amerindian root.
12. Price, "Maroons and their Communities", 608. Rout, *The African Experience in Spanish America*, 110, describes one such community in San Basilio in Colombia that survived and enabled its inhabitants to live autonomously for nearly 200 years, from 1599 to 1790. For a very useful survey of the literature in recent years on this subject, see Price, *Maroon Societies*, new introduction, 1–32.
13. See Rout, *The African Experience in Spanish America*, 99–104, for some of these punishments in Spanish America. Price summarizes: "similar punishments for *marronage* – from castration to being slowly roasted to death – are reported from many different regions" ("Maroons and their Communities", 609).
14. *Ibid.*
15. Bradley, *Slavery and Rebellion in the Roman World 140 BC–70 BC*, 1–17. This is connected with his differentiation of the ancient slave uprisings from revolution: "Indeed, with account duly taken of the cleavage that must be interposed between rebellion and revolution" (*ibid.*, 15).
16. *Ibid.*, emphasis added.
17. Bradley, *Slavery and Rebellion*, 81, emphasis added.
18. κατέσφαξαν ὀγδοήκοντα ὄντες, καὶ ὅτι πλῆθος ἀγείρουσι (Diodorus, 36.4).
19. Bradley, *Slavery and Rebellion*, 99, emphasis added.
20. Vogt, *Ancient Slavery and the Ideal of Man*, 40, emphasis added. Bradley has something very similar in the last paragraph of his book:

> But without an erosion in society at large of the concept of the necessity and immanence of slavery, indeed of the naturalness of slavery – without, that is, the emergence of the kind of egalitarian ideals that led to abolitionism in the modern world but that were conceptually unknown in antiquity – resistance on a massive, violent scale could not bring about any amelioration of the lives of those slavery oppressed.
> (*Slavery and Rebellion*, 126)

Earlier he had said more categorically: "What can be termed a maroon dimension to their resistance is indeed detectable in the historical record, and once exposed, it confirms *the absence of any ideological theory or impulse* behind the

slave movements" (*ibid.*, 104, emphasis added). See also Vogt, *Ancient Slavery and the Ideal of Man*, 73–82.
21. Bradley, *Slavery and Rebellion*, 103, emphasis added.
22. Schwartz, "Resistance and Accommodation in Eighteenth-century Brazil", 631–2 (appendix 2) reproduces the document.
23. *Ibid.*, 629.
24. *Ibid.*, 632.
25. Appian, *Civil Wars*, 1.120.
26. Laurent Dubois, *The Avengers of the New World: The Story of the Haitian Revolution* (Cambridge, MA: Harvard University Press, 2004). See also C. L. R. James, *The Black Jacobins: Toussaint L'Ouverture and the San Domingo Revolution* (Harmondsworth: Penguin, [1938] 2001), 73. See also Davis, *The Problem of Slavery in the Age of Revolution*, 137–48, on the shifting alliances of this period.
27. Schwartz, *Slaves, Peasants and Rebels*, 125.
28. Cicero, *Letters to Friends*, 15.4.10. Strabo may be describing something similar, when he writes:
    > Near the mountain ridges of the Taurus lies the piratical stronghold of Zenicetus – I mean Olympus (τὸ Ζηνικέτου πειρατήριόν ἐστιν ὁ Ὄλυμπος), both mountain and fortress, whence are visible all Lycia and Pamphilia and Pisidia and Milyas; but when the mountain was captured by Isauricus Zenicetus burnt himself up with his whole house. To him belonged also Corycus and Phaselis and many places in Pamphilia: but all were taken by Isauricus. (Strabo, *Geography*, 14.5.7)

    Publicus Servilius Isauricus was praetor in 54 BCE, and consul with Julius Caesar in 48 BCE. He wrote to Cicero while governor of Asia in 46 BCE.
29. Louis Robert and Jeanne Robert, *Claros I: Décrets Hellénististiques* (Paris: Editions de Recherche sur les Civilisations, 1989), 13, line 37. See also Christian Mileta, "Eumenes III und die Sklaven: Neue Ueberlegungen zum Charakter des Aristonikusaufstandes" *Klio* **80** (1998), 47–65, esp. 54–5. Robert and Robert, *Claros I*, date the inscription to the time of Aristonicus, although Jean-Louis Ferrary, "Le statut des cités libres dans l'empire romain à la lumière des inscriptions de Claros", *CRAI* (1991), 557–77, thinks it could be later than this. This inscription will be discussed in Chapter 4.
30. This expression is reminiscent of a quotation from Anaxandrides in Athenaeus: "Slaves my good sir, have no citizenship anywhere, yet Fortune shifts their bodies in all kinds of ways" [Οὐκ ἔστι δούλων, ὠγάθ', οὐδαμοῦ πόλις, / τύχη δὲ πάντῃ μεταφέρει τὰ σώματα] (*Deipnosophistae*, 6.263b–c).
31. Bradley, *Slavery and Rebellion*, 6–7.
32. Athenaeus, *Deipnosophistae*, 6.272f.
33. Florus, *Epitome of Roman History*, 2.7.1. In the following chapter Florus describes the war explicitly as a disgrace: "Enimero et servilium armorum dedecus feras" (*ibid.*, 2.8.1).
34. Athenaeus, *Deipnosophistae*, 6.265c.
35. *Ibid.*
36. However, the editors carry on: "But then few would claim even to have read

him" (David Braund and John Wilkins [eds], *Athenaeus and his World* [Exeter: Exeter University Press, 2000]), 1.
37. Frank Walbank observes that Athenaeus sometimes depicts Rome and Romans in an unfavourable light ("Athenaeus and Polybius", in *Athenaeus and his World*, 161–9, esp. 168).
38. Thucydides, *History of the Peloponnesian War*, 1.101.
39. Compare this to the early moments of the Spartacan rebellion and their use of such weapons (Plutarch, *Life of Crassus*, 8–9).
40. Diodorus, 34/35.2.17.
41. Livy, *Summaries*, 56.
42. Orosius, *History Against the Pagans*, 5.6.6.
43. It seems to me that accurate numbers are irrecoverable now. But even today different estimates of large numbers are often not at all similar. What concerns me with the revolts from antiquity is the perception by the authorities of the numbers involved. In the case of demonstrations in the twenty-first century, police estimates are always very much lower than those of the organizers of the event.
44. Diodorus, 34/35.2.18.
45. It was the successful siege of Enna and Tauromenium by the Romans that ended the slave war.
46. Diodorus, 34/35.2.46.
47. ὀνειδίζοντες αὐτῶν τὴν ὑπερηφανίαν καὶ τὴν ὑπερβολὴν τῆς εἰς τὸν ὄλεθρον προαγούσης ὕβρεως (*ibid.*)
48. Liv Mariah Yarrow, *Historiography at the End of the Republic: Provincial Perspectives on Roman Rule* (Oxford: Oxford University Press, 2006), 336–41, suggests that Diodorus does not present a sympathetic picture of the slaves as much as a critical one of the free-born poor. Her conclusion, while perhaps having some relation to the narratives of the other historians she discusses, is not an accurate representation of the picture drawn by Diodorus: "Yet when we hear of the horrors committed during the slave revolts and the gruesome nature of a certain culture, it is hard not to see in the historians more basic message: it could be worse than the Romans .... Rome can offer stability if those in the provinces are willing to cooperate" (*ibid.*, 340–41).
49. "In hoc autem servilis tumultus excitatio quanto rarior ceteris tanto truculentior est, quia intentione commovetur libera multitudo ut patriam augeat, servilis ut perdat" (Orosius, *History Against the Pagans*, 5.6.6).
50. Benjamin Farrington, *Diodorus Siculus: Universal Historian* (Swansea: University of Wales, Swansea, 1937), 24.
51. Bradley, *Slavery and Rebellion*, 125, emphasis added.
52. Gerald Verbrugghe, "Sicily 210–70 BC: Livy, Cicero and Diodorus", *Transactions of the American Philological Association* **103** (1972), 535–59; "The 'Elogium' from Polla and the First Slave War", *Classical Philology* **68** (1973), 25–35; "Slave Rebellion or Sicily in Revolt?", *Kokalos* **20** (1974), 46–60.
53. Verbrugghe, "Sicily 210–70 BC".
54. *Ibid.*, 540–5.
55. Diodorus, 34/35.2.3.

56. Verbrugghe, "Slave Rebellion or Sicily in Revolt?", 49–50.
57. Bradley discusses this, writing: "Admittedly, the fact that Eunus minted coins could be urged as evidence of an aspiration on his part toward a highly formalised monarchy" (*Slavery and Rebellion*, 120). He goes on to admit that Demeter "had been used earlier in Sicilian history for political and even anti-Roman purposes". Even so, he argues, "it would be illogical to assume at once that a rebellion of slaves was now a rising against Rome rule" (*ibid.*). Instead, he urges the reader to think that the representations of natural products on the coins reflected the slaves' wish to have enough to eat.
58. Livy, *Summaries*, 56, 58–9.
59. Livy, *Summaries*, 56. The threat was clearly a great one, and the suggestion by Otto Rossbach (ed.), *T. Livi periochae omnium librorum* (Leipzig: Teubner, 1910) for changing "*saepe*" (often) to "*saeve*" (fiercely) in the last sentence, because otherwise it is rather flat, on the contrary makes it less significant. It would only be expected for slaves to fight *saeve*, but surely less so for them to fight *saepe*. See Livy, *History of Rome, Volume XIV: Summaries, Fragments, Julius Obsequens*, Julius Obsequens, A. C. Schlesinger (trans.), index by Russel M. Geer (Loeb Classical Library) (Cambridge, MA: Harvard University Press, 1959), 59, n.7.
60. Strabo, *Geography*, 14.1.38. This is discussed at greater length in Chapter 4.
61. Mileta, "Eumenes III und die Sklaven". The mention of the city of slaves appears among the problems facing the city for which the man honoured by the inscription, Polemaios, had help from the Romans. στοιχοῦσαν δὲ τῆι περὶ αὐτὸν ὑποστάσει λαβὼν καὶ τὴν παρὰ τῆς συγκλήτου μαρτυρίαν, γινομένης ἁρπαγῆς καὶ ἐφόδου μεθ'ὅπλων καὶ ἀδικημάτων ἐπὶ τ(ῆ)ς ὑπαρχούσ(η)ς (ἡ)μεῖν χώρας ἐπὶ Δούλων πολέως (Robert & Robert, *Claros I*, 13, col. 2, line 37; discussion, 36–8). Ferrary, "Le statut des cités libres", suggests that this decree dates to a slightly later period, but this does not affect the argument here. That these rebels survived in the area some time after the fall of Aristonicus is a perfectly reasonable suggestion.
62. See Farrington, *Diodorus Siculus*, 25–35, for a discussion of this episode.
63. Ἐν τε ταῖς ἑορταῖς καὶ ταῖς εὐχίαις λέγεσθαί τε καὶ ἀδεσθαι παρ' αὐτοῖς εἰς τὸν ἥλιον, ἀφ' οὗ τάς τε νησους καὶ ἑαυτοὺς προσαγορεύουσι (Diodorus, 2.59.7). There are seven islands of about the same size, the same distance from each other and following the same customs and laws (*ibid.*, 2.58.7).
64. *Ibid.*, 2.55-60. The details we are given indicate that this is fantasy rather than reality: they were all the same shape and size, had flexible bones and were very strong. They had big ears, which they could close up; they had a forked tongue with which they could talk with two voices, conversing with two different people at the same time. Their islands were neither hot nor cold, the days were the same length as the nights and there was an abundance of food and drink. They brought up their children together and did not divide off into family units. Although their homes were richly endowed with all they needed they were not idle and they all took turns to work at some craft, except old people. Any disabled people or those beyond a certain age (although they lived to be very old, some as much as 150 years old) killed themselves for the good of

the community. The significance for Aristonicus' followers is that there was no place for slaves in this description. See Doyne Dawson, *Cities of the Gods: Communist Utopias in Greek Thought* (Oxford: Oxford University Press, 1992) on utopias in antiquity. He mentions this one briefly (*ibid.*, 172).

65. Plutarch, *Life of Tiberius Gracchus*, 20. See Farrington, *Diodorus Siculus*, 34–5, for an exposition of the view that there were ideological reasons for Blossius' connection with Tiberius Gracchus and Aristonicus. See also Donald R. Dudley, "Blossius of Cumae", *Journal of Roman Studies* 31 (1941), 94–9, who argues that we cannot generalize about Stoicism from Blossius' actions, but that we can see Blossius as an opponent to Roman imperialism. See W. W. Tarn, "Alexander Helios and the Golden Age", *Journal of Roman Studies* 22 (1932), 135–60, for a vivid exposition of the grand plans of Aristonicus and Blossius. It is possible that academics' views of the influence of philosophers on society is influenced by their idea of their own importance in the world.

66. Diodorus, 36.4.1–2.
67. *Ibid.*, 36.4.3–4.
68. See Chapter 4 for a discussion on the qualities attributed to the leaders by our sources.
69. *Ibid.*, 36.4.8.
70. *Ibid.*, 36.4.7.
71. Christian Mileta, "Quellenkritische Beobachtungen zur Vorgeschichte und zur Natur des Sizilischen Sklavenkriege in den Diodor-Fragmenten", in *Akten des 6. Oesterreichischen Althistorikertages Innsbruck 1996*, P. W. Haider (ed.), 91–112 (Innsbruck: Studien Verlag, 1998), 99.
72. Bradley, *Slavery and Rebellion*, 75.
73. The effect would be rather similar to the theatrical shows mocking the Romans put on by Eunus outside one of the cities.
74. Diodorus, 36.4.8.
75. ἡ δὲ τύχη καθάπερ ἐπίτηδες αὔξουσα τὰς τῶν δραπετῶν δυνάμεις ὁμονοῆσαι τοὺς τούτων ἡγημόνας ἐποίησεν (*ibid.*, 36.7.2).
76. παρέδωκεν εἰς φυλακήν (*ibid.*, 36.7.2).
77. The praetor was Gaius Claudius Glaber. Plutarch calls him Clodius and writes that it was merely a hill (*Life of Crassus*, 9). Appian calls him Varinius Glaber and tells us it was Mount Vesuvius (*Civil Wars*, 14, 116).
78. Baldwin, "Two Aspects of the Spartacus Slave Revolt", agreeing with Plutarch, challenges the idea that the Romans did not take these revolts seriously.
79. For a modern echo of this in the 1831 rebellion of slaves in Virginia led by Nat Turner see Douglas R. Egerton, "Nat Turner in a Hemispheric Context", in *Nat Turner: A Slave Rebellion in History and Memory*, K. S. Greenberg (ed.), 134–47 (Oxford: Oxford University Press, 2003), 145: "Nor was there anything absurd about Turner's stated expectation that his army could obtain weapons as they marched".
80. Appian, *Civil Wars*, 1.14.117.
81. ᾔδει δὲ καὶ ἔναγχος τὴν Ἰταλίαν σχεδὸν ἅπασαν ἀπὸ Ῥωμαίων ἀποστᾶσαν ὑπὸ ἔχθους, καὶ ἐπὶ πλεῖστον αὐτοῖς πεπολεμηκυῖαν, Σπαρτάκῳ τε μονομάχῳ συστᾶσαν ἐπ' αὐτούς, ἀνδρὶ ἐπ' οὐδεμιᾶς ἀξιώσεως ὄντι (Appian,

Mithridatic Wars, 109: 519-20). However, Baldwin, "Two Aspects of the Spartacus Slave Revolt", 294, cites the lack of Italian support as the reason why Spartacus' enterprise was doomed from the start.

82. On the nature of command see Zeev Rubinsohn, "A Note on Plutarch, Crassus X.1", *Historia* **19** (1970), 624-27, and B. A. Marshall, "Crassus' Ovation in 71 BC", *Historia* **21** (1972), 669-73.
83. Philip de Souza, *Piracy in the Graeco-Roman World* (Cambridge: Cambridge University Press, 1999), 133, points out that no other source mentions the pirates and that the episode could have been included to discredit Spartacus, although it is not clear why it would have done.
84. Suetonius, *Life of Augustus*, 3.1.
85. Suetonius states that the Senate ordered Augustus' father to pass through Thurii on the way to his province of Macedonia, because a group of outlawed slaves who had fought under Spartacus and Catiline were holding possession of the area (*Life of Augustus*, 3). This seems to be another example of a maroon community, causing no little damage to Roman morale. As a child the future Emperor Augustus was nicknamed Thurinus because his father had got rid of these slaves, although Suetonius gives an alternative reason, which was that some of his ancestors had come from the region (*ibid.*, 6).
86. Bradley, *Slavery and Rebellion*, 100.
87. This may seem puzzling because in *Slavery and Rebellion*, ch. 1, he shows very clearly the dissonance between the reports from the masters and the slaves in the modern world. However, his purpose there is not to point out that dissonance, but to illustrate the phenomenon of maroon communities.
88. *Ibid.*, 101. Elsewhere Bradley writes:
    It does, however, require stress that the escalation of the revolt of gladiators into a sustained war of servile resistance *cannot possibly have been* what Spartacus and his immediate companions had hoped to achieve when they made their escape from Capua. The sources have *little to say about the motivations* of the rebel slaves, but everything that is said pertains only to the gladiators' circumstances.
    (*Ibid.*, 98, emphasis added)
    Armin Jähne, *Spartacus: Kampf der Sklaven* (Berlin: Deutscher Verlag der Wissenschaften, 1986) likewise stresses that Spartacus and his followers only wanted their freedom ("Ziel und Programm", in *ibid.*, 157). Bradley remarks:
    There is no evidence to suggest that Spartacus and his followers, any more than the slaves at Enna or Halicyae in Sicily, purposely set out *from the beginning* to raise a general rebellion of slaves throughout central and southern Italy. Indeed, the peculiarity of their circumstances, once contrasted with those of other slaves, precludes any such thought.
    (*Slavery and Rebellion*, 98, emphasis added).
    If we translate *"vindicari"* in the more usual way, as discussed earlier, Florus (2.8) tells us that the slaves, having started out wanting merely to escape, turned their thoughts to revenge when they realized how many of them there were.
89. The Roman soldiers under Sulla remembered the recent slave war ten years earlier when they called Fimbria "Athenion", as if he were a slave leader (Appian,

Mithridatic Wars, 59). The episode is mentioned by Bradley, *Slavery and Rebellion*, 90.
90. *Ibid.*, 104, emphasis added.
91. *Ibid.* In arguing that all the slaves ever wanted was their freedom and nothing more, he ignores evidence he uses himself. He comments that the case of Spartacus was not a unique case of a gladiator rebelling (*ibid.*, 89); in 21 CE some gladiators joined Sacrovir's revolt (Tacitus, *Annals*, 3.43). As Bradley observes, this was a revolt not simply against slavery but against Roman rule, and yet he argues in earlier chapters that the slaves in Sicily could not have been intending to fight for an independent Sicily, but had merely been trying to escape and in the process had acquired too many followers.
92. Bradley, *Slavery and Rebellion*, 90–92, concludes: "The violence of the revolt was the product of the violence slave owners themselves had long fostered in their slaves and for which they themselves had set the example" (*ibid.*, 92).

4. The role of the leader

1. Thomas Grünewald, *Bandits in the Roman Empire: Myth and Reality*, J. Drinkwater (trans.) (London: Routledge, 2004) (originally published in German as *Räuber, Rebellen, Rivalen, Rächer* [Stuttgart: Franz Steiner, 1999]), suggests that the noble outlaws we find in the texts, such as Spartacus, are merely literary conventions (see e.g. *ibid.*, 13, 165–6). The translation does not help his case, perhaps, because in English the word "bandit" is more positive than the German "*Räuber*" that it translates. For instance, the sentence, "At the mention of 'bandit' ancient, like modern, readers anticipated grim exposes of the misdeeds of common, despicable thugs" (*ibid.*, 165) does not ring true. For modern, native English-speaking readers the mention of "bandit" carries at the very least some connotation of a romantic individualist. Grünewald is right, however, to draw attention to the common characteristics of some of these people. On the other hand, usually the descriptions are very slight and only consist of a couple of adjectives, so that no nuanced portrait is possible. In the case of slave leaders, only some are presented positively.
2. For that very reason when discussing rebel slaves it is a modern reaction to heroize the rebels since, whatever their motivation, they were participating in a fight against slavery on some level.
3. This is very similar to a contemporary description of the rebel leader Nat Turner, who, we are told, was "little more than a trickster who 'used all the arts familiar to such pretenders, to deceive, delude and overaw [the] minds' of his disciples" (quoted by Egerton, "Nat Turner in a Hemispheric Context", 138).
4. Appian, *Civil Wars*, 1.14.
5. It was not only slave leaders who had to be exceptional. The great enemy of Rome before this had been Hannibal, and in the historiography he is presented as exceptional. See, for instance, Cornelius Nepos' *Life of Hannibal*. On attitudes to slaves Herodotus relates an improbable story about Scythians returning home after a campaign lasting almost thirty years to find that slaves, or the

offspring of slaves, had taken over (*The Histories*, 4.1–4). They were unable to gain the upper hand until one of the Scythians suggested that instead of approaching them as equals, they should go with whips to remind them they were only slaves. This psychological analysis was successful and the Scythians regained their territory.

6. Cassius Dio, *Histories*, 76.10.1–7, which comes from Xiphilinos, *Epitome of Cassius Dio*, 318, 29–321, 24. R.st. The state of the text of Dio's *Histories* for this period is rather similar to that of Diodorus for the Sicilian wars. Indeed, the *Excerpts* of Constantine Porphyrogenitus are responsible for preserving some of Dio's text, as they had been for parts of Diodorus. The other epitomisers were Xiphilinos, from the eleventh century, and Zonaras in the twelfth. See Fergus Millar, *A Study of Cassius Dio* (Oxford: Clarendon Press, 1964), 1–4. The restored text was edited by U. P. Boissevain, *Cassii Dionis Cocceiani Historiarum Romanarum Quae Supersunt* (Berlin: Weidmann, 1955).

7. He reports that in the tenth anniversary of his reign, the emperor, Severus gave gold pieces to the people and praetorian guard, totalling 200 million sesterces. There were spectacles in Rome for the wedding of Severus' son and Plautianus' daughter. Fire erupting from Mount Vesuvius seemed to augur a change in the state, we read, and Plautianus was got rid of (Cassius Dio, *Histories*, 77.2). Plautianus had castrated 100 Roman nobles (*ibid.*, 76.14); we read of other vicious behaviour by him (*ibid.*, 75/76), and he gets his just deserts (*ibid.*, 77). We also read that the sons of Severus, Antoninus and Geta were friends of gladiators and charioteers (*ibid.*, 76/77.7), a sure sign of degeneracy. Just before he relates the story of Bulla Felix, we read that a man was executed because he was bald. Millar, *A Study of Cassius Dio*, 138–50, argues that there is "little justification for the view that Dio was hostile to Severus" (*ibid.*, 138), although he admits that there are hostile elements in his account (*ibid.*, 141–2).

8. Ἄγγελλε τοῖς δεσπόταις σου ὅτι τοὺς δούλους ὑμῶν τρέφετε, ἵνα μὴ λῃστεύωσι (Cassius Dio, *Histories*, 76.10.4–5). He had pretended to be a Roman official in order to free two of his men who had been captured. He promised a centurion that he would betray the chief, that is, himself, if the centurion followed him. The gullible Roman did and was duly captured. Bulla then dressed himself up as a Roman magistrate and put on a mock trial to judge the soldier. It is then that he told him to pass on the message to feed their slaves.

9. Οὔτε δὲ ἑωρᾶτο ὁρώμενος οὔτε εὑρίσκετο εὑρισκόμενος οὔτε κατελαμβάνετο ἁλισκόμενος· τοσαύτῃ καὶ μεγαλοδωρίᾳ καὶ σοφίᾳ ἐχρῆτο (*ibid.*, 76.10.2).

10. *Ibid.*, 76.10.7.

11. Athenaeus, *Deipnosophistae*, 6.266b.

12. *Ibid.*, 6.266c–d.

13. *Ibid.*, 6.265e–266b.

14. Readers in antiquity might have wondered at the arrogance of these slaves in setting themselves up as kings, and been frightened by their ability and planning; they might have realized the necessity, stressed by the agricultural writers (see e.g. Cato, *On Agriculture* 5.3–5; Columella, *On Agriculture*, 1.8.6),

of keeping one's slaves away from religion as far as possible, especially those slaves in positions of authority.

15. Appian, *Civil Wars*, 1.117, 1.116. This passed into tradition, so that Pliny writes:
    But we know that Spartacus forbade anyone in his camp to possess gold or silver, so much stronger at that time was the moral fibre of our slaves. The orator Messala has recorded that the triumvir Antony used gold chamber pots for all the calls of nature, a charge that would have shamed even Cleopatra. Previously foreigners held the record for extravagance.   (*Natural History*, 33.49)
16. Diodorus calls Eunus a τερατίας (Diodorus, 34/35.2.8).
17. καὶ τὴν ἀνταπόδοσιν τοῖς παρὰ τὰ δεῖπνα δεξιωσαμένοις ἐν γέλωτι οὐ χωρὶς σπουδῆς ἐποιήσατο τῆς χάριτος (*ibid.*, 34/35.2.9). Photius gives some precise details, so we learn that Eunus killed his owners and that there names were Antigenes and Pytho.
18. Diodorus, 34/35.2.41.
19. Bradley, *Slavery and Rebellion*, 124.
20. καὶ παραδοθεὶς εἰς φυλακὴν καὶ τοῦ σώματος αὐτοῦ διαλυθέντος εἰς φθειρῶν πλῆθος οἰκείως τῆς περὶ αὐτὸν ῥᾳδιουργίας κατέστρεψε τὸν βίον ἐν τῇ Μοργαντίνῃ [Remanded to prison, where his flesh disintegrated into a mass of lice, he met such an end as befitted his knavery and died at Morgantina] (Diodorus, 34/35.2.23). In 1982 two articles appeared independently, without reference to each other, on the subject of this gruesome form of death. Thomas W. Africa, "Worms and the Death of Kings: A Cautionary Note on Disease and History", *Classical Antiquity* 1 (1982), 1–17, gives an overview of the sort of people who suffered such a fate but A. Keaveney and J. A. Madden, "Phthiriasis and its Victims", *Symbolae Osloenses* 57 (1982), 87–99, differentiate between lice and worms, and say that Eunus suffered from scabies. Eunus' namesake, Antiochus IV Epiphanes, the monster of the Maccabean histories, died in a similarly horrible way. A fuller description of his death is given in 2 Maccabees 9:5, 8–9 – he had worms crawling from his eyes and he stank so much that no one could come near him (2 Maccabees 9:9-10) – than Diodorus gives of Eunus' and it bears more similarity with Plutarch's gory details of Sulla's demise (Plutarch, *Life of Sulla*, 36).
21. The only other woman who makes an appearance on the side of rebels is the wife of Spartacus, mentioned by Plutarch (*Life of Crassus*, 8).
22. The first chapter of Diodorus, 34/35.1, that is the chapter immediately preceding the narrative of the slave war, is also from Photius and has details about the real king Antiochus and his "merciful" treatment of the Jews. The Hellenistic king had a counsellor called Achaeus, so this slave may also have changed his name.
23. *Ibid.*, 34/35.2.21.
24. There is a sentence in the *Excerpts*, unconnected to the main narrative about the slave war, about the Syrian runaways cutting off not just the hand but also the arms of their captives, but what this refers to is not at all clear (οἱ Σύροι οἱ δραπέται [the Syrian runaways], 34/35.8). If this sentence is taken to refer to

the slaves, it may account for why it has been supposed in the past that most of the slaves were from Syria. However, Diodorus does not generally call the rebels "runaways" but uses different terms to describe them, and at no other point does he include the country of origin to describe them. Also, if this did refer to the slaves on Sicily it would be unusual, since only in the initial attack on Enna, described by Photius, are the slaves described as acting with great brutality (*ibid.*, 34/35.2.12). That is not to say that Diodorus did not thus describe them, but only that in what we have left this is not typical. More usually, it is the masters who are described as behaving in a violent and cruel manner.

25. Diodorus calls him Komanos, whereas Valerius Maximus (*Memorable Deeds and Sayings*, 9.12.1) mentions Cleon's brother as being called Komas. He killed himself rather than answer questions. In Photius' account there are also more details about people's names than we find in the later summary: Kleon's brother, the betrayer, Sarapion, and the Roman commander.
26. Diodorus, 34/35.2.21.
27. We learn from Diodorus (34/35.2.14) that the ex-slaves Hermeias and Zeuxis killed Damophilus, but only from the *Excerpts* (*ibid.*, 34/35.2.39) that it was Hermeias who escorted Damophilus' daughter to safety.
28. *Ibid.*, 34/35.2.43.
29. *Ibid.*, 36.4.8.
30. *Ibid.*
31. *Ibid.*, 36.4.3.
32. *Ibid.*, 36.5.2.
33. *Ibid.*, 36.5.3. Farrington's observation that the slaves wanted to take control of the island (*Diodorus Siculus*, 24), referred to earlier, is more than mere speculation in this case, as Diodorus reports that Athenion considered that Sicily belonged to him.
34. Bradley, *Slavery and Rebellion*, 77.
35. Diodorus writes: "on hearing the news of Eunus' success, and of the victories of the fugitives fighting with him, he [Cleon] rose in revolt" (Diodorus, 34/35.2.43).
36. ἡ δὲ τύχη καθάπερ ἐπίτηδες αὔξουσα τὰς τῶν δραπετῶν δυνάμεις ὁμονοῆσαι τοὺς τούτων ἡγημόνας ἐποίησεν (*ibid.*, 36.7.2).
37. παρέδωκεν εἰς φυλακήν (*ibid.*, 36.7.2).
38. τήβενναν τε περιπόρφυρον περιεβάλλετο καὶ πλατύσημον ἔδυ χιτῶνα κατὰ τοὺς χρηματισμούς, καὶ ῥαβδούχους εἶχε μετὰ πελέκεων τοὺς προηγουμένους, καὶ τἄλλα πάντα ὅσα ποιοῦσί τε καὶ ἐπικοσμοῦσι βασιλείαν ἐπετήδευε (*ibid.*, 36.7.4). The description sounds more like that of a Roman official than of a king, since the terms are direct translations of the Roman garments, the *toga praetexta* and the *tunica laticlavia*. The use of the *toga praetexta* was reserved for magistrates and high priests. Livy (*History of Rome*, 34.7.2) purports to report the speech by Lucius Valerius, tribune of the plebs in 195 BCE, where he put forward a motion to repeal the Lex Oppia. This speech gives precise details as to who wore the *toga praetexta*. The *tunica laticlavia*, the tunic with broad purple stripes, was the dress of the senatorial class. Equestrians wore narrow stripes on their tunics. See Shelley Stone, "The Toga: From National

to Ceremonial Costume", in *The World of Roman Costume*, J. L. Sebesta & L. Bonfante (eds), 13-45 (Madison, WI: University of Wisconsin Press, 1994), 13, 15, for details on Roman dress. Salvius dedicated a robe bordered with purple, presumably a *toga praetexta*, to the Palikoi in gratitude for his victory over the Romans (Diodorus, 36.7.1).

39. *Ibid.*, 36.8.1. As Shaw points out, the figures only add up to 16,000 but 17,000 is in the manuscript (*Spartacus and the Slave Wars*, 118, n.9). It is interesting to note that Bithynians were part of this force, and that indirectly, according to Diodorus, it was the request to the king of Bithynia for troops that set this war off.
40. Diodorus, 36.9.
41. He was the son of Manius Aquillius, who finished the war against Aristonicus, taking over from Marcus Perperna. The fact that the Senate sent a consul shows the increased anxiety about the conflict.
42. ὁ μὲν οὖν κατὰ Σικελίαν τῶν οἰκετῶν πόλεμος, διὰ μείνας ἔτη σχεδόν που τέτταρα, τραγικὴν ἔσχε τὴν καταστροφήν (Diodorus, 36.10.3). Diodorus (as reported by Photius) uses the word "*katastrophe*" twice in a very short space, once to describe the fate of the slaves, and the second time to describe the end of the war generally.
43. Florus, *Epitome of Roman History*, 2.7. He gives Spartacus a separate chapter (*ibid.*, 2.8).
44. "Vixdum respiraverat insula, cum statim Servilio praetore a Syro reditur ad Cilicem" (*ibid.*, 2.7.9). Thus in the picture presented by Florus there was very little time between the two wars.
45. "... non minorem quam ille fanaticus prior conflavit exercitum, acriusque multo, quasi et illum vindicaret, vicos, oppida, castella diripiens, in servos infestius quam in dominos quasi in transfugas, saeviebat" (Florus, *Epitome of Roman History*, 2.7.10). Florus saw a connection between the two outbreaks and attributed vengeance to Athenion's actions. See also Cassius Dio, *Roman History*, fragments of Book 27.93,4 (5.88), for a brief comment about Athenion and the damage he and his men caused.
46. "quippe dum circa adprehendendum eum a multitudine contenditur, inter rixantium manus praeda lacerata est" (Florus, *Epitome of Roman History*, 2.7.12).
47. Diodorus, 36.7.4. One might argue that these details represent the assumptions of our sources, who expected the slaves to organize themselves in ways recognizable to the Roman state. Jack Goody's point about people on the edge of society could well be true of the slaves:
    In fact many communities living on the margins of great states, or any centralized polity, deliberately rejected centralized authority (for example, the Robin Hoods of all around the globe) while some, for other reasons altogether, organized themselves in different, "acephalous" ways. The peoples of the margins, of the deserts, of the woods and of the hills would always provide a different model for government than the centralized peoples of the plains. (*The Theft of History* [Cambridge: Cambridge University Press, 2006], 91)

48. "simulatoque impio testamento filium eius Aristonicum, quia patrium regnum petiverat, hostium more per triumphum duxere" (Sallust, *Histories*, 4.69.8–9).
49. J. C. Dumont, "À propos d'Aristonicus", *Eirene* 5 (1966), 189–96, esp. 189, remarks that the inscription recording the Senate's ratification of the will of Attalus confirms the truth of the will. For the text of this decree see Robert K. Sherk, *Roman Documents from the Greek East: Senatus consulta and Epistulae to the Age of Augustus* (Baltimore, MD: Johns Hopkins Press, 1969), no. 11, 59–62.
50. See R. Develin, *Justin: Epitome of the Philippic History of Pompeius Trogus*, J. C. Yardley (trans.) (Atlanta, GA: Scholars Press, 1994), 1–11. Sallust is hardly anti-Roman, but the letter attributed to Mithridates certainly is.
51. Justin, *Epitome of the Philippic History of Pompeius Trogus*, 36.4.1–4.
52. *Ibid.*, 36.4.4.
53. *Ibid.*, 36.4.5–12. This Crassus was consul in 131 BCE; T. R. S. Broughton, *The Magistrates of the Roman Republic*, 3 vols (New York: American Philological Association, 1951–86), vol. 1, 500, 503. For clarification on this confusing family, see the family tree of the Licinii in Hubert Cancik, Helmut Schneider and Manfred Landfester (eds), *Brill's New Pauly: Encyclopaedia of the Ancient World*, 20 vols with index (Brill: Leiden, 2006).
54. Justin, *Epitome of the Philippic History of Pompeius Trogus*, 36.4.9. Aristonicus also minted his own coins, of which there are some remaining; see J. P. Adams, "Aristonikos and the Cistophoroi", *Historia* **29** (1980), 302–14, and E. S. G. Robinson, "Cistophoroi in the name of King Eumenes", *Numismatic Chronicle* **14** (6th series) (1954), 1–8.
55. Justin, *Epitome of the Philippic History of Pompeius Trogus*, 36.4.12.
56. *Ibid.*, 1.35.7, emphasis added.
57. Vladimir Vavrinek, "Aristonicus of Pergamum: Pretender to the Throne or Leader of a Slave Revolt?", *Eirene* **13** (1975), 109–29. Vavrinek is only one of many to consider the question of Aristonicus' motives. Dumont, for instance argues that the Pergamene decree referred to earlier shows that Aristonicus had wealthy supporters, and therefore they would not have been anti-slavery. He simply says that Strabo was mistaken about Heliopolis ("À propos d'Aristonicus", 195, n. 33). He concludes that the uprising had no utopian objectives but nevertheless bears witness to the antagonism between slaves and masters (*ibid.*, 196).
58. Vavrinek, "Aristonicus of Pergamum", 115.
59. See for instance Christopher L. Brown and Philip D. Morgan (eds), *Arming Slaves from Classical Times to the Modern Age* (New Haven, CT: Yale University Press, 2006) on slaves being armed in order to fight for their masters throughout the ages. See also Peter Hunt, *Slaves, Warfare and Ideology in the Greek Historians* (Cambridge: Cambridge University Press, 1998).
60. Diodorus, 36.2.3.
61. *Ibid.*, 36.1.1–2.
62. τῷ δὲ ἔρωτι δουλεύων, ἐπεχείρησε πράξει παραλογωτάτῃ. (*ibid.*, 36.2a.1, emphasis added to English translation).

63. H. H. Scullard, *From the Gracchi to Nero*, 5th edn (London: Routledge [1959] 1982), 93. Also: "The brave undertaking of the slaves has about it a touch of the tragedy of any attempt to achieve the impossible" (Vogt, *Ancient Slavery and the Ideal of Man*, 91).
64. Baldwin, "Two Aspects of the Spartacus Slave Revolt", 289–90. He allows the possibility that Sallust may not have been entirely hostile to Spartacus, while categorizing all the rest as pro-Roman.
65. Theresa Urbainczyk, *Spartacus* (London: Duckworth, 2004). What follows is an elaboration of that argument.
66. J. G. Griffith, "Spartacus and the Growth of Historical and Political Legends", in *Spartacus: Symposium rebus Spartaci gestis dedicatum 2050 A.*, C. M. Danov and A. Fol (eds), 64–70 (Sofia: Academie Bulgare des Sciences, 1981), 64.
67. *Ibid.*, 69–70.
68. Shaw, *Spartacus and the Slave Wars*. He places the main texts first and then the more minor ones. Giulia Stampacchia, *La Tradizione della guerra di Spartaco da Sallustio a Orosio* (Pisa: Giardini, 1976) has a very useful collection of sources.
69. Sosipater Charisius, *Ars Grammatica* 1.133.
70. Diodorus, 38/39.21.
71. *Ibid.*
72. Baldwin, "Two Aspects of the Spartacus Slave Revolt", 294.
73. Patrick McGushin, *Sallust: The Histories*, 2 vols (Oxford: Clarendon Press, 1992, 1994) has provided a translation and done a thorough investigation into the fragments, rearranging them from the previous order devised by B. Maurenbrecher, *C. Sallusti Crispi Historiarum Reliquiae* (Stuttgart: Teubner, 1891), and adding a helpful commentary.
74. "ingens ipse virium atque animi" (Sallust, *Histories*, 3.91 [Maurenbrecher], 3.61 [McGushin]). However, another suggestion is that this refers to Mithridates; see Sallust, *Histories*, 147 [Maurenbrecher].
75. Sallust, *Histories*, 3.98 [Maurenbrecher], 3.66 [McGushin].
76. "Crassus obtrectans potius collegae, quam boni aut mali publici gnavos aestimator" (*ibid.*, 4.56 [McGushin, his translation]; 4.51 [Maurenbrecher]).
77. Donald C. Earl, *The Political Thought of Sallust* (Cambridge: Cambridge University Press, 1961), 116, 120.
78. Eutropius, *Breviarium*, 6.7, cf. Livy, *Epitome*, XCV–XCVII, as observed by H. W. Bird in *Eutropius: Breviarium*, H. W. Bird (trans. with intro and comm.) (Liverpool: Liverpool University Press, 1993), 33–4, 102 n.11.
79. Plutarch was born before 40 CE and died after 120 CE, Appian was born around 90 CE and died around 160 CE. For Plutarch's influence through the ages, see D. A. Russell, *Plutarch* (London: Duckworth, 1973), 143–63.
80. ἡ γυνὴ δ'ὁμόφυλος οὖσα τοῦ Σπαρτάκου, μαντικὴ δὲ καὶ κάταχος τοῖς περὶ τὸν Διόνυσον ὀργιασμοῖς (Plutarch, *Life of Crassus*, 8). Pierre Piccinin, "Le Dionysisme dans le *bellum Spartacium*", *La Parola del Passato* **56**(4) (2001), 272–96, argues that the cult of Dionysus is important for our understanding of the uprising. The leaders of the Sicilian revolts have religious authority yet this is the only mention of any connection of Spartacus with a divinity. The

suppression of the Bacchanalian cults in the early second century in Italy, which would indeed appear to have involved slaves, seems to have taken up much energy on the part of the Roman authorities. Mithridates took the name Dionysus, see Brian C. McGing, *The Foreign Policy of Mithridates VI Eupator King of Pontus* (Leiden: Brill, 1986), 102. According to the *Oxford Classical Dictionary*, "Dionysus' cults and myths are often violent and bizarre, a challenge to the established social order". The coins of Aristonikos have the head of Dionysus on them, although Robinson, "Cistophoroi in the name of King Eumenes", 6, attributes this to Eumenes II having a personal interest in this god.

81. Ἔφραζε τὸ σημεῖον εἶναι μεγάλης καὶ φοβερᾶς περὶ αὐτὸν εἰς εὐτυχὲς τέλος ἐσομένης δυνάμεως (Plutarch, *Life of Crassus* [Loeb], 336); Ἔφραζε τὸ σημεῖον εἶναι μεγάλης καὶ φοβερᾶς περὶ αὐτὸν εἰς ἀτυχὲς τέλος ἐσομένης δυνάμεως (*ibid.*, [Teubner], 136). The Penguin translation by Rex Warner reads "he would have a great and terrible power which would end in misfortune" (Plutarch, *The Fall of the Roman Republic: Six Lives* [Harmondsworth: Penguin, 1972], 122). The Loeb reads "the sign of a great and formidable power which would attend him to a fortunate issue". The Loeb text has the word "*eutyches*" whereas Warner (Penguin) is translating "*atyches*". Shaw, *Spartacus and the Slave Wars*, 132 n.2, takes the same reading as Warner, but this is not necessarily correct and reveals the preference of the translator, since in fact the manuscripts – even the most reliable manuscript of Plutarch S, the second oldest, the *Codex Seitenstettensis* – have "*eutyches*". In the second Teubner edition, which Bernadotte Perrin (Loeb), describes as showing more boldness and greater freedom in the admission of conjecture (p. xvii), Sintenis changed his reading to "*atyches*", although in his first he had "*eutyches*". We are told that "*atyches*" is merely a marginal reading in one manuscript from the fifteenth century (*ibid.* [Teubner], 136). I would argue strongly that there is no good reason to accept the reading "*atyches*", and certainly "*eutyches*" fits Plutarch's general portrayal of Spartacus more closely. My thanks to the late Professor Neville Birdsall for his help with this matter.

82. εἰ δὲ καὶ τὸ περὶ τοὺς Εἵλωτας ἀναγκάσει τις ἡμᾶς εἰς τὴν Λυκούργου θέσθαι πολιτείαν, ὠμότατον ἔργον καὶ παρανομώτατον, μακρῷ τινι τὸν Νουμᾶν ἑλληνικώτερον γεγονέναι νομοθέτην φήσομεν, ὅς γε κἀ τοὺς ὡμολογημένους δούλους ἔγευσε τιμῆς ἐλευθέρας, ἐν τοῖς Κρονίοις ἑστιᾶσθαι μετὰ τῶν δεσποτῶν ἀναμεμιγμένους ἐθίσας (Plutarch, *Comparison of Lycurgus and Numa*, 1, emphasis added to English translation).

83. ἦν δὲ πολύφιλος καὶ διὰ φιλοξενίαν εὐτράπεζος, ἀεὶ μὲν Ἑλλήνων καὶ φιλολόγων περὶ αὐτὴν ὄντων, ἁπάντων δὲ τῶν βασιλέων καὶ δεχομένων παρ' αὐτῆς δῶρα καὶ πεμπόντων (Plutarch, *Life of Gaius Gracchus*, 19).

84. Compare Plutarch's gruesome description of the revolting death of Sulla (his flesh disintegrating into a mass of foul-smelling worms), a man who had made the streets of Athens run with blood, with that of Appian (*Civil Wars*, 1.12. 105), where he has a brief fever and dies the same day, Appian commenting that he was fortunate in life and death. S. C. R. Swain, "Hellenic Culture and the Roman Heroes of Plutarch", *Journal of Hellenic Studies* **110**

(1990), 126–45, discusses Plutarch's method of using Greek culture to evaluate character.
85. Jähne writes that Plutarch depicts the character of Spartacus favourably in order to build up Crassus by giving him a worthy opponent (*Spartacus*, 12). There is no evidence that Plutarch wanted to glorify Crassus.
86. Christoph F. Konrad, *Plutarch's Sertorius: A Historical Commentary* (Chapel Hill, NC: University of North Carolina Press, 1994), 47, notes that Plutarch describes Sertorius as having a sharp, quick mind and that this is his usual way of praising a good general. This quality is often paired with daring and bravery. Konrad gives several examples, and notes that although he describes Spartacus in this way, he does not do so for Crassus.
87. Plutarch, *Life of Crassus*, 2.
88. Frances B. Titchener, "Why did Plutarch Write about Nicias?", *Ancient History Bulletin* 5(5–6) (1991), 153–8, argues that Plutarch could find very little good to say about Nicias but needed a parallel for Crassus. "I would suggest that the Nikias-Crassus pair was amongst those that were intended to portray examples to be avoided rather than imitated" (A. G. Nikolaidis, "Is Plutarch Fair to Nikias?", *Illinois Classical Studies* 13[2] [1988], 319–33, esp. 331).
89. In a long note at the end of the *Life of Crassus* in their translation of Plutarch, the Langhorne brothers declared: "There have been more execrable characters, but there is not, perhaps, in the history of mankind, one more contemptible than Crassus. His ruling passion was the most sordid lust of wealth and the whole of his conduct, political, popular, and military was subservient to this" (*Plutarch's Lives*, J. Langhorne & W. Langhorne (trans.) [London: T. Longman [1770] 1904], 299–300).
90. "Cicero was Plutarch's kind of man" (C. Pelling, "Plutarch: Roman Heroes and Greek Culture", in *Philosophia Togata: Essays on Philosophy and Roman Society*, T. Griffin & J. Barnes [eds], 199–232 [Oxford: Clarendon Press, 1989], 217).
91. Timothy Duff, *Plutarch's Lives: Exploring Vice and Virtue* (Oxford: Clarendon Press, 1999), 270. He goes on to point out that Plutarch appears to contradict the lives in his comparison by elevating Crassus' military exploits and finding things to praise in them. It could surely be the case that Romans are allowed to be superior in military matters and that it would not look good if the comparisons were totally one-sided. Plutarch does try to be even-handed on the surface. However, there is no doubting the fact that he has contempt for Crassus. See also C. Pelling, "Plutarch and Roman Politics", in *Essays on Plutarch's Lives*, B. Scardigli (ed.), 319–59 (Oxford: Clarendon Press, 1995), 322–3, on the *Life of Crassus*.
92. "Most *Lives* also utilize 'internal comparisons' whereby the hero is compared with other leading figures in the narrative" (J. L. Moles [trans. with intro. and comm.], *Plutarch: The Life of Cicero* [Warminster: Aris & Phillips, 1988], 19).
93. Οὐ μόνον φρόνημα μέγα καὶ ῥώμην ἔχων ἀλλὰ καὶ συνέσει καὶ πρᾳότητι τῆς τύχης ἀμείνων καὶ τοῦ γένους ἑλληνικώτερος. Τούτῳ δὲ λέγουσιν, ὅτε πρῶτον εἰς Ῥώμην ὤνιος ἤχθη (Plutarch, *Life of Crassus*, 8, Shaw's translation in *Spartacus and the Slave Wars*). The sentence before is ἀνὴρ Θρᾷξ τοῦ νομαδικοῦ γένους [Spartacus was a Thracian, born among a pastoral nomadic

people]. Konrat Ziegler, "Die Herkunft des Spartacus", *Hermes* **83** (1955), 248–50, argues that the Greek text should read Μαιδικοῦ rather than νομαδικοῦ, so that we should read this as that he was from the Maidi tribe in Thrace. Zivka Velkova, "Der Name Spartakus", in *Spartacus*, Danov and Fol (eds) (1981), 195–8, gives information on other instances of this typically Thracian name, which occurs in a surprising number of places, and is also the name of some Bosporean rulers (see Diodorus, 12.31.1, 12.36.1, 14.93.1, 20.100.7), although on inscriptions and coins the name is spelled "Spartokos". Jähne, *Spartacus*, 173, for instance, refers to Theodor Mommsen's theory that Spartacus came from Bosporus (*Römische Geschichte*, Book 5 [1885]). T. Todorov, "De l'Origine de Spartacus", in *Spartacus*, Danov and Fol (eds) (1981), 199–201, argues that Spartacus was not Maidic but Odrysian. J. Kolendo, "Comment Spartacus devient-il esclave?", in *Spartacus*, Danov and Fol (eds) (1981), 71–7, suggests that Spartacus had been a mercenary soldier in the auxiliary troops of the Roman army but fell foul of the authorities and became a slave.

94. In the *Life of Cato the Elder*, 23, Plutarch describes Cato's contempt for Greeks and their culture. Plutarch says "he was opposed on principle to the study of philosophy, and because his patriotic fervour made him regard the whole of Greek culture and its methods of education with contempt". He also did not trust Greek physicians and treated himself and his family with his own methods. Plutarch describes these and then adds mischievously, "However his self-sufficiency in these matters seems to have been justly punished, for he lost both his wife and his son by disease" (*ibid.*, 24). A little earlier his brutal nature was revealed in the callous way he treated his slaves and Plutarch ends this chapter with a damning note on his character: "But he certainly went too far when he ventured once to declare that the man who deserved the highest praise, indeed who should be honoured almost as a god, was the one who at the end of his life was found to have added to his property more than he had inherited" (*ibid.*, 21). This is discussed by Pelling, "Plutarch: Roman Heroes and Greek Culture", 214–15.

95. The killing of his horse is discussed by Stampacchia, *La Tradizione della guerra*, 146–7 in connection with religious sacrifice, and see also Antonio Guarino, *Spartakus: Analyse eines Mythos*, B. Gullath (trans.) (Munich: Deutscher Taschenbuch, 1980), 66.

96. This is highlighted by the way Plutarch describes the death of this pair: Spartacus died fighting and his body was never found; Crassus' body on the other hand suffered maltreatment after his undignified death, and his head was used as a prop in a production of Euripides' play, the *Bacchae* at the Parthian court. See Plutarch, *Life of Crassus*, 31–3.

97. On Appian's work see Emilio Gabba, *Appiano e la Storia delle Guerre civili* (Florence: La Nuova Italia, 1956); P. J. Cuff, "Prolegomena to a Critical Edition of Appian BC 1", *Historia* **16** (1967), 177–88; and Alain M. Gowing, *The Triumviral Narratives of Appian and Cassius Dio* (Ann Arbor, MI: University of Michigan Press, 1992).

98. Appian, *Civil Wars*, 1.14, 116.

99. Mount Vesuvius was a suitable place, perhaps, because the revolt is rather

like a volcano, a comparison made by Orosius in his account of the second Sicilian war. Florus says that Vesuvius was suitable for such ravening monsters ("prima sedes velut rabidis beluis mons Vesuvius placuit") (Florus, *Epitome of Roman History*, 2.8), but H. T. Wallinga, "Bellum Spartacium: Florus' Text and Spartacus' Objective", *Athenaeum* **70**(80) (1992), 25–43, esp. 31–4, points out that Vesuvius is hardly suitable since it was seen as a paradise, being so fertile.

100. Shaw, *Spartacus and the Slave Wars*, 140 n.6, writes that Appian is confused: the praetor Gaius Claudius Glaber was sent out.
101. Appian, *Civil Wars*, 1.14.119.
102. *Ibid.*, 1.14.119.
103. See Marshall, "Crassus' Ovation in 71 BC", on Crassus' attitude to Pompey, and Aulus Gellius, *Attic Nights*, 5.6.20–23, on Crassus' crown of laurel.
104. Grünewald's dismissal of our accounts is too extreme: "when it came to dealing with bandits Roman historians became novelists ... The *latro* was no more than an imaginary character in this imaginary state, a character who had never actually drawn breath, a myth" (*Bandits in the Roman Empire*, 164–6). While it may be true that some of the heroic features are overdrawn, it is not true to say that there were no individuals who performed the actions of Eunus, Salvius or Spartacus. Rather than rejecting all our sources as fiction, it is more productive to ask why such favourable pictures were drawn and what role these heroes play in the representation of Roman history.
105. Richard J. A. Talbert, "The Role of Helots in the Class Struggle at Sparta", *Historia* **38** (1989), 22–40, esp. 30.
106. Hesychius of Alexandria, *Hesychii Alexandrini Lexicon*, 2 vols, K. Latte (ed.) (Haunia: Ejnar Munksgaard Editore, 1953, 1966). This word occurs in vol. 2, p. 676.
107. Talbert, "The Role of Helots", 39.
108. Michael Whitby also challenges the conventional view of the Spartans as constantly afraid of their own workforce, who rebel on every conceivable opportunity: "I prefer the alternative of a Sparta whose citizens were sufficiently arrogant to believe the myths of their own superiority" ("Two Shadows: Images of Spartans and Helots", in *The Shadow of Sparta*, A. Powell & S. Hodkinson [eds], 87–126 [London: Routledge, 1994], 111). His argument is that although the Spartans may have cruelly exploited their helots, they were not afraid of them. Unfortunately for him as well, this means disregarding virtually all the ancient evidence, including the testimony of Thucydides and Aristotle, no mean opponents as he himself admits: "Thus the two most intelligent ancient sources, Thucydides and Aristotle, support the negative interpretation. But intelligent judgments need not be right or universally valid and this may be true of Sparta" (*ibid.*, 108). He doubts the reality of the slaughter of 2,000 helots related by Thucydides, *History of the Peloponnesian War* (Whitby, "Two Shadows", 98) and refers to Talbert, "The Role of Helots", as if the latter had some arguments in favour of his view apart from the fact that he did not believe it. In fact, all Talbert writes is: "Assuming that the story is to be credited at all" ("The Role of Helots", 24).

109. The Bacchanalian conspiracies mentioned by Livy in his account of the early second century may be apposite here. The authorities viewed them as religious groups, but also involving slaves.

5. The ideology of the slaves

1. Similarly, modern scholars have marvelled at the lack of prospects for the Nat Turner rebellion: "Although Nat may not yet have recognised it, his rebellion was already disintegrating ... In fact, few uprisings have ever been so ill prepared and unplanned" (T. C. Parramore, "Covenant in Jerusalem", in *Nat Turner: A Slave Rebellion in History and Memory*, K. S. Greenberg [ed.], 58–76 [Oxford: Oxford University Press, 2003], 61). For a general discussion of the dismissal of this rebellion see Egerton, "Nat Turner in a Hemispheric Context".
2. Thucydides, *History of the Peloponnesian War*, 5.102. The Melians, of course, were then annihilated by the Athenians, but most readers understand the reasoning for their holding out. And, in fact, they are successful at first.
3. οἱ ἄνθρωποι ἐπιθυμοῦσι μὲν ἐλεύθεροι εἶναι μάλιστα πάντων, καὶ φασὶ τὴν ἐλευθερίαν μέγιστον τῶν ἀγαθῶν, τὴν δὲ δουλείαν αἴσχιστον καὶ δυστυχέστατον ὑπάρχειν (Dio Chrysostom, *On Slavery and Freedom*, 1.1).
4. W. L. Westermann, "Between Slavery and Freedom", *American Historical Review* 50(2) (1945), 213–27, quotes Abraham Lincoln observing the same thing, and he points out that things have not improved since 1864 and that we still mean different things by it. "There are few words more vague in their connotations, more expansible and more subject to distortion than these two – freedom and slavery" (*ibid.*, 213).
5. Genovese, *From Rebellion to Revolution*, starts with the rousing statement: "Enslavement in any form has figured as the antithesis of that individual autonomy considered the essence of freedom in modern societies. The revolt against slavery thus emerged as the basic assertion of human dignity and of humanity itself" (*ibid.*, 3). Few today would disagree with this formulation of the issue. Jean-Jacques Rousseau started *The Social Contract* with a discussion of slavery, with the assumption that this was bad and freedom was good: "Man was born free, and he is everywhere in chains" (*The Social Contract*, M. Cranston [trans.] [Harmondsworth: Penguin, 1968], 1.1). He goes on: "To renounce freedom is to renounce one's humanity, one's rights as a man and equally one's duties" (*ibid.*, 1.4). See Paul Cartledge, *The Greeks: A Portrait of Self and Others*, 2nd edn (Oxford: Oxford University Press, 2002), 156–66, on Greek ideas of freedom. Kurt A. Raaflaub, *The Discovery of Freedom in Ancient Greece*, rev. and updated, R. Franciscono (trans.) (Chicago, IL: University of Chicago Press, 2004) gives an idea of the complexity of the topic. For some caustic remarks on the importance of the contribution of the Greeks to our notion of freedom see Goody, *The Theft of History*, 55–8.
6. See Price, "Maroons and their Communities", which gives a brief overview of the violent rebellions in this period before going on to talk about maroons and their communities. Rout, *The African Experience in Spanish America*,

ch. 4, gives a fascinating list and description of the continual slave uprisings, some impressively large and longlasting, in South and Central America in the same period. See also Schwartz, *Slaves, Peasants and Rebels*, 106–7, for a list of maroon communities in Bahia, Brazil 1614–1826.
7. See Weiler, *Die Beendigung des Sklavenstatus*, 115–45, on the wish for freedom, and the assumption among the owners that this is what slaves wanted. Price remarks: "During the past several decades, historical scholarship has done much to dispel the myth of the 'docile slave'" ("Maroons and their Communities", 608).
8. Plato, *Republic*, Book 9, 578e–579b.
9. In the dialogue *Gorgias* Plato puts into the mouth of Callicles the sentiments expressed in Book 1 of the *Republic*: that justice is a trick played on the stronger, whereas nature intended the stronger to win, not be restrained by rules and convention. He goes on to say:

> But I fancy, when some man arises with a nature of sufficient force, he shakes off all that we have taught him, bursts his bonds and breaks free; he tramples underfoot our codes and juggleries, our charms and laws which are all against nature; our slave rises in revolt and shows himself our master, and there dawns the full light of natural justice.
> (Plato, *Gorgias*, 484A)

Earlier, Callicles had asked: "For how can a man be happy if he is a slave to anybody at all?" (*ibid.*, 481E).
10. Xenophon, *Hiero*, 3.4.5. The Greek word is πίστις, the primary meaning of which is trust in others.
11. πολῖται γὰρ δορυφοροῦσι μὲν ἀλλήλους ἄνευ μισθοῦ ἐπὶ τοὺς δούλους (*ibid.*, 3.4.3).
12. Lysias, Speech 7, emphasis added.
13. See Seneca, *Epistulae*, 47.5, and Macrobius, *Saturnalia*, 1.11.13, discussed by J. Christes, "Sklaverei in griechischen Sprichwörtern und Sentenzen", in *Funfzig Jahre Forschungen zur antiken Sklaverei an der Mainzer Akademie 1950–2000: Miscellanea zum Jubiläum*, H. Bellen & H. Heinen (eds), 429–46 (Stuttgart: Franz Steiner, 2001), 442.
14. "Quos viceris amicos tibi esse cave credas. Inter dominum et servum nulla amicitia est" (Quintus Curtius Rufus, *History of Alexander*, 7.8.28).
15. Vogt, *Ancient Slavery and the Ideal of Man*, 130.
16. "Among domestic slaves in particular, there were many who reciprocated their master's good will and concern for them by industrious and dedicated work; there were always slaves who were dependable" (*ibid.*, 129–45, esp. 130). Fridolf Kudlien, *Sklaven-Mentalität im Spiegel antiker Wahrsagerei* (Stuttgart: Franz Steiner, 1991), similarly emphasizes this aspect of slavery; his work is discussed carefully by McKeown, *The Invention of Ancient Slavery?*, 30–41.
17. Vogt quotes a passage from Velleius Paterculus' *Roman History* that says that the wives of the proscribed were very loyal, the freedmen quite loyal, the slaves fairly loyal but the sons not at all: "id tamen notandum est fuisse in proscriptos uxorum fidem summam, libertorum mediam, servorum aliquam, filiorum

nullam" (2,67,2). Velleius' main point is that the sons were treacherous, not that the slaves were not.
18. One might see a similarity with the fate of women in antiquity, whose voices are also not heard. When one reads Pliny the Younger's description of the devotion of his wife, it is not difficult to imagine that his own wife may not have used the same terms to describe her own feelings:
> She is highly intelligent and extremely frugal; she loves me, which is a sign of chastity. Her love for me has made her take up books. She reads and rereads my writings and even memorises them ... When I read my own work aloud, she sits discreetly behind a curtain and soaks up the praise. She accompanies herself on the lyre as she sings my verses, with no instructor but love, the best teacher of all. (*Letters*, 4.19)

19. For a useful collection of the sources on Spartacus, see Stampacchia, *La Tradizione della guerra*. See *ibid.*, 163–7, for the passages by Cicero.
20. Aristotle, *Politics*, 1.3, emphasis added. This is discussed by Giuseppe Cambiano, who writes: "The opponents of slavery did not hold a current opinion: in that sense their view was paradoxical. Almost certainly they were either isolated intellectuals or members of some exclusive group; nor is there any evidence to show that they were slaves themselves" ("Aristotle and the Anonymous Opponents of Slavery", in *Classical Slavery*, M. L. Finley [ed.], 28–52 [London: Cass, 1987], 29). And yet this group was rather more numerous than the group that thought that women might have had some intellectual capacities, judging by the relative space Aristotle devoted to a defence of slavery and to the situation of women. He felt no need to explain or justify this latter phenomenon and it seems to me that he would not have spent as much time as he did on slavery if these "isolated intellectuals" had not raised the issue. See also Nicholas D. Smith, "Aristotle's Theory of Natural Slavery", in *A Companion to Aristotle's Politics*, D. Keyt and F. D. Miller (eds), 142–55 (Oxford: Blackwell, 1991) on Aristotle's theory of natural slavery, and Malcolm Schofield, *Saving the City: Philosopher-Kings and Other Classical Paradigms* (London: Routledge, 1999), 115–50, esp. 133–7, on the opponents of slavery. Schofield, however, is more interested in Aristotle's argument than in what the passage may tell us about other views.
21. Plutarch, *Comparison of Lycurgus and Numa*, 1.5. This idea of a golden age when men had no slaves and had been happy was a commonplace in antiquity; see Vogt, *Ancient Slavery and the Ideal of Man*, 27–8. Dawson gives details of some utopias without slaves; see for instance *Cities of the Gods*, 135–6, 142, 158 n.50, 152, 178. See Norman Cohn, *The Pursuit of the Millennium*, rev. and expanded (Oxford: Oxford University Press [1957], 1970), 187–90, on the ancient background to the millenarianism of the Middle Ages. Virgil's fourth eclogue and Horace's sixteenth epode both evoke the age of Saturn, where men are delivered from all evils, and nature supplies all human needs, and in *Aeneid* Book 6, Virgil has Anchises prophesy the new golden age brought in by Augustus. N. A. Mashkin, "Eschatology and Messianism in the Final Period of the Roman Republic", *Philosophy and Phenomenological Research* **10**(2) (1949), 206–28, argues that during the period of the late Republic, doctrines of the end of injustice with the miraculous coming of happier times flourished, and it was

documents such as these that Augustus had destroyed when he came to power. Suetonius tells us that "Augustus collected all the copies of Greek and Latin prophetic verse then current, the work of either anonymous or unrespected authors, and burned more than two thousand. He kept only the Sibylline books and edited even these" (*Life of Augustus*, 31). Augustus seems to have been fond of book-burning. Appian tells us that in 36 BCE, after defeating Sextus Pompeius, he commanded that all records of his earlier career be burned (*Roman History*, 5.132.548).
22. Herodotus, *Histories*, 6.137.
23. "Italiae cultures primi Aborigines fuere, quorum rex Saturnus tantae justitiae fuisse dicitur, ut neque servierit quisquam sub illo neque quicquam privatae rei habuerit, sed omnia communia et indivisa omnibus fuerint, veluti unum cunctis patrimonium esset" (Justin, *Epitome of the Philippic History of Pompeius Trogus*, 43.1.3).
24. Diodorus, 2.55–60. At first there appears to be only one island but later he says the people worship the sun after whom they name the islands and themselves, so that this utopia is referred to as the Isles of the Sun (*ibid.*, 2.59.7).
25. *Digest*, 1.5, emphasis added.
26. Peter Garnsey, *Ideas of Slavery from Aristotle to Augustine* (Cambridge: Cambridge University Press, 1996), 243.
27. *Ibid.*, 84.

6. Sympathy for the slaves: Diodorus Siculus

1. For the reappraisal see Kenneth Sacks, *Diodorus Siculus and the First Century* (Princeton, NJ: Princeton University Press, 1990). For a typical view, see the entry in the second edition of the *Oxford Classical Dictionary*, which ends: "Despite his universal conception of history and his aim of writing for the Graeco-Roman world, his work is undistinguished, with confusion arising from the different traditions and chronologies, a compilation only as valuable as its authorities, but thus valuable to us" (A. H. McDonald, "Diodorus Siculus", in *Oxford Classical Dictionary*, 2nd edn, N. G. L. Hammond and H. H. Scullard [eds] [Oxford: Oxford University Press, 1970], 347). The more appreciative entry in the third edition is by Kenneth Sacks.
2. Diodorus, 1.1.1–1.5.3. For a useful introduction to Diodorus see P. J. Stylianou, *A Historical Commentary on Diodorus Siculus, Book 15* (Oxford: Oxford University Press, 1998), 1–139.
3. Diodorus, 1.1.3.
4. Stylianou, *A Historical Commentary on Diodorus Siculus*, 3–6.
5. For a discussion of the *proemia* see Sacks, *Diodorus Siculus and the First Century*, 9–22.
6. Diodorus, 1.1.3.
7. *Ibid.*, 1.4.
8. Sacks, *Diodorus Siculus and the First Century*, esp. ch. 5, 117–59. Sacks quotes Diodorus' comment on Rome's conquest of Greece:

The Greeks, after witnessing in person the butchery and beheading of their kinsmen and friends, the capture and looting of their cities, the abusive enslavement of whole populations, after, in a word, losing both their liberty and the right to speak freely exchanged the height of prosperity for the most extreme misery.   (Diodorus, 32.26.2)

He describes it as one of the strongest indictments of Roman warfare and imperial rule found in ancient literature (Sacks, *Diodorus Siculus and the First Century*, 138-9).

9. καὶ γὰρ τῶν Σικελιωτῶν οἱ πολλοὺς πλούτους κεκτημένοι διημιλλῶντο πρὸς τὰς τῶν Ἰταλιωτῶν ὑπερηφανίας τε καὶ πλεονεξίας καὶ κακουργίας (Diodorus 34/35.2.27). At the start of *Diodorus Siculus*, Farrington quotes a passage from Diodorus that sums up Diodorus' sentiments quite succinctly: ἁλίσκονται δ', οἶμαι, τῶν ἡμέρων ἀνδρῶν αἱ ψυχαὶ μάλιστά πως ἐλέῳ διὰ τὴν κοινὴν τῆς φύσεως ὁμοπάθειαν [The souls of gentle men are, I suppose, most open to pity owing to the fellowship of all nature in suffering] (13.24).

10. Sacks, *Diodorus Siculus and the First Century*, 151-4. Hermann Strasburger, "Poseidonios on Problems of the Roman Empire", *Journal of Roman Studies* 55 (1965), 40-53, takes the Diodoran passages to be from Posidonius but nevertheless his conclusion is that Posidonius saw the Roman Empire as bringing peace and stability.

11. Sacks, *Diodorus Siculus and the First Century*, 151-2; see also *ibid.*, 51-2, on Diodorus stressing the relationship between rulers and subjects.

12. Diodorus, 1.1.4.

13. *Ibid.*, 37.2.1. Describing the cause of the Marsic War, Diodorus writes: αἰτίαν δὲ πρώτην γενέσθαι τοῦ πολέμου τὸ μεταπεσεῖν τοὺς Ῥωμαίους ἀπὸ τῆς εὐτάκτου καὶ λιτῆς ἀγωγῆς καὶ ἐγκρατοῦς δι' ἧς ἐπὶ τοσοῦτον ηὐξήθησαν, εἰς ὀλέθριον ζῆλον τρυφῆς καὶ ἀκολασίας [The primary cause of the war was that the Romans abandoned the disciplined, frugal, and stern manner of life that had brought them to such greatness, and fell into the pernicious pursuit of luxury and licence] (*ibid.*, 37.2.1).

14. See N. G. Wilson, *Photius: The Bibliotheca* (London: Duckworth, 1994), 13-17, for a brief description of the work, and Warren T. Treadgold, *The Nature of the Bibliotheca of Photius* (Washington, DC: Centre for Byzantine Studies, Dumbarton Oaks, 1980) for a longer one. The full title of the work is *Inventory and enumeration of the books that we have read, of which our beloved brother Tarasius requested a general analysis.*

15. See Treadgold, *The Nature of the Bibliotheca of Photius*, 1-15.

16. Mileta, "Quellenkritische Beobachtungen zur Vorgeschichte", describes how epitomisers worked. They had writers write a preliminary detailed summary and then another editor worked through this and decided which passages to keep or delete. He suggests that the excerptors employed by Constantine used a copy of Photius' summary, and were consciously trying to do something different with his work, that is, they were using Photius but with their own themes in mind.

17. *Ibid.* and Mileta, "Verschwoerung oder Eruption". Wiedemann, *Greek and*

Roman Slavery, 200–207, includes both versions, although this is not the case for the second slave war (see *ibid.*, 208–15; also Shaw, *Spartacus and the Slave Wars*, 80–94). Shaw also does not always indicate the different versions for the second war (*ibid.*, 115–20).

18. See Moses I. Finley, *A History of Sicily: Ancient Sicily to the Arab Conquest* (London: Chatto & Windus, 1968), 188–9, for a concise summary of events. In 827 CE a Byzantine general had rebelled and set himself up as emperor, calling in help from the Aghlabid emir. Palermo fell in 831 CE, Enna in 859, Syracuse in 878 and Taormina in 902.
19. Diodorus, 34/35.2.9–10.
20. *Ibid.*, 34/35.2.35.
21. The view that there were dangers in excess was a commonplace in ancient philosophy and was not held only by the Stoics.
22. Athenaeus, *Deipnosophistae*, 12.542.
23. *Ibid.*, 12.541.
24. Ὅτι ὁ αὐτὸς Δαμόφιλος διὰ τὴν εὐθάδειαν καὶ τὴν ὠμότητα τῶν τρόπων οὐκ ἦν ἡμέρα καθ'ἣν οὐκ ἠκίζετό τινας τῶν οἰκετῶν ἐπ'αἰτίαις οὐ δικαίαις (Diodorus, 34/35.2.37).
25. ἐξ ὧν ἐδείκνυτο τῶν δούλων οὐχὶ ὠμότης εἶναι φύσεως τὰ γινόμενα εἰς τοὺς ἄλλους, ἀλλὰ τῶν προϋπηργμένων εἰς αὐτοὺς ἀδικημάτων ἀνταπόδοσις (*ibid.*, 34/35.2.13).
26. *Ibid.*, 34/35.2.40.
27. ἐρράγη ποτὲ σὺν καιρῷ τὸ μῖσος [an outbreak of hatred] (*ibid.*, 34/35.2.26).
28. ἐξ οὗ χωρὶς παραγγέλματος πολλαὶ μυριάδες συνέδραμον οἰκετῶν ἐπὶ τὴν τῶν δεσποτῶν ἀπώλειαν (*ibid.*, 34/35.2.26).
29. *Ibid.*, 34/35.2.33.
30. πάντες δε τὸ κράτιστον τῶν ὅπλων τὸν θυμὸν ἀνελάμβανον κατὰ τῆς ἀπωλείας τῶν ὑπερηφάνων κυρίων (*ibid.*, 34/35.2.24b).
31. This description is somehow reminiscent of a passage from the narrative of the ex-slave Frederick Douglass. When he fought back against his "nigger breaker" of a master and refused to be broken, he introduced the episode with the words "You have seen how a man was made a slave; you shall see how a slave was made a man" (*Narrative of the Life of Frederick Douglass, an American Slave Written by Himself*, B. Quarles [ed.] [Cambridge, MA: Belknap Press, [1845] 1988], 97).
32. ὀνειδίζοντες αὐτῶν τὴν ὑπερηφανίαν καὶ τὴν ὑπερβολὴν τῆς εἰς τὸν ὄλεθρον προαγούσης ὕβρεως (*ibid.*, 34/35.2.46).
33. *Ibid.*, 34/35.2.47.
34. *Ibid.*, 34/35.9.
35. *Ibid.*, 5.3.5–6, 14.63, 14.70–71.

7. The secret of the success of the Spartan helots

1. Athenaeus, *Deipnosophistae*, 6.265c.
2. Pollux, *Onomasticon*, 3.83. See, however, "It was generally conceded that the

bondage of the half-free Helots of Lacedaimonia was more onerous than full enslavement at Athens or about Delphi" (Westermann, "Between Slavery and Freedom", 217–18).
3. Jean Ducat, *Les Hilotes*, Bulletin de Correspondance Hellénique, supplement 20 (Athens: École Française d'Athènes, 1990), 44–51.
4. See Weiler, *Die Beendigung des Sklavenstatus*, 15–54, on the terms used and the relatively late emergence of the term from which the English "slave" derives (*ibid.*, 15–16). For Greek words, see, for example, the astonishingly complicated discussion by Marie-Madeleine Mactoux, "Pour une approche nouvelle du champ lexical de l'esclavage chez les orateurs attiques", in *Actes du colloque sur l'esclavage, Nieborów 2–6 XII 1975* (conference proceedings), I. Bieżuńska-Małowist and J. Kolendo (eds), 75–124 (Warsaw: History Institute, University of Warsaw, 1979). For a more straightforward article about Latin words, see Luigi Capogrossi Colognesi, "La denominazione degli schiavi e dei padroni nel latino del terzo e del secondo secolo a.C.", in *Actes du colloque sur l'esclavage*, Bieżuńska-Małowist and Kolendo (eds), 171–206.
5. See Glenn R. Morrow, *Plato's Law of Slavery and its Relation to Greek Law* (Urbana, IL: University of Illinois Press, 1939), 25–46.
6. οὕτω καὶ τὸ κτῆμα ὄργανον πρὸς ζωήν ἐστι, καὶ ἡ κτῆσις πλῆθος ὀργάνων ἐστι, καὶ ὁ δοῦλος κτῆμά τι ἔμψυχον (Aristotle, *Politics*, 1.2.4–5).
7. *Ibid.*
8. See Cambiano, "Aristotle and the Anonymous Opponents", for a discussion on Aristotle's views on slavery. See also W. W. Fortenbaugh, "Aristotle on Slaves and Women", in *Articles on Aristotle, 2: Ethics and Politics*, J. Barnes, M. Schofield and R. Sorabji (eds), 135–9 (London: Duckworth, 1977) and Smith, "Aristotle's Theory of Natural Slavery".
9. The solution of Nino Luraghi, "Helotic Slavery Reconsidered", in *Sparta: Beyond the Mirage*, A. Powell and S. Hodkinson (eds), 227–48 (Swansea: Classical Press of Wales, 2002) does not result in a radically different situation. Even under his scenario, where the helots were *not* the native peoples of the land who had been enslaved but rather Spartans who had fallen into debt, the result is nevertheless a feeling of unity among the enslaved, which normally does not obtain in the ancient Greek world, and against which thinkers such as Plato and Aristotle had warned. See also Kurt A. Raaflaub, "Freedom for the Messenians? A Note on the Impact of Slavery and Helotage on the Greek Concept of Freedom", in *Helots and their Masters in Laconia and Messenia: Histories, Ideologies, Structures*, N. Luraghi and S. E. Alcock (eds), 169–90 (Cambridge, MA: Harvard University Press, 2003) on freedom for the Messenians.
10. This treaty is reproduced in Thucydides, *History of the Peloponnesian War*, 5.23.2.
11. Strabo uses the term δοῦλοι to describe the situation of the helots (8.5.4).
12. Detlef Lotze, *Metaxy eleutheron kai doulon: Studien zur Rechtsstellung unfreier Landbevolkerungen in Griechenland* (Berlin: Akademie-Verlag, 1959) (reprinted New York: Arno Press, 1979) discusses the status of helots and other similar peoples. In his conclusion (*ibid.*, 79) he describes the situation of helotry as a form of collective slavery.

13. Even if the suggestion of Luraghi, "Helotic Slavery Reconsidered", that in fact originally they had been poorer members of the Spartan citizen body were the case, this does not alter the picture hugely for my purposes here.
14. "Serf" is a term accepted by Stephen Hodkinson, "Spartiates, Helots and the Direction of the Agrarian Economy: Towards an Understanding of Helotage in Comparative Perspective", in *Helots and their Masters*, Luraghi and Alcock (eds), 248–85; see *ibid.*, 249 n.2 for further reading. M. I. Finley, *The Ancient Economy*, updated 2nd edn (Berkeley, CA: University of California Press [1973] 1999), 184–5, objects to the use of the term "serfdom" as involving much more than being tied to the soil, and injecting notions properly belonging to feudal Europe into the discussion. However see the riposte in Ste Croix, *The Class Struggle in the Ancient Greek World*, 137–40. The evidence in Luraghi, "Helotic Slavery Reconsidered", seems compelling, and his close analysis of the sources shows far more similarity to regular slavery than is usually presented by modern scholars when considering helots. See Michael L. Bush, "Introduction", in *Serfdom and Slavery: Studies in Legal Bondage*, M. L. Bush (ed.), 1–17 (Harlow: Longman, 1996) and Stanley L. Engerman, "Slavery, Serfdom and Other Forms of Coerced Labour: Similarities and Differences", also in *Serfdom and Slavery*, M. L. Bush (ed.), 18–41, for clear discussions on the differences between slavery and serfdom (and the problems of defining the terms). The helots do not fit neatly into their definitions of serfs. One crucial difference between slaves and serfs is that serfs do not belong completely to their masters but there is a force above them, either a prince or the state. With Sparta's political system, one can see how the term "serf" then became attached to the helots. And yet the differences between medieval serfdom and the situation in Sparta are also marked. For example: "slaves were essentially objects of force. This meant that, when engaged in large-scale production, slavery was highly dependent upon a superstructure of physical control" (Bush, "Introduction", 3). As we have seen, this superstructure of control was more evident in Sparta than elsewhere. An illustration of the complications of the case of the helots is provided by Hodkinson, *Property and Wealth in Classical Sparta* (London: Duckworth, 2000), who wishes to show that helots were privately owned rather than public property. He quotes Aristotle, *Politics*, 2.2.5 (1263a30), which says that the Spartans used each other's slaves practically as their own, without commenting on the fact that Aristotle uses the word δοῦλος, which rather undermines Hodkinson's own argument that the helots were not technically slaves (Hodkinson, *Property and Wealth in Classical Sparta*, 114–15).
15. See Isocrates, *Panathenaicus*, 181, quoted later in this chapter.
16. οἱ δὲ Λακεδαιμόνιοι πάντας τοὺς δούλους εἵλωτας καλοῦσιν (*Herodiani Technici Reliquiae*, vol. 1, A. Lentz [ed.], Grammatici Graeci, 3.1 [Hildesheim: Georg Olms, [1867] 1965]], vol. 1, p. 244, lines 18–22).
17. ὥστε τοὺς λέγοντας ἐν Λακεδαίμονι καὶ τὸν ἐλεύθερον μάλιστα ἐλεύθερον εἶναι καὶ τον δοῦλον μάλιστα δοῦλον οὐ φαύλως τεθεωρήκεναι τὴν διαφοράν (Plutarch, *Life of Lycurgus*, 28.5).
18. ὡς μάλιστα δοῦλοί τε ἐν Λακεδαίμονι καὶ ἐλεύθεροι ... οὕτω σύμπαντες

οἱ Σπαρτιᾶται τὴν ἐλευθερίαν ἀφῄρηντο συζῶντες ἐχθεῖ τῷ παρὰ τῶν οἰκετῶν (Libanius, *About Slavery*, 25.63). Note that Libanius refers to slaves.
19. Plutarch, *Life of Cleomenes*, 9.
20. τιμῶσι δὲ τὸν φόβον οὐχ ὥσπερ οὓς ἀποτρέπονται δαίμονας ἡγούμενοι βλαβερόν ἀλλὰ τὴν πολιτείαν μάλιστα συνέχεσθαι φόβῳ νομίζοντες (*ibid.*, 9.1-2). It perhaps should be noted that they also had temples to Death and Laughter as well as to Fear, although Plutarch does not give a theory as to why. See Ephraim David: "To sum up, laughter was used at Sparta as an important instrument for the consolidation of the social hierarchy, the promotion of harmony among the homoioi and the cultivation of the norms and values comprising their social code" ("Laughter in Spartan Society", in *Classical Sparta: Techniques Behind her Success*, A. Powell [ed.], 1–25 [London: Routledge, 1989], 17). On Spartan religion see also Robert Parker, "Spartan Religion", in *Classical Sparta*, A. Powell (ed.), 142–72.
21. Plutarch, *Comparison of Lycurgus and Numa*, 1.5.
22. οὐδ'αὖ ἀνδραπόδων κτήσει τῶν τε ἄλλων καὶ τῶν εἱλωτικῶν, οὐδὲ μὴν ἵππων (Plato, *Alcibiades*, 1.122d).
23. Pausanias, *Guide to Greece*, 3.20.6. Another suggestion for the origin of the term is that it is from the passive of the verb "to take", αἱρέω. The situation of the helots was so well known that there was a verb in Greek, εἱλωτεύω, meaning to serve as a helot. See the discussion in Ste Croix, *The Class Struggle in the Ancient Greek World*, 149, and, more recently, Paul Cartledge, "Raising Hell? The Helot Mirage – A Personal Re-view", in *Helots and their Masters*, Luraghi and Alcock (eds), 12–30.
24. Φύλαρχος δ'ἐν ἕκτῃ ἱστοριῶν καὶ Βυζαντίους φησὶν οὕτω Βιθυνῶν δεσπόσαι ὡς Λακεδαιμονίους τῶν εἱλώτων (Athenaeus, *Deipnosophistae*, 6.271b).
25. *Ibid.*, 6.263c-d. Compare Talbert, "The Role of Helots", 30, for a similar view about the abilities of the helots. Sacks, *Diodorus Siculus and the First Century*, argues that Diodorus' anti-Roman sentiments as manifested in his accounts of the Sicilian slave wars are his own opinions, and not those of Posidonius, who has normally been posited as his source for these years. This passage tends to confirm that Posidonius does not share Diodorus' general sympathy for slaves.
26. Athenaeus, *Deipnosophistae*, 6.263f. The Greek word for "lot" is κλῆρος. The passage runs: κλαρώτας, φησί, Κρῆτες καλοῦσι τοὺς δούλους ἀπὸ τοῦ γενομένου περὶ αὐτῶν κλήρου. What is worth noting here is that although these are a different phenomenon from, say, Athenian slaves, Ephorus calls them slaves. Plutarch tells us explicitly that Lycurgus had gone to Crete in his journey to investigate good government but makes no remarks about treatment of slaves there (*Life of Lycurgus*, 4).
27. Athenaeus, *Deipnosophistae*, 6.264a-b.
28. *Ibid.*, 6.264d-e. This is also from Plato's *Laws*, where the roving bands of Italy are also mentioned (*Laws*, Book 6, 777C).
29. Isocrates, *Panathenaicus*, 181. See Vivienne Gray, "Images of Sparta: Writer and Audience in Isocrates' *Panathenaicus*", in *The Shadow of Sparta*, A. Powell

& S. Hodkinson (eds), 223-71 (London: Routledge, 1994) on the nature of the criticism of Sparta in this speech.
30. Plutarch, *Life of Lycurgus*, 28.
31. Plutarch, *Comparison of Lycurgus and Numa*, 1.5.
32. Dio Chrysostom, *On Slavery and Freedom II*, 28.
33. Thomas Figueira, "The Evolution of the Messenian Identity", in *Sparta: New Perspectives*, S. Hodkinson & A. Powell (eds), 211-44 (Swansea: Classical Press of Wales, 1999). In the third century BCE, Nabis freed thousands of "slaves": presumably helots. See Paul Cartledge and Antony Spawforth, *Hellenistic and Roman Sparta: A Tale of Two Cities* (London: Routledge, 1989), 69-70. An overview of the earlier debate on Nabis is comprehensively covered by Oliva, *Sparta and her Social Problems*, 274-98.
34. See Aristotle, *Politics*, 7.7, "proving" that the Greeks are the "natural master race".

8. Slave revolts in the ancient historiography

1. Finley, *Ancient Slavery and Modern Ideology*, 65. Schwartz makes a similar comment about Brazil: "For almost four centuries slavery played such a central role in the historical development of the country that it was virtually impossible to separate any aspect of human experience from it" (*Slaves, Peasants and Rebels*, 161). Schwartz also discusses issues pertinent to this book:
    This tension and contrast between slavery as a pervasive system and the actions of slaves, masters and others in shaping its contours is really an aspect of a long and unresolved debate among historians and sociologists over the roles of human action or "agency" and social, political, and economic structures in explaining society. Did Napoleon make his age or was he the product of his times? (*Ibid.*, 162)
2. Gad Heuman and James Walvin (eds), *The Slavery Reader* (London: Routledge, 2003), 545. This is a book primarily concerned with Atlantic slavery.
3. S. A. Cook, F. E. Adcock and M. Charlesworth (eds), *The Cambridge Ancient History*, vol. 9, 1st edn (Cambridge: Cambridge University Press, 1932); J. A. Crook, A. Lintott and E. Rawson (eds), *The Cambridge Ancient History*, vol. 9, 2nd edn (Cambridge: Cambridge University Press, 1994).
4. Cook, Adcock and Charlesworth (eds), *The Cambridge Ancient History*, vol. 9, 11-16 and 151-7 (both chapters by Hugh Last).
5. Crook, Lintott and Rawson (eds), *The Cambridge Ancient History*, vol. 9, 25-7 (by Andrew Lintott) refers very obliquely to slave revolts when discussing "The Agrarian Problem"; see, for example: "Hence Gracchus deplored not only the injustice which was being done to those who fought for Rome but the danger of replacing potential warriors with slaves, who could not be used for military service but might on the contrary rebel" (*ibid.*, 54).
6. *Ibid.*, 215-23 (by Robin Seager); only pages 221-3 are about Spartacus.
7. Cook, Adcock and Charlesworth (eds), *The Cambridge Ancient History*, vol. 9, 329-32 (by Hugh Last). Aristonicus similarly had a subsection to himself (*ibid.*,

102–7), whereas in the second edition he merits only a paragraph by Andrew Lintott (Crook, Lintott and Rawson [eds], *The Cambridge Ancient History*, vol. 9, 34).
8. Harriet L. Flower (ed.), *The Cambridge Companion to the Roman Republic* (Cambridge: Cambridge University Press, 2004).
9. Klaus Bringmann, *A History of the Roman Republic*, W. J. Smyth (trans.) (Cambridge: Polity, 2007) (first published in German in 2002).
10. Pierre Piccinin, "Les Italiens dans le Bellum Spartacium, *Historia* **53** (2004), 173–99, esp. 198.
11. W. Zeev Rubinsohn, "Was the Bellum Spartacium a Servile Insurrection?", *Rivista di filologia e d'instruzione classica* **99** (1971), 290–99. Guarino, *Spartakus*, sets out to show that the story of Spartacus was just a myth, not based on reality. Guarino accepts nothing from our sources that does not fit his theory so he is able to argue that Spartacus was not a threat (*ibid.*, 79), and not even a slave (*ibid.*, 52); that Spartacus was not his real name (*ibid.*, 78); that Sicily and Italy at this time were independent of each other (*ibid.*, 80); and he concludes that it was not a slave war (*ibid.*, 89).
12. A further and connected strand to this dismissal of the ancient slave revolts is to argue that the one clear example of revolt, that of the helots, is not a slave revolt: that the helots were not slaves.
13. Griffith, "Spartacus and the Growth", 69. Griffith starts his article on Spartacus with the observation that, "authoritative works in English, the fruits of a long tradition of rigorous historical criticism, say little about him". He concludes it, as one might expect, by saying that they are correct in their allocation, or lack of allocation, of space (*ibid.*, 64, 69–70).
14. As discussed earlier, it is certainly not true that people could not imagine a slave-free society, since this kind of golden age was a topos in Greek and Roman literature.
15. Mary Beard and Michael Crawford, *Rome in the Late Republic*, 2nd edn (London: Duckworth, [1985] 1999). This is a usefully clear and concise introduction to this period of history, often used in undergraduate courses.
16. Appian, *Civil Wars*, 1.2.
17. Polybius, *The Histories*, 1.1.
18. *Ibid.*, 1.3.
19. *Ibid.*, 1.5.
20. Appian, *Civil Wars*, 1.6.
21. See, for instance, Plutarch, *Life of Julius Caesar*, 60. Later, Appian writes something similar: "Thus the Romans, after having government by kings for above sixty Olympiads and a democracy under consuls chosen yearly, for 100 Olympiads, resorted to kingly government again" (*Civil Wars*, 1.99) and in the next chapter we learn that Sulla had twenty-four axes carried in front of him: the same number as the kings had had (*ibid.*, 1.100).
22. *Ibid.*, 1.7.
23. *Ibid.*, 1.9.
24. *Ibid.*
25. *Ibid.*, 1.10. In fact the ancients did enlist slaves in their armies; see Peter Hunt,

"Arming Slaves and Helots in Classical Greece", in *Arming Slaves from Classical Times to the Modern Age*, C. L. Brown & P. D. Morgan (eds), 14–39 (New Haven, CT: Yale University Press, 1998) and *Slaves, Warfare and Ideology*.
26. Appian, *Civil Wars*, 1.18. The murder on the Capitol is the subject of *ibid.*, 1.17.
27. *Ibid.*, 1.34.
28. Appian, *Mithridatic Wars*, 1.39.
29. Appian, *Civil Wars*, Book 1, is full of interesting details about the relationships between slave and free. In 1.42, he tells us that the Romans captured Slabiae, Minervium and Salernum and remarks that the prisoners and slaves from these places were taken into the military service. He adds that Sextus Caesar also enrolled the ordinary people and the slaves in the places he captured, although he executed the important Roman citizens there.
30. *Ibid.*, 1.49.
31. *Ibid.*, 1.58.
32. *Ibid.*, 1.60.
33. *Ibid.*, 2.20–23. Here I wish to stress how Appian saw the situation. For him the involvement of slaves was extremely significant. For a more sophisticated analysis, see Wilfried Nippel, "Policing Rome", *Journal of Roman Studies* 74 (1984), 20–29, and *Aufruhr und "Polizei" in der Römischen Republik* (Stuttgart: Klett-Cotta, 1988).
34. Appian, *Civil Wars*, 1.65.
35. *Ibid.*, 1.69.
36. *Ibid.*, 1.70. Shortly afterwards we read that these slaves who had answered Cinna's call and were now in his army were particularly bloodthirsty, plundering and killing those they met in the street, "some of them attacking their own masters particularly" (*ibid.*, 1.74). So, showing his true Roman colours, he rounded them up and had them killed, Appian commenting rather unjustly: "Thus did the slaves receive fit punishment for their repeated treachery to their masters". (They also disobeyed Cinna when he ordered them to stop their violence but they were not then his slaves.) Shortly after this, however, Sulla prepared to return from the east where he was fighting Mithridates, and those on Cinna's side panicked, Cinna himself being killed by his own men (*ibid.*, 1.78).
37. *Ibid.*, 1.100.
38. *Ibid.*, 1.104.
39. "a Caesare Augusto in saeculum nostrum haud multo minus anni ducenti, quibus inertia Caesarum quasi consenuit atque decoxit, nisi quod sub Traiano principe movit lacertos et praeter spem omnium senectus imperii quasi reddita iuventute reviruit" (Florus, *Epitome of Roman History*, Preface to Book 1). There is, however, the question of what he means: 200 years from the time of the birth of Augustus, his assumption of the title of Augustus or his death? If he means from the time of Augustus' birth in 63 BCE then Florus was writing towards the end of the reign of Hadrian (117–28 CE), but if he means from the death of Augustus, then it would be 214 CE (that is, during the reign of Caracalla 211–17 CE) According to the *Oxford Classical Dictionary*, Florus wrote no earlier than Antoninus Pius (138–61 CE), which seems a safe enough statement. Trajan ruled from 98–117 CE.

NOTES, CHAPTER 8

40. Florus, *Epitome of Roman History*, 2.7, 2.8.
41. "tractatum etiam in senatu, an, quia condidisset imperium, Romulus vocaretur; sed sanctius et reverentius visum est nomen Augusti, ut scilicet iam tum, dum colit terras, ipso nomine et titulo consecraretur" (*ibid.*, 2.34). The work thus starts with the words Populus Romanus and ends with consecraretur, referring to Augustus. The nature of the work is thus very clear.
42. *Ibid.*, 2.6.
43. By the time Florus was writing, this was of course the case.
44. *Ibid.*, 2.7.
45. *Ibid.*, 2.8.
46. Hannibal is represented as doing the same. This episode is so well known that it makes its way into Pliny, *Natural History*, 8.18.
47. "Et quod sub gladiatore duce oportuit, sine missione pugnatum est. Spartacus ipse in primo agmine fortissime dimicans quasi imperator occisus est" (*ibid.*, 2.8.14). "Missio" is a technical term meaning release from the contest for a wounded gladiator.
48. *Ibid.*, 2.9.
49. *Ibid.*, 1.47.
50. *Ibid.*, 1.47, emphasis added.
51. "quam eo magnitudinis crescere, ut viribus suis conficeretur" [than to increase to such greatness that they were ruined by their own strength] (*ibid.*, 1.47).
52. *Ibid.*
53. *Ibid.*
54. *Ibid.*
55. Orosius, *History Against the Pagans*, 5.24.3. It is interesting to note that T. Rice Holmes, *The Roman Republic and the Founder of the Empire: From the Origins to 58 BC*, vol. 1 (Oxford: Oxford University Press, 1923), 157, seems to have chosen to follow this account most closely in his emphasis on the brutality of the slaves, which is not prominent in the earlier accounts.
56. Orosius, *History Against the Pagans*, 5.24.3.
57. *Ibid.*, 5.24.20.
58. See, for instance, Aptheker, *American Negro Slave Revolts*, and Jordan, *Tumult and Silence at Second Creek*, who quotes from the private correspondence of a white woman in Mississippi: "It [news of the slave conspiracy] is kept very still, not to be in the papers ... don't speak of it only cautiously" (*ibid.*, 26).
59. Beard and Crawford, *Rome in the Late Republic*, 85.
60. *Ibid.*, 10, emphasis added.
61. Augustine, *City of God*, 4.5.
62. *Ibid.*
63. *Ibid.*, 4.4.

Bibliography

Primary sources

Athenaeus, *Deipnosophistae* [*The Banqueting Sophists*] (also known as *The Deipnosophists*, which is the title of the Loeb Classical Library translation), purports to give the conversation of a group of philosophers as they dine. In 15 books, translations from the Loeb Classical Library edition, 7 vols, Charles Burton Gulick (trans.) (Cambridge, MA: Harvard University Press, 1927-41). The Loeb Classical Library is now publishing a new edition and translation by S. Douglas Olson entitled *The Learned Banqueters* (2006-).

Appian, *Roman History*, 4 vols, Horace White (trans.), Loeb Classical Library. The *Civil Wars* are in vols 3 and 4 (1972-9). The most recent edition is Paul Goukowsky, *Appien: Histoire romaine* (Greek text, French translation, notes), Collection Budé (1997-). A more recent English translation is Appian, *The Civil Wars*, John Carter (trans. with intro. and notes) (Harmondsworth: Penguin, 1996).

Augustine, *City of God*, Henry Bettenson (trans.) (Harmondsworth: Penguin, [1972] 1984). Latin text can be found in *The City of God Against the Pagans*, 7 vols, George E. McCracken *et al.* (ed. and trans.) in the Loeb Classical Library (1957-72).

Cassius Dio, *Roman History*, 9 vols, Ernest Carey & Herbert B. Foster (trans.), Loeb Classical Library (1914-27). The state of Dio's text for the episode about Bulla Felix is rather similar to that of Diodorus for the Sicilian slave wars. Indeed, the *Excerpts* of Constantine Porphyrogenitus are responsible for preserving some of Dio's text, as they had been for parts of Diodorus. The other epitomizers were Xiphilinos, from the eleventh century and Zonaras in the twelfth. The restored text was edited by U. P. Boissevain, *Cassii Dionis Cocceiani Historiarum Romanarum Quae Supersunt* (Berlin: Weidmann, 1955).

Diodorus Siculus, *The Library of History*, in 40 books. Translations come from *Diodorus Siculus*, 12 volumes, Loeb Classical Library (1933-67). Volume 12 is translated by Francis R. Walton. The Loeb edition indicates which passages have been extracted from the *Biblioteca* of Photius and which from the *Excerpts* of

Constantine. Passages relevant to the slave wars can also be found with a more up to date translation in Shaw, *Spartacus and the Slave Wars*, which also contains extracts from the most important primary sources for the two Sicilian slave wars and that of Spartacus.

Eutropius, *Breviarium*, H. W. Bird (trans. with intro. and comm.) (Liverpool: Liverpool University Press, 1993).

Florus, *Epitome of Roman History*, Edward Seymour Forster (trans.), Loeb Classical Library (1966).

Justin, *Epitome of the Philippic History of Pompeius Trogus*, J. C. Yardley (trans.) and R. Develin (intro. and notes) (Atlanta, GA: Scholars Press, 1994).

Livy, *History of Rome* or *ab Urbe Condita Libri,* originally 142 books. Many of the 142 books are not extant but there are summaries. One composed in the fourth century CE is known as the *Periochae* (which is Greek for summaries). Another, the *Oxyrhynchus Epitome*, was found on a papyrus in Egypt. The Loeb Classical Library edition is a translation in 14 volumes; the last volume translated by A. C. Schlesinger has the summaries of Livy and the text of Julius Obsequens (1959). A recent translation for the summaries is Livy *Rome's Mediterranean Empire Books 41–45 and the Periochae*, Jane D. Chaplin (trans.) (Oxford: Oxford University Press, 2007).

Many of Plutarch's *Lives* can be found translated in the Penguin editions: *The Rise and Fall of Athens: Nine Greek Lives*, Ian Scott-Kilvert (trans.) (1960); *The Age of Alexander: Nine Greek Lives*, Ian Scott-Kilvert (trans.) (1973); *The Makers of Rome: Nine Lives*, Ian Scott-Kilvert (trans.) (1965); and *The Fall of the Roman Republic: Six Lives*, Rex Warner (trans.) (1972). However for the *Comparison*, which is still extant for many of the lives, the Loeb Classical Library in 11 volumes is necessary. Volume 3 contains the *Lives of Nicias and Crassus*, Bernadotte Perrin (trans.) (1916). The full list for the others is:

- *Parallel Lives, I: Theseus and Romulus. Lycurgus and Numa. Solon and Publicola*
- *Parallel Lives, II: Themistocles and Camillus. Aristides and Cato Major. Cimon and Lucullus*
- *Parallel Lives, III: Pericles and Fabius Maximus. Nicias and Crassus*
- *Parallel Lives, IV: Alcibiades and Coriolanus. Lysander and Sulla*
- *Parallel Lives, V: Agesilaus and Pompey. Pelopidas and Marcellus*
- *Parallel Lives, VI: Dion and Brutus. Timoleon and Aemilius Paulus*
- *Parallel Lives, VII: Demosthenes and Cicero. Alexander and Caesar*
- *Parallel Lives, VIII: Sertorius and Eumenes. Phocion and Cato the Younger*
- *Parallel Lives, X: Agis and Cleomenes. Tiberius and Gaius Gracchus. Philopoemen and Flamininus*
- *Parallel Lives, XI: Aratus. Artaxerxes. Galba. Otho. General Index*

Orosius, *History against the Pagans*. The most recent English translation is in *The Fathers of the Church: Iberian Fathers, vol. 3, Pacian of Barcelona, Orosius of Braga*, C. L. Hanson (ed. and trans.) (Washington, DC: Catholic University of America Press, 1999).

Strabo, *Geography*, in 17 books, Horace Leonard Jones (trans.), 8 vols, Loeb Classical Library (1917–1932). The most recent Greek text is *Strabons Geographika*, S. L. Radt (ed. and trans. [German]), vols 1–10 (currently in the process of publication) (Göttingen: Vandenhoeck & Ruprecht, 2002–). A recent French translation is *Strabon: Géographie*, vols 1–9, containing Books 1–12, G. Aujac, F. Lasserre, R. Baladié, R. (eds and trans.) (Paris: Les Belles Lettres, 1966–96).

Secondary sources

Adams, J. P. 1980. "Aristonikos and the Cistophoroi". *Historia* **29**: 302–14.
Africa, T. W. 1961. "Aristonicus, Blossius and the City of the Sun". *International Review of Social History* **6**: 110–24.
Africa, T. W. 1982. "Worms and the Death of Kings: A Cautionary Note on Disease and History". *Classical Antiquity* **1**: 1–17.
Andreau, J. & R. Descat 2006. *Esclavage en Grèce et à Rome*. Paris: Hachette.
Aptheker, H. [1943] 1993. *American Negro Slave Revolts*, 6th edn. New York: International Publishers.
Baldwin, B. 1967. "Two Aspects of the Spartacus Slave Revolt". *Classical Journal* **62**: 289–94.
Bales, K. 1999. *Disposable People: New Slavery in the Global Economy*. Berkeley, CA: University of California Press.
Bales, K. 2005. *Understanding Global Slavery: A Reader*. Berkeley, CA: University of California Press.
Bales, K. 2007. *Ending Slavery: How We Free Today's Slaves*. Berkeley, CA: University of California Press.
Beard, M. & M. Crawford [1985] 1999. *Rome in the Late Republic*, 2nd edn. London: Duckworth.
Bellen, H. & H. Heinen (eds) 2003. *Bibliographie zur antiken Sklaverei: Forschungen zur antiken Sklaverei, Beiheft 4*, 2 vols. Stuttgart: Franz Steiner.
Bieżuńska-Małowist, I. 1979. "Les recherches polonaises sur l'esclavage dans l'antiquité". See Bieżuńska-Małowist & Kolendo (1979), 47–55.
Bieżuńska-Małowist, I. & J. Kolendo (eds) 1979. *Actes du colloque sur l'esclavage, Nieborów 2–6 XII 1975* (conference proceedings). Warsaw: History Institute, University of Warsaw.
Bieżuńska-Małowist, I. & M. Małowist (eds) 1987. *Niewolnictwo*. Warsaw: Czytelnik.
Birgalias, N. 2002. "Helotage and Spartan Social Organisation". In *Sparta: Beyond the Mirage*, A. Powell & S. Hodkinson (eds), 249–66. Swansea: Classical Press of Wales.
de Blois, L. & R. J. van der Spek 1997. *An Introduction to the Ancient World*. London: Routledge.
Bradley, K. 1984. *Slaves and Masters in the Roman Empire: A Study in Social Control*. Brussels: Collection Latomus.
Bradley, K. 1989. *Slavery and Rebellion in the Roman World 140 BC–70 BC*. London: Batsford.

Bradley, K. 1994. *Slavery and Society at Rome*. Cambridge: Cambridge University Press.
Braund, D. & J. Wilkins (eds) 2000. *Athenaeus and his World*. Exeter: Exeter University Press.
Brennan, T. C. 2000. *The Praetorship in the Roman Republic*, 2 vols. Oxford: Oxford University Press.
Bringmann, K. 2007. *A History of the Roman Republic*, W. J. Smyth (trans.). Cambridge: Polity. First published in German in 2002.
Brisson, J.-P. 1959. *Spartacus*. Paris: Club Français du Livre.
Broughton, T. R. S. 1951–86. *The Magistrates of the Roman Republic*, 3 vols. New York: American Philological Association.
Brown, C. L. & P. D. Morgan (eds) 2006. *Arming Slaves from Classical Times to the Modern Age*. New Haven, CT: Yale University Press.
Brunt, P. A. 1971 *Social Conflicts in the Roman Republic*. London: Chatto & Windus.
Brunt, P. A. & J. M. Moore 1967. *Res Gestae Divi Augusti: The Achievements of the Divine Augustus*. Oxford: Oxford University Press.
Bücher, K. 1874. *Die Aufstände der unfreien Arbeiter 143–129*. Frankfurt: C. Adelmann.
Bush, M. L. (ed.) 1996. *Serfdom and Slavery: Studies in Legal Bondage*. Harlow: Longman.
Bush, M. L. 1996. "Introduction". In *Serfdom and Slavery: Studies in Legal Bondage*, M. L. Bush (ed.), 1–17. Harlow: Longman.
Bussi, S. 2001. *Economia e demografia della schiavitù in Asia Minore ellenistico-romana*. Milan: LED.
Cambiano, G. 1987. "Aristotle and the Anonymous Opponents of Slavery". In *Classical Slavery*, M. L. Finley (ed.), 28–52. London: Cass.
Cancik, H., H. Schneider & M. Landfester 2006. *Brill's New Pauly: Encyclopaedia of the Ancient World*, 20 vols. Brill: Leiden.
Capogrossi Colognesi, L. 1979. "La denominazione degli schiavi e dei padroni nel latino del terzo e del secondo secolo a.C.". See Bieżuńska-Małowist & Kolendo (1979), 171–206.
Capozza, M. 1966. *Movimenti servili nel mondo romano in età repubblicana. I. Dal 501 al 184 a. Cr.* Rome: Università degli Studi di Padova, Istituto di Storia antica, 5.
Cartledge, P. 1991. "Richard Talbert's Revision of the Spartan-Helot Struggle: A Reply". *Historia* **40**: 379–381.
Cartledge, P. 2001. "Rebels and Sambos in Classical Greece: A Comparative View". Reprinted in his *Spartan Reflections*, 127–52 (London: Duckworth, 2001). Originally published in *Crux: Essays in Greek History Presented to G. E. M. de Ste Croix*, P. Cartledge & D. Harvey (eds), 16–46 (Exeter: Imprint Academic, 1985).
Cartledge, P. 2002. *The Greeks: A Portrait of Self and Others*, 2nd edn. Oxford: Oxford University Press.
Cartledge, P. 2003. "Raising Hell? The Helot Mirage – A Personal Re-view". See Luraghi & Alcock (2003), 12–30.
Cartledge, P. & A. Spawforth 1989. *Hellenistic and Roman Sparta: A Tale of Two Cities*. London: Routledge.
Christes, J. 1979. *Sklaven und Freigelassene als Grammatiker und Philologen in Antiken Rom*. Wiesbaden: Franz Steiner.

Christes, J. 2001. "Sklaverei in griechischen Sprichwörtern und Sentenzen". In *Funfzig Jahre Forschungen zur antiken Sklaverei an der Mainzer Akademie 1950–2000: Miscellanea zum Jubiläum*, H. Bellen & H. Heinen (eds), 429–46. Stuttgart: Franz Steiner.
Cohn, N. [1957] 1970. *The Pursuit of the Millennium*, rev. and expanded. Oxford: Oxford University Press.
Cook, S. A., F. E. Adcock & M. Charlesworth (eds) 1932. *The Cambridge Ancient History*, vol. 9, 1st edn. Cambridge: Cambridge University Press.
Crawford, M. 1992. *The Roman Republic*, 2nd edn. London: Fontana.
Crook, J. A., A. Lintott & E. Rawson (eds) 1994. *The Cambridge Ancient History*, vol. 9, 2nd edn. Cambridge: Cambridge University Press.
Cuff, P. J. 1967. "Prolegomena to a Critical Edition of Appian BC 1". *Historia* **16**: 177–88.
Dahomay, J. 2003. "Slavery and Law: Legitimations of an Insurrection". In *The Abolitions of Slavery: From the L. F. Sonthonax to Victor Schoelcher, 1793, 1794, 1848*, M. Dorigny (ed.), 3–16. Oxford: Berghahn.
Danov, C. M. 1981. "Zur Geschichte des Spartacusaufstandes". See Danov & Fol (1981), 9–13.
Danov, C. M. & A. Fol (eds) 1981. *Spartacus: Symposium rebus Spartaci gestis dedicatum 2050 A*. Sofia: Academie Bulgare des Sciences.
David, E. 1989. "Laughter in Spartan Society". In *Classical Sparta: Techniques Behind her Success*, A. Powell (ed.), 1–25. London: Routledge.
Davis, D. B. 1975. *The Problem of Slavery in the Age of Revolution*. Ithaca, NY: Cornell University Press.
Dawson, D. 1992. *Cities of the Gods: Communist Utopias in Greek Thought*. Oxford: Oxford University Press.
de Souza, P. 1999. *Piracy in the Graeco-Roman World*. Cambridge: Cambridge University Press.
Develin, R. 1994. *Justin: Epitome of the Philippic History of Pompeius Trogus*, J. C. Yardley (trans.). Atlanta, GA: Scholars Press.
Dorigny, M. (ed.) 2003. *The Abolitions of Slavery: From the L. F. Sonthonax to Victor Schoelcher, 1793, 1794, 1848*. Oxford: Berghahn. Originally published in French as *Les abolitions de l'esclavage* (Paris: de l'Unesco et Presses Universitaires de Vincennes, 1995).
Douglass, F. [1845] 1988. *Narrative of the Life of Frederick Douglass, an American Slave Written by Himself*, B. Quarles (ed.). Cambridge, MA: Belknap Press.
Dubois, L. 2004. *The Avengers of the New World: The Story of the Haitian Revolution*. Cambridge, MA: Harvard University Press.
Ducat, J. 1990. *Les Hilotes*. Bulletin de Correspondance Hellénique, supplement 20. Athens: École Française d'Athènes.
Ducat, J. 2002. "The Obligations of Helots", S. Coombes (trans.). See Whitby (2002), 196–211.
Dudley, D. R. 1941. "Blossius of Cumae". *Journal of Roman Studies* **31**: 94–9.
Duff, T. 1999. *Plutarch's Lives: Exploring Vice and Virtue*. Oxford: Clarendon Press.
Dumont, J. C. 1966. "À propos d'Aristonicus". *Eirene* **5**: 189–96.

Earl, D. C. 1961. *The Political Thought of Sallust*. Cambridge: Cambridge University Press.

Egerton, D. R. 2003. "Nat Turner in a Hemispheric Context". In *Nat Turner: A Slave Rebellion in History and Memory*, K. S. Greenberg (ed.), 134-47. Oxford: Oxford University Press.

Engerman, S. L. 1996. "Slavery, Serfdom and Other Forms of Coerced Labour: Similarities and Differences". In *Serfdom and Slavery: Studies in Legal Bondage*, M. L. Bush (ed.), 18-41. Harlow: Longman.

Ève, P. 2003. "Forms of Resistance in Bourbon, 1750-1789". In *The Abolitions of Slavery: From the L. F. Sonthonax to Victor Schoelcher, 1793, 1794, 1848*, M. Dorigny (ed.), 17-39. Oxford: Berghahn.

Farrington, B. 1937. *Diodorus Siculus: Universal Historian*. Swansea: University of Wales, Swansea.

Fast, H. 1951. *Spartacus*. New York: Howard Fast.

Ferrary, J.-L. 1991. "Le statut des cités libres dans l'empire romain à la lumière des inscriptions de Claros". *CRAI* (1991): 557-77.

Figueira, T. 1999. "The Evolution of the Messenian Identity". In *Sparta: New Perspectives*, S. Hodkinson & A. Powell (eds), 211-44. Swansea: Classical Press of Wales.

Finley, M. I. 1959. "Was Greek Civilisation Based on Slave Labour?". *Historia* **8**: 145-64. Reprinted in *Slavery in Classical Antiquity: Views and Controversies*, M. I. Finley (ed.), 53-72 (Cambridge: Heffer, 1960).

Finley, M. I. (ed.) 1960. *Slavery in Classical Antiquity: Views and Controversies*. Cambridge: Heffer.

Finley, M. I. 1968. *A History of Sicily: Ancient Sicily to the Arab Conquest*. London: Chatto & Windus.

Finley, M. I. [1973] 1999. *The Ancient Economy*, updated 2nd edn. Berkeley, CA: University of California Press.

Finley, M. I. 1980. *Ancient Slavery and Modern Ideology*. Harmondsworth: Penguin.

Flower, H. L. (ed.) 2004. *The Cambridge Companion to the Roman Republic*. Cambridge: Cambridge University Press.

Forbiger, A. (trans.) [1855-98] 2005. *Strabo: Geographica* [in German]. Berlin: Wiesbaden.

Forrest, W. G. G. & T. C. W. Stinton 1962. "The First Sicilian Slave War". *Past and Present* **22**: 87-92.

Fortenbaugh, W. W. 1977. "Aristotle on Slaves and Women". In *Articles on Aristotle, 2: Ethics and Politics*, J. Barnes, M. Schofield & R. Sorabji (eds), 135-9. London: Duckworth.

Fuks, A. 1968. "Slave War and Slave Troubles in Chios in the Third Century BC". *Athenaeum* **46**: 102-11.

Gabba, E. 1956. *Appiano e la Storia delle Guerre civili*. Florence: La Nuova Italia.

Garnsey, P. 1996. *Ideas of Slavery from Aristotle to Augustine*. Cambridge: Cambridge University Press.

Genovese, E. D. 1979. *From Rebellion to Revolution: Afro-American Slave Revolts in the Making of the Modern World*. Baton Rouge, LA: Louisiana State University Press.

Giannini, A. 1966. *Paradoxographorum Graecorum Reliquiae*. Milan: Istituto Editoriale Italiano.
Golden, M. 1992. "The Uses of Cross-cultural Comparison in Ancient Social History". *Classical Views/Echos du monde classique* **36**(11): 309–11.
Gomme, A. W. 1945. *A Historical Commentary on Thucydides, Volume 1: Introduction, and Commentary on Book 1*. Oxford: Oxford University Press.
Goody, J. 2006. *The Theft of History*. Cambridge: Cambridge University Press.
Gowing, A. M. 1992. *The Triumviral Narratives of Appian and Cassius Dio*. Ann Arbor, MI: University of Michigan Press.
Gray, V. 1994. "Images of Sparta: Writer and Audience in Isocrates' *Panathenaicus*". In *The Shadow of Sparta*, A. Powell & S. Hodkinson (eds), 223–71. London: Routledge.
Green, P. 1961. "The First Sicilian Slave War". *Past and Present* **20**: 10–29.
Greenberg, K. S. (ed.) 2003. *Nat Turner: A Slave Rebellion in History and Memory*. Oxford: Oxford University Press.
Griffith, J. G. 1981. "Spartacus and the Growth of Historical and Political Legends". See Danov & Fol (1981), 64–70.
Groag, E., A. Stein, L. Petersen, *et al.* (eds) 1933. *Prosopographia Imperii Romani Saeculi* I, II, III, 2nd edn. Berlin: Walter De Gruyter.
Grünewald, T. 2004. *Bandits in the Roman Empire: Myth and Reality*, J. Drinkwater (trans.). London: Routledge. Originally published in German as *Räuber, Rebellen, Rivalen, Rächer* (Stuttgart: Franz Steiner, 1999).
Guarino, A. 1980. *Spartakus: Analyse eines Mythos*, B. Gullath (trans.). Munich: DTV Deutscher Taschenbuch. Originally published in Italian as *Spartaco: Analisi di un Mito* (Naples: Liguori, 1979).
Harris, P. 2007. *An Introduction to Law*, 7th edn. Cambridge: Cambridge University Press.
Heinen, H. 2007. *Handwörterbuch der antiken Sklaverei*. Stuttgart: Franz Steiner.
Henry, R. (ed.) 1960. *Photius: Bibliothèque*, 8 vols. Paris: Les Belles Lettres.
Heuman, G. & J. Walvin (eds) 2003. *The Slavery Reader*. London: Routledge.
Hodkinson, S. 1992. "Sharecropping and Sparta's Economic Exploitation of the Helots". In *Philolakon: Studies in Honour of Hector Catling*, J. M. Sanders (ed.), 123–34. London: British School at Athens.
Hodkinson, S. 2000. *Property and Wealth in Classical Sparta*. London: Duckworth.
Hodkinson, S. 2003. "Spartiates, Helots and the Direction of the Agrarian Economy: Towards an Understanding of Helotage in Comparative Perspective". See Luraghi & Alcock (2003), 248–85.
Hornblower, S. 1991. *A Commentary on Thucydides, Volume 1*. Oxford: Oxford University Press.
Hunt, P. 1998. *Slaves, Warfare and Ideology in the Greek Historians*. Cambridge: Cambridge University Press.
Hunt, P. 2006. "Arming Slaves and Helots in Classical Greece". In *Arming Slaves from Classical Times to the Modern Age*, C. L. Brown & P. D. Morgan (eds), 14–39. New Haven, CT: Yale University Press.
Huxley, G. L. 1962. *Early Sparta*. London: Faber.

Jähne, A. 1986. *Spartacus: Kampf der Sklaven*. Berlin: Deutscher Verlag der Wissenschaften.
James, C. L. R. [1938] 2001. *The Black Jacobins: Toussaint L'Ouverture and the San Domingo Revolution*. Harmondsworth: Penguin.
Jordan, W. D. 1993. *Tumult and Silence at Second Creek: An Inquiry into a Civil War Slave Conspiracy*. Baton Rouge. LA: Louisiana State University Press.
Keaveney, A. & J. A. Madden 1982. "Phthiriasis and its Victims". *Symbolae Osloenses* **57**: 87–99.
Kiechle, F. 1969. *Sklavenarbeit und technischer Fortschritt in römischen Reich*. Wiesbaden: Franz Steiner.
Kolendo, J. 1981. "Comment Spartacus devient-il esclave?". See Danov & Fol (1981), 71–7.
Konrad, C. F. 1994. *Plutarch's Sertorius: A Historical Commentary*. Chapel Hill, NC: University of North Carolina Press.
Kudlien, F. 1991. *Sklaven-Mentalität im Spiegel antiker Wahrsagerei*. Stuttgart: Franz Steiner.
Langauer, W. & J. Kochanowicz 1989. "Nowa książka o niewolnictwo". *Historyka* **19**: 119–28.
Lentz, A. [1867] 1965. *Herodiani Technici Reliquiae*, vol. 1 (Grammatici Graeci, 3.1). Hildesheim: Georg Olms.
Lotze, D. 1959. *Metaxy eleutheron kai doulon: Studien zur Rechtsstellung unfreier Landbevolkerungen in Griechenland*. Berlin: Akademie-Verlag. Reprinted (New York: Arno Press, 1979).
Lukes, S. 1974. *Power: A Radical View*. Basingstoke: Macmillan.
Luraghi, N. 2002. "Becoming Messenian". *Journal of Hellenic Studies* **122**: 45–69.
Luraghi, N. 2002. "Helotic Slavery Reconsidered". In *Sparta: Beyond the Mirage*, A. Powell & S. Hodkinson (eds), 227–48. Swansea: Classical Press of Wales.
Luraghi, N. 2002. "Helots called Messenians? A Note on Thuc. 1.101.2". *Classical Quarterly* **52**: 588–92.
Luraghi, N. 2003. "The Imaginary Conquest of the Helots". See Luraghi & Alcock (2003), 109–41.
Luraghi, N. & S. E. Alcock (eds) 2003. *Helots and their Masters in Laconia and Messenia: Histories, Ideologies, Structures*. Cambridge, MA: Harvard University Press.
Mactoux, M. M. 1979. "Pour une approche nouvelle du champ lexical de l'esclavage chez les orateurs attiques". See Bieżuńska-Małowist & Kolendo (1979), 75–124.
Marshall, B. A. 1972. "Crassus' Ovation in 71 BC". *Historia* **21**: 669–73.
Mashkin, N. A. 1949. "Eschatology and Messianism in the Final Period of the Roman Republic". *Philosophy and Phenomenological Research* **10**(2): 206–28.
Matthews, J. 1989. *The Roman Empire of Ammianus*. London: Duckworth.
Maurenbrecher, B. 1891. *C. Sallusti Crispi Historiarum Reliquiae*. Stuttgart: Teubner.
Mazza, M. 1985. "Sul lavoro servile nella Sicilia romana". In *Antike Abhängigkeitsformen in den griechischen Gebieten ohne Polisstruktur und den römischen Provinzen*, Proceedings of the Symposium on Slavery, Jena 1981, H. Kreissig & F. Kühnert (eds), 103–20. Berlin: Akademie-Verlag.

McGing, B. C. 1986. *The Foreign Policy of Mithridates VI Eupator King of Pontus.* Leiden: Brill.
McGushin, P. 1992, 1994. *Sallust: The Histories*, 2 vols, trans. with intro. and comm. Oxford: Clarendon Press.
McKeown, N. 2007. *The Invention of Ancient Slavery?* London: Duckworth.
Mileta, C. 1998. "Eumenes III und die Sklaven: Neue Ueberlegungen zum Charakter des Aristonikusaufstandes". *Klio* **80**: 47–65.
Mileta, C. 1998. "Quellenkritische Beobachtungen zur Vorgeschichte und zur Natur des Sizilischen Sklavenkriege in den Diodor-Fragmenten". In *Akten des 6. Oesterreichischen Althistorikertages Innsbruck 1996*, P. W. Haider (ed.), 91–112. Innsbruck: Studien Verlag.
Mileta, C. 1998. "Verschwoerung oder Eruption? Diodor und die byzantinischen Exzerptoren ueber den Ersten Sizilischen Sklavenkrieg". In *Dissertatiunculae criticae, Festschrift fuer Guenther Christian Hansen*, C.-F. Collatz, J. Dummer, J. Kollesch, M.-L. Werlitz (eds), 133–53. Würzburg: Königshausen & Neumann.
Millar, F. 1964. *A Study of Cassius Dio.* Oxford: Clarendon Press.
Moles, J. L. 1988. *The Life of Cicero*, trans. with intro. and comm. Warminster: Aris & Phillips.
Morrow, G. R. 1939. *Plato's Law of Slavery and its Relation to Greek Law.* Urbana, IL: University of Illinois Press.
Nikolaidis, A. G. 1988. "Is Plutarch Fair to Nikias?". *Illinois Classical Studies* **13**(2): 319–33.
Nippel, W. 1984. "Policing Rome". *Journal of Roman Studies* **74**: 20–29.
Nippel, W. 1988. *Aufruhr und "Polizei" in der Römischen Republik.* Stuttgart: Klett-Cotta.
Oliva, P. 1971. *Sparta and her Social Problems.* Prague: Academia.
Parker, R. 1989. "Spartan Religion". In *Classical Sparta: Techniques Behind her Success*, A. Powell (ed.), 142–72. London: Routledge.
Parramore, T. C. 2003. "Covenant in Jerusalem". In *Nat Turner: A Slave Rebellion in History and Memory*, K. S. Greenberg (ed.), 58–76. Oxford: Oxford University Press.
Patterson, O. 1970. "Slavery and Slave Revolts: A Socio-Historical Analysis of the First Maroon War, Jamaica 1655–1740". *Social and Economic Studies* **19**(3): 289–325.
Patterson, O. 1977. "Slavery". *Annual Review of Sociology* **3**: 407–49.
Patterson, O. 1982. *Slavery and Social Death: A Comparative Study.* Cambridge, MA: Harvard University Press.
Patterson, O. 2003. "Reflections on Helotic Slavery and Freedom". See Luraghi & Alcock (2003), 289–309.
Pavlovskaja, A. I. 1979. "Les recherches des historiens soviétiques sur l'esclavage en Grèce et dans le monde hellenistique". See Bieżuńska-Małowist & Kolendo (1979), 23–33.
Pelling, C. 1989. "Plutarch: Roman Heroes and Greek Culture". In *Philosophia Togata: Essays on Philosophy and Roman Society*, T. Griffin & J. Barnes (eds), 199–232. Oxford: Clarendon Press.
Pelling, C. 1995. "Plutarch and Roman Politics". In *Essays on Plutarch's Lives*, B. Scardigli (ed.), 319–59. Oxford: Clarendon Press.

Piccinin, P. 2001. "Le Dionysisme dans le *bellum Spartacium*". *La Parola del Passato* 56(4): 272–96.
Piccinin, P. 2004. "Les Italiens dans le Bellum Spartacium". *Historia* 53: 173–99.
Powell, A. (ed.) 1989. *Classical Sparta: Techniques Behind her Success*. London: Routledge.
Powell, A. & S. Hodkinson 1994. *The Shadow of Sparta*. London: Routledge.
Powell, A. & S. Hodkinson (eds) 2002. *Sparta: Beyond the Mirage*. Swansea: Classical Press of Wales.
Powell, A. & K. Welch (eds) 2002. *Sextus Pompeius*. London: Duckworth.
Price, R. [1979] 1996. *Maroon Societies: Rebel Slave Communities in the Americas* (with new introduction). Baltimore, MD: Johns Hopkins University Press.
Price, R. 2003. "Maroons and their Communities". In *The Slavery Reader*, G. Heuman & J. Walvin (eds), 608–25. London: Routledge.
Raaflaub, K. A. 2003. "Freedom for the Messenians? A Note on the Impact of Slavery and Helotage on the Greek Concept of Freedom". See Luraghi & Alcock (2003), 169–90.
Raaflaub, K. A. 2004. *The Discovery of Freedom in Ancient Greece*, rev. and updated, R. Franciscono (trans.). Chicago, IL: University of Chicago Press. First published in German as *Die Entdeckung der Freiheit* (Munich: C. H. Beck, 1985).
Raskolnikoff, M. 1975. *La recherche soviétique et l'histoire économique et sociale du monde hellénistique et romain*. Strasbourg: Association pour l'étude de la civilisation romaine.
Rice Holmes, T. 1923. *The Roman Republic and the Founder of the Empire: From the Origins to 58 BC*, vol. 1. Oxford: Oxford University Press.
Rickman, G. 1980. *The Corn Supply of Ancient Rome*. Oxford: Clarendon Press.
Robert, L. & J. Robert 1989. *Claros I: Décrets Hellénististiques*. Paris: Editions de Recherche sur les Civilisations.
Robinson, E. S. G. 1954. "Cistophoroi in the name of King Eumenes". *Numismatic Chronicle* 14 (6th series): 1–8.
Rossbach, O. (ed.) 1910. *T. Livi periochae omnium librorum*. Leipzig: Teubner.
Rousseau, J.-J. [1762] 1968. *The Social Contract*, M. Cranston (trans.). Harmondsworth: Penguin.
Rout, L. B. 1976. *The African Experience in Spanish America: 1502 to the Present Day*. Cambridge: Cambridge University Press.
Rubinsohn, W. Z. 1971. "Was the Bellum Spartacium a Servile Insurrection?". *Rivista di filologia e d'instruzione classica* 99: 290–99.
Rubinsohn, W. Z. 1987. *Spartacus' Uprising and Soviet Historical Writing*, J. G. Griffith (trans.) Oxford: Oxbow Books.
Rubinsohn, W. Z. 1993. *Die grossen Sklavenaufstände der Antike: 500 Jahre Forschung*, Darmstadt: Wissenschaftliche Buchgesellschaft.
Rubinsohn, Z. 1970. "A Note on Plutarch, Crassus X.1". *Historia* 19: 624–27.
Russell, D. A. 1973. *Plutarch*. London: Duckworth.
Sacks, K. 1990. *Diodorus Siculus and the First Century*. Princeton, NJ: Princeton University Press.
Scardigli, B. (ed.) 1995. *Essays on Plutarch's Lives*. Oxford: Clarendon Press.

Schofield, M. 1999. *Saving the City: Philosopher-Kings and Other Classical Paradigms*. London: Routledge.
Schwartz, S. B. 1992. *Slaves, Peasants and Rebels: Reconsidering Brazilian Slavery*. Urbana, IL: University of Illinois Press.
Schwartz, S. B. 2003. "Resistance and Accommodation in Eighteenth-century Brazil". In *The Slavery Reader*, G. Heuman & J. Walvin (eds), 626–34. London: Routledge.
Scullard, H. H. [1959] 1982. *From the Gracchi to Nero*, 5th edn. London: Routledge.
Shaw, B. D. 2001. *Spartacus and the Slave Wars: A Brief History with Documents*. Boston, MA: Bedford/St Martin's.
Sherk, R. K. 1969. *Roman Documents from the Greek East: Senatus consulta and Epistulae to the Age of Augustus*. Baltimore, MD: Johns Hopkins Press.
Smith, N. D. 1991 "Aristotle's Theory of Natural Slavery". In *A Companion to Aristotle's Politics*, D. Keyt & F. D. Miller (eds), 142–55. Oxford: Blackwell.
Štaerman, E. M. 1971. "Der Klassenkampf der Sklaven zur zeit des roemischen Kaeserreiches". *Jahrbuch fuer Wirtschaftsgeschichte* **2**: 307–35.
Štaerman, E. M. 1979. "L'étude de l'esclavage dans les prvinces romaines". See Bieżuńska-Małowist & Kolendo (1979), 35–46.
Stampacchia, G. 1976. *La Tradizione della guerra di Spartaco da Sallustio a Orosio*. Pisa: Giardini.
Stanev, N. 1981. "Un heros condamné: configurations a l'appréciation de la posterité". See Danov & Fol (1981), 95–101.
Ste Croix, G. E. M. de 1981. *The Class Struggle in the Ancient Greek World: From the Archaic Age to the Arab Conquests*. London: Duckworth.
Ste Croix, G. E. M. de 2002. "The Helot Threat". See Whitby (2002), 190–95. First published in *Origins of the Peloponnesian War* (London: Duckworth, 1972).
Stone, S. 1994. "The Toga: From National to Ceremonial Costume". In *The World of Roman Costume*, J. L. Sebesta & L. Bonfante (eds), 13–45. Madison, WI: University of Wisconsin Press.
Strasburger, H. 1965. "Poseidonios on Problems of the Roman Empire". *Journal of Roman Studies* **55**: 40–53.
Stylianou, P. J. 1998. *A Historical Commentary on Diodorus Siculus, Book 15*. Oxford: Oxford University Press.
Swain, S. C. R. 1990. "Hellenic Culture and the Roman Heroes of Plutarch". *Journal of Hellenic Studies* **110**: 126–45. Reprinted in *Essays on Plutarch's Lives*, B. Scardigli (ed.), 229–64 (Oxford: Clarendon Press, 1995).
Talbert, R. J. A. 1989. "The Role of Helots in the Class Struggle at Sparta". *Historia* **38**: 22–40.
Tarn, W. W. 1932. "Alexander Helios and the Golden Age". *Journal of Roman Studies* **22**: 135–60.
Thompson, F. H. 2003. *The Archaeology of Greek and Roman Slavery*. London: Duckworth.
Titchener, F. B. 1991. "Why did Plutarch Write about Nicias?". *Ancient History Bulletin* **5**: 153–8.
Todorov, T. 1981. "De l'Origine de Spartacus". See Danov & Fol (1981), 199–201.

Treadgold, W. T. 1980. *The Nature of the Bibliotheca of Photius*. Washington, DC: Centre for Byzantine Studies, Dumbarton Oaks.

Urbainczyk, T. 2004. *Spartacus*. London: Duckworth.

van Wees, H. 2003. "Conquerors and Serfs: Wars of Conquest and Forced Labour in Archaic Greece". See Luraghi & Alcock (2003), 33–80.

Vavrinek, V. 1975. "Aristonicus of Pergamum: Pretender to the Throne or Leader of a Slave Revolt?". *Eirene* **13**: 109–29.

Velkova, Z. 1981. "Der Name Spartakus". See Danov & Fol (1981), 195–8.

Verbrugghe, G. P. 1972. "Sicily 210–70 BC: Livy, Cicero and Diodorus". *Transactions of the American Philological Association* **103**: 535–59.

Verbrugghe, G. P. 1973. "The 'Elogium' from Polla and the First Slave War". *Classical Philology* **68**: 25–35.

Verbrugghe, G. P. 1974. "Slave Rebellion or Sicily in Revolt?". *Kokalos* **20**: 46–60.

Verbrugghe, G. P. 1975. "Narrative Pattern in Posidonius' History". *Historia* **24**: 198–204.

Vidal-Naquet, P. 1986. *The Black Hunter: Forms of Thought and Forms of Society in the Greek World*. Baltimore, MD: Johns Hopkins University Press.

Vogt, J. 1975. *Ancient Slavery and the Ideal of Man*, T. Wiedemann (trans.). Oxford: Blackwell. Originally published in German as *Sklaverei und Humanität: Studien zur antiken Sklaverei und ihrer Erforschung* (Wiesbaden: Steiner, 1965).

Walbank, F. 2000. "Athenaeus and Polybius". In *Athenaeus and his World*, D. Braund & J. Wilkins (eds), 161–9. Exeter: Exeter University Press.

Wallinga, H. T. 1992. "Bellum Spartacium: Florus' Text and Spartacus' Objective". *Athenaeum* **70**(80): 25–43.

Weber, M. 1976. *The Agrarian Sociology of Ancient Civilisations*, R. I Frank (trans.). London: New Left Books.

Weiler, I. 2003. *Die Beendigung des Sklavenstatus im Altertum. Ein Beitrag zur vergleichenden Sozialgeschichte*. Stuttgart: Franz Steiner.

Welwei, K.-W. 1974. *Unfreie im antiken Kriegsdienst*. Wiesbaden: Franz Steiner.

Welwei, K.-W. 2004. "War die *Krypteia* ein grausames Terrorinstrument? Zur Entstehung einer Fiktion". *Laverna* **15**: 33–46.

Westermann, A. 1839. ΠΑΡΑΔΟΞΟΓΡΑΦΟΙ *Scriptores Rerum Mirabilium Graeci*. London.

Westermann, W. L. 1945. "Between Slavery and Freedom". *American Historical Review* **50**(2): 213–27.

Whitby, M. 1994. "Two Shadows: Images of Spartans and Helots". In *The Shadow of Sparta*, A. Powell & S. Hodkinson (eds), 87–126. London: Routledge.

Whitby, M. (ed.) 2002. *Sparta*. Edinburgh: Edinburgh University Press.

Wiedemann, T. 1981. *Greek and Roman Slavery*. London: Routledge.

Wilson, N. G. 1994. *Photius: The Bibliotheca*. London: Duckworth.

Wyke, M. 1997. *Projecting the Past*. London: Routledge.

Yarrow, L. M. 2006. *Historiography at the End of the Republic: Provincial Perspectives on Roman Rule*. Oxford: Oxford University Press.

Yavetz, Z. 1988. *Slaves and Slavery in Ancient Rome*. New Brunswick, NJ: Transaction.

Ziegler, K. 1955. "Die Herkunft des Spartacus". *Hermes* **83**: 248–50.

Index

Achaeus 55, 56
Acragas (Agrigentum) 12, 39, 86, 89
Africanus, Publius 13
Agrigentum *see* Acragas
Agyrium 81
Alexander the Great 70, 77, 114–15
Alexandria 71, 73
Andreau, J. 117, 119, 124
Antiochus *see* Eunus
Aptheker, H. 6, 7, 118, 120, 121
Appian Way 2
Appian 13, 22, 34, 46–8, 51
   on the Roman Republic 102–7
   on Spartacus 71–3
Aquillius, Manius 59, 62
armies *see* slave armies
Athenaeus 18, 25, 27, 29, 37, 53–4
   on helots 95, 96
   and Posidonius 83, 85–6
   quotes Theopompus 91
Arethusa, fountain of 89
Aristonicus 14, 15, 16, 36, 43, 60–61, 87–8
   in Appian's history 105
   in Augustine's *City of God* 123
Aristotle 24, 73, 78, 79
   describes slaves as animate tools 92
   advises that slaves should not speak a common language 99, 123–4
Athenion 32, 45–6, 54, 57–60
Athens 12, 24
   Laurion silver mines of 18

Athenians and Pelasgians 79
Antony, Mark 70
Attalus III 15, 61, 62
   in Florus' history 110
Attica 12, 18, 25, 126, 127
attitudes to slave revolts
   ancient 1–9, 81–90, 100–115
   modern 1–9, 100–115
Augustine 112, 113–15, 123
Augustus 22, 48, 66, 93, 104
   in Florus' history 108–9, 110
   nicknamed Thurinus as a child 135

Baldwin, B. 64, 65, 126
Bales, K. 4, 119, 121
Beard, M. 103, 112–13
Blossius 43
Bradley, K. 18, 31–3, 40, 45, 48–50, 55, 58, 117, 121
Brazil 31–5, 120
Brundisium 23
Bulla Felix 52–3, 126

Cassius governor of Cisalpine Gaul 46
Caecilius of Kale Akte 18, 37
Caesar, Julius 23, 50, 81, 104, 113
   in Florus' history 110
Cambridge Ancient History 100–101
Cambridge Companion to the Roman Republic 101
Capozza, M. 122

173

Capua   17, 22, 23, 48, 49, 71
Caribbean   6, 31
Cartledge, P.   119
Cassius Dio   52, 53
Catiline   23
   in Florus' history   108
Cato the Elder   99, 145
Chios   29-31, 37, 38, 53-4, 74
   Chians   91
Cicero   23, 36, 37, 41, 43, 65, 68-70
   using Spartacus as a comparison   78
Cilicia   11, 36, 37, 43, 110
   Cilician   56, 57, 60
   Cilician pirates   48
Cimbri   17, 19
Cinadon   26
Citizens of the City of the Sun *see* Heliopolitae
City of God see Augustine
City of the Sun *see* Heliopolitae
Claros   43
Cleon   12, 42, 54, 56, 58
   brother of   139
Cleopatra   70
Colophon   36, 43
Communist Manifesto   2, 118
Constantine Porphyrogenitus, *Excerpts* of   45, 55, 56, 63
   and the text of Diodorus' history   83-90, 122
Cossinius   46
Cornelia, mother of the Gracchi   68
Crassus, Marcus Licinius   22, 34, 47, 48, 61-2, 66-72, 102
   in Orosius' history   112
Crassus, Publius Licinius   61-2
Crawford, M.   103, 112-13
Crixus   22, 46, 51, 71
Crucifixion   2, 48, 60, 71, 112
Curtisius, Titus   23
Curtius Rufus, Quintus   77

Dahomay, J.   3, 118
Damophilus   11, 84-5
   daughter of   82, 85, 86-7, 89
Deipnosophistae see Athenaeus

Delos   12, 18
Demeter   42
Demosthenes   25, 26
Descaut, R.   117, 119, 124
Digest   7, 79
Dio Cassius *see* Cassius Dio
Dio Chrysostom   76, 98
Diodorus Siculus *passim* but see especially 81-90
Dionysus   67, 143
Drimakos   30-31, 37, 38, 44, 53-4, 56, 74
Dubois, L.   35
Ducat, J.   92
Duff, T.   70

Engels, F.   2
Enna   11, 12, 38, 39, 44
   Damophilus and Megallis from   84
Ephesus   25
Equites   11, 17
Eumenes   11, 15, 16
Epaminondas   27
Eunus   11, 41, 42, 45, 52, 54, 55, 56, 58, 60
   death of   138
   as king   75
   remembers favour   89
   slaves approach   84
   from Syria   83
Eutropius   66
Excerpts see Constantine

Farrington, B.   40
Figueira, T.   98
Finley, M. I.   2, 3, 4, 8, 100, 118, 121
Flaccus, Gaius Fulvius   13, 42, 106
Florus   37, 52, 60, 62
   on the Roman Republic   107-11, 112, 113
Forrest, W. G. G.   122
freedom   1-9, 75-80
Frontinus   66

Genovese, E.   3, 4, 5, 6, 9, 13, 51, 118, 120

INDEX

Glaber, Varinius 71
gladiators 8, 21, 22, 23, 49, 67, 71
goals of slaves *see* intentions of slaves
Gracchus, Gaius 11
  in Florus' history 108
  his reforms 41
  the Gracchi brothers 111, 123
Gracchus, Tiberius 13, 43, 100, 103, 104, 105, 113
  in Florus' history 108
  in the Epitome of Livy 125
Green, P. 121, 122
Gregory of Nyssa 79
Griffith, J. G. 64, 101–2
Grünewald, T. 136, 146
Guide to Greece see Pausanias

Hermeias 85, 87, 139
Herodian 94
Haiti 8 *see also* St Domingue
Halicyae 19, 20, 21, 44
Hannibal 10, 136
Heliopolis 43, 125 *see also* Heliopolitae
Heliopolitae 15–16, 43
helots 3, 24–8, 37–8, 68, 73–4, 91–9
  aims of 75
  leaders of 73–4
  status of 91–9
Herakleia 21
Herdonius 60
Herodotus 79, 136–7
Hesychius of Alexandria 73
historians 1–9, 81–90, 100–115
Hypsaeus, Lucius 39

Iambulus 43, 79
ideology 75–80
Ilhéus, Eugeno Santa of 33–4
intentions of slaves 75–80
Ithome, Mount 24, 27, 38, 128

Jamaica 5–6, 32, 120
Jugurtha 16
Justin 61, 79

Kubrick, S. 67

Laureion *see* Athens
leaders *see* slave leaders *and* Athenion, Cleon, Crixus, Eunus, Oenomaus, Salvius, Spartacus, Varius
Leucae 15
Leuctra 27, 98
Libanius 94
Lilybaeum 57
Livy 12, 13, 39, 41, 42, 66, 107–8, 125
Louverture, Toussaint *see* Toussaint Louverture
Lucullus, Lucius Licinius 17, 58, 59
  son of, with same name 48
Lycurgus 68, 78, 97–8
Lysias 77

McGushin, P. 65
McKeown, N. 2, 117, 148
Macrobius 77
Mamertium 39
Marius 19, 68, 70, 100, 107
  in Florus' history 108, 110
maroons (maroon communities) 31–8, 43, 120, 127–30, 135
Marx, K. 2, 118
Marxists 3
Maurenbrecher, B. 65
Megallis 11, 84–5
  daughter of 82, 85, 86–7
Messenia 95, 98–9
Messenians 25–7, 29, 96, 97, 98
  Messenian city of Helos 94
Mileta, C. 45, 84
Minturnae 12
Minutius, Titus Vettius 17, 60–61, 63, 125–6
Mithridates 10, 15, 22, 47, 61, 123
  takes name Dionysus 143
Morgantina 44, 45, 55, 56, 57, 126
Mummius 47
Myron of Priene 27

Naupactus 25, 26, 38
Nero 24
Nerva, Licinius 19, 44
Nicias 67–70
Nicomedes, king of Bithynia 19

INDEX

Nuceria 17
Numa 68, 78–9, 98
Nymphodorus of Syracuse 30, 31, 37, 38, 53, 54

Obsequens, Julius 12, 13, 123
Octavian, Octavius *see* Augustus
Oenomaus 22, 51, 66, 71
Orosius 12, 28, 39, 40
  on Roman Republic 111–12
outbreak 10–28

Palikoi, sanctuary of 19
Patterson, O. 4, 5, 119, 120
Pausanias 94, 98
Peloponnesian War 25, 127
Pergamum 12, 14, 15, 16, 42, 61, 111
Perperna, Marcus 60, 62
  perhaps grandson of preceding 72
Photius 19, 39, 45, 54, 55, 56, 63
  and Diodorus' history 83–8, 122
Piccinin, P. 101
Plato 29
  Alcibiades of 94
  Gorgias of 148
  Laws of 96
  Republic of 76–7
  thinks slaves should not share a common language 99, 123–4
play, slaves stage 39–40, 89
Plutarch 16, 22, 46, 48, 51, 53, 64–71, 72
  on Cato 99
  Comparison of Lycurgus and Numa 78–9
  on helots 94, 97–8
  views on Romans 83
Pompey, Gn. 22, 23, 48, 71, 72, 101, 102, 103, 113
  in Appian's history 106–7
  in Florus' history 110
Pliny the Elder 138
Polybius 103–4
Popillius, Publius 13
Porphyrogenitus *see* Constantine
Posidonius 18, 83, 85–6, 95, 126
Praeneste 24

Price, R. 31–2
Pylos 25, 26
Pollux of Naucratis 91–2, 94

resistance of slaves 1–9, 75–80
revolt of slaves 1–9
  frequency of 1–9, 100–115
  in historiography 81–90, 100–115
  outbreak of 10–28
  maintenance of 29–50
revolution 3, 32–5
Rubinsohn, Z. 101
Rupilius, Publius 13, 56

Sacks, K. 81, 82–3, 86
Sacrovir 23
Ste Croix, G. E. M. de 118, 127
St Domingue 3, 34, 35, 119 *see also* Haiti
Sallust 15, 23, 65–6
Salvius 32, 44–6, 54, 56–9
  as king 75
Samians 25
Saramaka 36
Sarapion 56
Satyros 59
Schwartz, S. B. 34, 120, 156
Scullard, H. H. 103
Segesta 57
Seneca 77
Sertorius 21, 68, 70, 71, 72
  in the *Cambridge Ancient History* 101
  in Florus' history 108
Servilius, Gaius 59
Shaw, B. D. 64, 122
Siculus *see* Diodorus Siculus
Sicily *see* Sicilian slave war, First *and* Sicilian slave war, Second
  Spartacus aiming to go to 48
Sicilian slave war, First 10–14, 38–42, 54–7, 81–90
Sicilian slave war, Second 16–21, 43–6, 58–60
Sinuessa 12
slave armies
  formation of 10–28

176

INDEX

ideology of 75–80
leadership of 51–74
maintenance of 29–50
slave leaders 11–24, 51–74 *see also*
    Athenion, Cleon, Crixus, Eunus,
    Oenomaus, Salvius, Spartacus,
    Varius
slave revolts *see* revolt
slaves, slavery *passim*
snake 67
Social War 105–6
    in Florus' history 108, 109
Socrates 76, 94
Spain 72 *see also* Sertorius
Sparta 3, 24–8, 29 *see also*
    Spartans
Spartacus
    leads gladiators 8, 21–4
    leads slave army 46–50
    discussed by Bradley 33
    goal of 40
    as leader 51, 52, 56, 62, 64–73
    name and origins of 144–5
    referred to by Cicero 78
    in *Cambridge Ancient History* 101
    in *Cambridge Companion to the
    Roman Republic* 101
    in Appian's history 34, 71–2,
    105–6
    in Augustine 114
    in Florus' history 108–9
    in Orosius' history 112
    in Plutarch 67–71
Spartans 37, 38, 73–4, 91–9 *see also*
    Sparta
Stinton, T. C. W. 122
Strabo 15, 42, 43, 63, 93
Stylianou, P. J. 82
Suetonius 22, 48
Sulla 21, 70, 72, 104, 113
    in Appian's narrative 106, 107
sympathy for rebellious slaves 81–90, 91–9

Syria 83, 110 *see also* Syrian, Syrians
Syrian 42, 60
    Syrian runaways cutting off arms of
    their captives 138–9
Syrians 41, 56

Tacitus 23, 24
Talbert, R. 73
Tauromenium 39, 56, 87, 125
Theopompus 29, 37, 91
Thucydides 24, 25, 26, 29, 73, 92, 127, 128
    Melian debate of 75
Timaeus of Tauromenium 29
Titinius, Marcus 21, 44
Toussaint Louverture 2, 35
Triokala 58, 59
Turner, Nat 7
Tryphon *see* Salvius

Valerius, Publius 71
Varinius, Publius 46
Varius 19, 32
Varro 65
Vavrinek, V. 62–3
Velleius Paterculus 66
Verbrugghe, G. 41–2
Verres 65
Vesuvius 71
Via Appia *see* Appian Way
Vogt, J. 18, 33, 77–8, 121

Whitby, M. 146
Wilberforce, W. 33
Wiedemann, T. 121, 124, 130

Xenophon 26, 27
    Hiero of 77

Yarrow, L. M. 132
Yavetz, Z. 123

Zeuxis 85, 139